On Old Age

(De Senectute)

Cicero

LATIN TEXT ▓ NOTES ▓ VOCABULARY

Edited by

CHARLES E. BENNETT

(New Cicero)

Bolchazy-Carducci Publishers, Inc.
Wauconda, Illinois USA

Cover Design
by Adam Phillip Velez

Cover Illustration
by Leon Danilovics

On Old Age
De Senectute

© **copyright 2002 Bolchazy-Carducci Publishers, Inc.**

Bolchazy-Carducci Publishers, Inc.
1000 Brown Street
Wauconda, IL 60084 USA
http://www.bolchazy.com

First published by Allyn and Bacon, 1922
Reprinted with permission, 1985, 1990 and 2002

Printed in the United States of America
2002
by Bang Printing

ISBN 0-86516-001-5

On Old Age

(De Senectute)

Cicero

CICERO

CONTENTS

SOPHOCLES

PREFACE

The relevance of Cicero's *On Old Age* transcends time and a multiplicity of cultures. This masterpiece of antiquity examines, with superlative clarity, the challenging problems we must all face, individually, and as members of any society.

The paradox is obvious: we hope for old age simply because the alternative —premature death—is unacceptable to our species. Simultaneously, we dread old age because we believe, correctly or not, that it represents the threshold of extinction as well as a state of deprivation and debility — physical, mental, and sexual.

Cicero addresses this oppressive ambivalence as it applies to us as individual entities.

On Old Age also speaks lucidly of the emotional contradictions inherent to the aspects of approaching old age and the sociological problems induced by this phenomenon. In our own society, its adverse aspects are manifested in controversial and contradictory laws: early retirement, for example, mandated for many resourceful and capable individuals, is diametrically opposed by the common-sense practice of encouraging our elders to assume and retain the highest positions in our society. At the same time, it is obvious that early retirement—enforced—results in a reduction of productivity and a decrease in gross national product. As the working class is depleted by the increasing number of retirees, the burden of vastly expanded Social Security funding must be borne by fewer and fewer producers.

And finally, while we all hope to attain old age with its attendant comforts, we tolerate inhuman conditions in senior-citizen nursing homes ... which lie in the future for many thousands of us.

So, Cicero's *On Old Age* speaks directly to our times. *Tolle, lege,* therefore, with your students. Classicists who would choose to hide the light of this masterpiece under a bushel are taking an impassable route.

Your students will find Cicero's *On Old Age* totally compatible with the humanistic views of contemporary society. Too, they will find this ancient masterwork relatively easy to read in the original—and completely charming.

This reprinted edition contains the Latin text and notes edited by Charles E. Bennett, first published as part of *New Cicero* in 1922. This reprint contains also vocabulary and a list of proper names. Bennett's edition was chosen for this reprint because it was unanimously recommended by a number of classicists who were polled.

Chicago, 1980   Ladislaus J. Bolchazy

PLATO

M. TULLI CICERONIS
CATO MAJOR DE SENECTUTE LIBER
AD T. POMPONIUM ATTICUM

Dedication to Atticus

I. 1. Ō Tite, sī quid tē adjuerō cūramve levāssō,
Quae nunc tē coquit et versāt in pectore fīxa,
Ecquid erit praemī?

Licet enim mihi versibus eīsdem affārī tē, Attice, qui-
5 bus affātur Flāminīnum

Ille vir haud magnā cum rē, sed plēnus fidēī;

quamquam certō sciō nōn, ut Flāminīnum,

Sollicitārī tē, Tite, sīc noctēsque diēsque;

nōvī enim moderātiōnem animī tuī et aequitātem tēque
10 nōn cognōmen sōlum Athēnīs dēportāsse, sed hūmāni-
tātem et prūdentiam intellegō. Et tamen tē suspicor
eīsdem rēbus quibus mē ipsum interdum gravius com-
movērī, quārum cōnsōlātiō et major est et in aliud
tempus differenda. Nunc autem vīsum est mihi dē
15 senectūte aliquid ad tē cōnscrībere. **2.** Hōc enim
onere, quod mihi commūne tēcum est, aut jam urgen-
tis aut certē adventantis senectūtis et tē et mē ipsum
levārī volō; etsī tē quidem id modicē ac sapienter sīcut

120

omnia et ferre et lātūrum esse certō sciō. Sed mihi,
cum dē senectūte vellem aliquid scrībere, tū occurrē-
bās dignus eō mūnere, quō uterque nostrum commūniter ūterētur. Mihi quidem ita jūcunda hūjus librī
cōnfectiō fuit, ut nōn modo omnēs absterserit senectū- 5
tis molestiās, sed effēcerit mollem etiam et jūcundam
senectūtem. Numquam igitur laudārī satis dignē philosophia poterit, cui quī pāreat, omne tempus aetātis
sine molestiā possit dēgere. **3.** Sed dē cēterīs et
dīximus multa et saepe dīcēmus; hunc librum ad tē 10
dē senectūte mīsimus. Omnem autem sermōnem tribuimus nōn Tīthōnō, ut Aristō Cēus (parum enim
esset auctōritātis in fābulā), sed M. Catōnī senī, quō
majōrem auctōritātem habēret ōrātiō; apud quem Laelium et Scīpiōnem facimus admīrantēs, quod is tam 15
facile senectūtem ferat, eīsque eum respondentem.
Quī sī ērudītius vidēbitur disputāre, quam cōnsuēvit
ipse in suīs librīs, attribuitō litterīs Graecīs, quārum
cōnstat eum perstudiōsum fuisse in senectūte. Sed
quid opus est plūra? Jam enim ipsīus Catōnis sermō 20
explicābit nostram omnem dē senectūte sententiam.

*The young men express their admiration of the way Cato bears old
age. His explanation*

II. **4.** *Scipio.* Saepe numerō admīrārī soleō cum
hōc C. Laeliō cum cēterārum rērum tuam excellentem,
M. Catō, perfectamque sapientiam, tum vel maximē,
quod numquam tibi senectūtem gravem esse sēnserim, 25
quae plērīsque senibus sīc odiōsa est, ut onus sē Aetnā
gravius dīcant sustinēre.

Cato. Rem haud sānē difficilem, Scīpiō et Laelī,

admīrārī vidēminī. Quibus enim nihil est in ipsīs opis
ad bene beātēque vīvendum, eīs omnis aetās gravis
est; quī autem omnia bona ā sē ipsī petunt, eīs nihil
potest malum vidērī, quod nātūrae necessitās afferat.
5 Quō in genere est in prīmīs senectūs; quam ut adi-
pīscantur omnēs optant, eandem accūsant adeptam;
tanta est stultitiae incōnstantia atque perversitās.
Obrēpere ajunt eam citius, quam putāssent. Prīmum
quis coēgit eōs falsum putāre? Quī enim citius adu-
10 lēscentiae senectūs quam pueritiae adulēscentia obrē-
pit? Deinde quī minus gravis esset eīs senectūs, sī
octingentēsimum annum agerent quam sī octōgēsimum? Praeterita enim aetās quamvīs longa cum
efflūxisset, nūllā cōnsōlātiōne permulcēre posset stul-
15 tam senectūtem. 5. Quōcircā sī sapientiam meam
ᴧdmīrārī solētis (quae utinam digna esset opīniōne
vestrā nostrōque cognōmine!), in hōc sumus sapientēs,
quod nātūram optimam ducem tamquam deum sequimur eīque pārēmus; ā quā nōn vērī simile est, cum
20 cēterae partēs aetātis bene discrīptae sint, extrēmum
āctum tamquam ab inertī poētā esse neglēctum. Sed
tamen necesse fuit esse aliquid extrēmum et tamquam
in arborum bācīs terraeque frūctibus mātūritāte tem-
pestīvā quasi viētum et cadūcum, quod ferendum est
25 molliter sapientī. Quid est enim aliud Gigantum modō
bellāre cum dīs nisi nātūrae repugnāre?

They urge him to proceed

6. *Laelius.* Atquī, Catō, grātissimum nōbīs, ut etiam
prō Scīpiōne pollicear, fēceris, sī, quoniam spērāmus, —
volumus quidem certē, — senēs fierī, multō ante ā tē

didicerimus, quibus facillimē ratiōnibus ingravēscentem aetātem ferre possīmus.

Cato. Faciam vērō, Laelī, praesertim sī utrīque vestrum, ut dīcis, grātum futūrum est.

Laelius. Volumus sānē, nisi molestum est, Catō, 5 tamquam longam aliquam viam cōnfēcerīs, quā nōbīs quoque ingrediendum sit, istūc, quō pervēnistī, vidēre quāle sit.

III. 7. *Cato.* Faciam, ut poterō, Laelī. Saepe ənim interfuī querēlīs aequālium meōrum (parēs autem 10 vetere prōverbiō cum paribus facillimē congregantur), quae C. Salīnātor, quae Sp. Albīnus, hominēs cōnsulārēs, nostrī ferē aequālēs, dēplōrāre solēbant, tum quod voluptātibus carērent, sine quibus vītam nūllam putārent, tum quod spernerentur ab eīs ā quibus 15 essent colī solitī. Quī mihi nōn id vidēbantur accūsāre, quod esset accūsandum. Nam sī id culpā senectūtis accideret, eadem mihi ūsū venīrent reliquīsque omnibus majōribus nātū, quōrum ego multōrum cognōvī senectūtem sine querēlā, quī sē et libīdinum 20 vinculīs laxātōs esse nōn molestē ferrent nec ā suīs dēspicerentur. Sed omnium istīus modī querēlārum in mōribus est culpa, nōn in aetāte. Moderātī enim et nec difficilēs nec inhūmānī senēs tolerābilem senectūtem agunt, importūnitās autem et inhūmānitās omnī 25 aetātī molesta est.

8. *Laelius.* Est, ut dīcis, Catō; sed fortasse dīxerit quispiam tibi propter opēs et cōpiās et dignitātem tuam tolerābiliōrem senectūtem vidērī, id autem nōn posse multīs contingere. 30

Cato. Est istud quidem, Laelī, aliquid, sed nēquā-

quam in istō sunt omnia. Ut Themistoclēs fertur
Serīphiō cuidam in jūrgiō respondisse, cum ille dīxis-
set nōn eum suā sed patriae glōriā splendōrem asse-
cūtum: 'Nec hērculē,' inquit, 'sī ego Serīphius essem,
5 nec tū, sī Athēniēnsis essēs, clārus umquam fuissēs.'
Quod eōdem modō dē senectūte dīcī potest. Nec enim
in summā inopiā levis esse senectūs potest nē sapientī quidem nec īnsipientī etiam in summā cōpiā nōn
gravis. 9. Aptissima omnīnō sunt, Scīpiō et Laelī,
10 arma senectūtis artēs exercitātiōnēsque virtūtum,
quae in omnī aetāte cultae, cum diū multumque vīxe-
rīs, mīrificōs efferunt frūctūs, nōn sōlum quia numquam dēserunt nē extrēmō quidem tempore aetātis
(quamquam id quidem maximum est),. vērum etiam
15 quia cōnscientia bene āctae vītae multōrumque bene
factōrum recordātiō jūcundissima est.

Fabius Maximus as an example of the ideal old man

IV. 10. Ego Q. Maximum, eum quī Tarentum re-
cēpit, senem adulēscēns ita dīlēxī, ut aequālem; erat
enim in illō virō cōmitāte condīta gravitās, nec senec-
20 tūs mōrēs mūtāverat; quamquam eum colere coepī
nōn admodum grandem nātū, sed tamen jam aetāte
prōvectum. Annō enim post cōnsul prīmum fuerat,
quam ego nātus sum, cumque eō quārtum cōnsule
adulēscentulus mīles ad Capuam profectus sum quīn-
25 tōque annō post ad Tarentum. Quaestor deinde quadrienniō post factus sum, quem magistrātum gessī
cōnsulibus Tuditānō et Cethēgō, cum quidem ille admodum senex suāsor lēgis Cinciae dē dōnīs et mūneribus fuit. Hīc et bella gerēbat ut adulēscēns, cum

plānē grandis esset, et Hannibalem juvenīliter exsultantem patientiā suā molliēbat; dē quō praeclārē
familiāris noster Ennius:

> Ūnus homō nōbīs cunctandō restituit rem.
> Noenum rūmōrēs pōnēbāt ante salūtem.   5
> Ergō plūsque magisque virī nunc glōria clāret.

11. Tarentum vērō quā vigilantiā, quō cōnsiliō recē-
pit! cum quidem, mē audiente, Salīnātōrī, quī āmissō
oppidō fuerat in arce, glōriantī atque ita dīcentī:
'*Meā operā, Q. Fabī, Tarentum recēpistī,*' '*Certē,*' 10
inquit rīdēns, '*nam nisi tū āmīsissēs, numquam recē-
pissem.*' Nec vērō in armīs praestantior quam in
togā; quī cōnsul iterum, Sp. Carviliō collēgā quiē-
scente, C. Flāminiō tribūnō plēbis, quoad potuit, restitit
agrum Pīcentem et Gallicum virītim contrā senātūs 15
auctōritātem dīvidentī; augurque cum esset, dīcere
ausus est optimīs auspiciīs ea gerī, quae prō reī pūbli-
cae salūte gererentur; quae contrā rem pūblicam ferrentur, contrā auspicia ferrī. **12.** Multa in eō virō
praeclāra cognōvī; sed nihil admīrābilius, quam quō 20
modō ille mortem fīlī tulit, clārī virī et cōnsulāris.
Est in manibus laudātiō, quam cum legimus, quem
philosophum non contemnimus? Nec vērō ille in
lūce modo atque in oculīs cīvium magnus, sed intus
domīque praestantior. Quī sermō, quae praecepta, 25
quanta nōtitia antīquitātis, scientia jūris augurī!
Multae etiam, ut in homine Rōmānō, litterae; omnia
memoriā tenēbat nōn domestica sōlum, sed etiam
externa bella. Cūjus sermōne ita tum cupidē fruēbar,
quasi jam dīvīnārem, id quod ēvēnit, illō exstīnctō fore, 30
unde discerem, nēminem.

Other examples

V. 13. Quōrsus igitur haec tam multa dē Maximō?
Quia profectō vidētis nefās esse dictū miseram fuisse
tālem senectūtem. Nec tamen omnēs possunt esse
Scīpiōnēs aut Maximī, ut urbium expugnātiōnēs, ut
5 pedestrēs nāvālēsve pugnās, ut bella ā sē gesta, ut tri-
umphōs recordentur. Est etiam quiētē et pūrē atque
ēleganter āctae aetātis placida ac lēnis senectūs, quālem accēpimus Platōnis, quī ūnō et octōgēsimō annō
scrībēns est mortuus, quālem Īsocratis, quī eum
10 librum, quī Panathēnāicus īnscrībitur, quārtō et nōnā-
gēsimō annō scrīpsisse sē dīcit vīxitque quīnquennium
posteā; cūjus magister Leontīnus Gorgiās centum et
septem complēvit annōs neque umquam in suō studiō
atque opere cessāvit. Quī, cum ex eō quaererētur, cūr
15 tam diū vellet esse in vītā: '*Nihil habeō,*' inquit,
'*quod accūsem senectūtem.*' Praeclārum respōnsum et
doctō homine dignum. 14. Sua enim vitia īnsipi-
entēs et suam culpam in senectūtem cōnferunt; quod
nōn faciēbat is, cūjus modo mentiōnem fēcī, Ennius:

20   Sīcut fortis equos, spatiō quī saepe suprēmō
        Vīcit Olumpia, nunc seniō cōnfectus quiēscit.

Equī fortis et victōris senectūtī comparat suam.
Quem quidem probē meminisse potestis; annō enim
ūndēvīcēsimō post ejus mortem hī cōnsulēs, T. Flāmi-
25 nīnus et M'. Acīlius, factī sunt, ille autem Caepiōne
et Philippō iterum cōnsulibus mortuus est, cum ego
quīnque et sexāgintā annōs nātus lēgem Vocōniam
magnā vōce et bonīs lateribus suāsī. Sed annōs septuāgintā nātus (tot enim vīxit Ennius) ita ferēbat duo,

quae maxima putantur, onera, paupertātem et senectūtem, ut eīs paene dēlectārī vidērētur.

The charges brought against old age

15. Etenim, cum complector animō, quattuor reperiō causās, cūr senectūs misera videātur: ūnam, quod
āvocet ā rēbus gerendīs, alteram, quod corpus faciat 5
īnfīrmius, tertiam, quod prīvet omnibus ferē voluptātibus, quārtam, quod haud procul absit ā morte. Eārum,
sī placet, causārum quanta quamque sit jūsta ūna
quaeque, videāmus.

Old age is alleged to withdraw men from active pursuits

VI. Ā rēbus gerendīs senectūs abstrahit. Quibus? 10
An eīs, quae juventūte geruntur et vīribus? Nūllaene
igitur rēs sunt senīlēs, quae vel īnfīrmīs corporibus
animō tamen administrentur? Nihil ergō agēbat Q.
Maximus, nihil L. Paulus, pater tuus, socer optimī
virī, fīlī meī? Cēterī senēs, Fabriciī, Cūriī, Coruncā- 15
niī, cum rem pūblicam cōnsiliō et auctōritāte dēfendē-
bant, nihil agēbant? 16. Ad Appī Claudī senectūtem accēdēbat etiam, ut caecus esset; tamen is, cum
sententia senātūs inclīnāret ad pācem cum Pyrrhō
foedusque faciendum, nōn dubitāvit dīcere illa, quae 20
versibus persecūtus est Ennius:

> Quō vōbīs mentēs, rēctae quae stāre solēbant
> Antehāc, dēmentēs sēsē flexēre viāī?

cēteraque gravissimē; nōtum enim vōbīs carmen est;
et tamen ipsīus Appī exstat ōrātiō. Atque haec ille 25
ēgit septimō decimō annō post alterum cōnsulātum,
cum inter duōs cōnsulātūs annī decem interfuissent

cēnsorque ante superiōrem cōnsulātum fuisset; ex quō
intellegitur Pyrrhī bellō grandem sānē fuisse; et tamen
sīc ā patribus accēpimus. **17.** Nihil igitur afferunt,
quī in rē gerendā versārī senectūtem negant, similēs-
5 que sunt, ut sī quī gubernātōrem in nāvigandō nihil
agere dīcant, cum aliī mālōs scandant, aliī per forōs
cursent, aliī sentīnam exhauriant, ille autem clāvum
tenēns quiētus sedeat in puppī. Nōn facit ea, quae
juvenēs, at vērō multō majōra et meliōra facit. Nōn
10 vīribus aut vēlōcitāte aut celeritāte corporum rēs magnae geruntur, sed cōnsiliō, auctōritāte, sententiā; quibus nōn modo nōn orbārī, sed etiam augērī senectūs
solet. **18.** Nisi forte ego vōbīs, quī et mīles et tribūnus et lēgātus et cōnsul versātus sum in variō genere
15 bellōrum, cessāre nunc videor, cum bella nōn gerō;
at senātuī, quae sint gerenda, praescrībō, et quō modō;
Karthāginī male jam diū cōgitantī bellum multō ante
dēnūntiō; dē quā verērī nōn ante dēsinam, quam illam
excīsam esse cognōverō. **19.** Quam palmam utinam
20 dī immortālēs, Scīpiō, tibi reservent, ut avī reliquiās
persequāre! Cūjus ā morte tertius hīc et trīcēsimus
annus est, sed memoriam illīus virī omnēs excipient
annī cōnsequentēs. Annō ante mē cēnsōrem mortuus
est, novem annīs post meum cōnsulātum, cum cōnsul
25 iterum mē cōnsule creātus esset. Num igitur, sī ad
centēsimum annum vīxisset, senectūtis eum suae pae-
nitēret? Nec enim excursiōne nec saltū nec ēminus
hastīs aut comminus gladiīs ūterētur, sed cōnsiliō,
ratiōne, sententiā. Quae nisi essent in senibus, nōn
30 summum cōnsilium majōrēs nostrī appellāssent senātum. **20.** Apud Lacedaemoniōs quidem eī, quī am-

plissimum magistrātum gerunt, ut sunt, sīc etiam
nōminantur senēs. Quodsī legere aut audīre volētis
externa, maximās rēs pūblicās ab adulēscentibus labe-
factātās, ā senibus sustentātās et restitūtās reperiētis.

Cedo, quī vestram rem pūblicam tantam āmīsistis tám cito? 5

Sīc enim percontantur in Naevī poētae Lupō; respondentur et alia et hōc in prīmīs:

Prōvéniēbant ōrátōrēs noví, stultī, adulēscéntulī.

Temeritās est vidēlicet flōrentis aetātis, prūdentia
senēscentis. 10

Loss of memory

VII. **21.** At memoria minuitur. Crēdō, nisi eam
exerceās, aut etiam sī sīs nātūrā tardior. Themistoclēs omnium cīvium percēperat nōmina; num igitur
cēnsētis eum, cum aetāte prōcessisset, quī Aristīdēs
esset, Lȳsimachum salūtāre solitum? Equidem nōn 15
modo eōs nōvī, quī sunt, sed eōrum patrēs etiam et
avōs, nec sepulcra legēns vereor, quod ajunt, nē memoriam perdam; hīs enim ipsīs legendīs in memoriam
redeō mortuōrum. Nec vērō quemquam senem audīvī
oblītum, quō locō thēsaurum obruisset; omnia, quae 20
cūrant, meminērunt, vadimōnia cōnstitūta, quis sibi,
cui ipsī dēbeant. **22.** Quid jūris cōnsultī, quid ponti-
ficēs, quid augurēs, quid philosophī senēs? Quam
multa meminērunt! Manent ingenia senibus, modo
permaneat studium et industria, neque ea sōlum in 25
clārīs et honōrātīs virīs, sed in vītā etiam prīvātā et
quiētā.

The poet Sophocles and others

Sophoclēs ad summam senectūtem tragoediās fēcit;
quod propter studium cum rem neglegere familiārem
vidērētur, ā fīliīs in jūdicium vocātus est, ut,
quem ad modum nostrō mōre male rem gerentibus
5 patribus bonīs interdīcī solet, sīc illum quasi dēsipi-
entem ā rē familiārī removērent jūdicēs. Tum senex
dīcitur eam fābulam, quam in manibus habēbat et
proximē scrīpserat, Oedipum Colōnēum, recitāsse jūdi-
cibus quaesīsseque, num illud carmen dēsipientis vidē-
10 rētur. Quō recitātō sententiīs jūdicum est līberātus.
23. Num igitur hunc, num Homērum, num Hēsiodum,
Simōnidem, Stēsichorum, num, quōs ante dīxī, Īso-
cratēn, Go giān, num philosophōrum prīncipēs, Pȳtha-
goram, Dēmocritum, num Platōnem, num Xenocratēn,
15 num posteā Zēnōnem, Cleanthem aut eum, quem vōs
etiam vīdistis Rōmae, Diogenem Stōicum, coēgit in
suīs studiīs obmūtēscere senectūs? An in omnibus hīs
studiōrum agitātiō vītae aequālis fuit? **24.** Age, ut
ista dīvīna studia omittāmus, possum nōmināre ex
20 agrō Sabīnō rūsticōs Rōmānōs, vīcīnōs et familiārēs
meōs, quibus absentibus numquam ferē ūlla in agrō
majōra opera fiunt, nōn serendīs, nōn percipiendīs,
nōn condendīs frūctibus. Quamquam in aliīs minus
hōc mīrum est; nēmō enim est tam senex, quī sē an-
25 num nōn putet posse vīvere; sed īdem in eīs ēlabōrant,
quae sciunt nihil ad sē omnīnō pertinēre:

Serít arborḗs, quae alterī saeclō prṓsint,

ut ait Stātius noster in Synephēbīs. **25.** Nec vērō
dubitat agricola, quamvīs sit senex, quaerentī, cui

serat, respondēre: '*Dīs immortālibus, quī mē nōn acci-*
pere modo haec ā majōribus voluērunt, sed etiam posterīs
prōdere.'

VIII.   Et melius Caecilius dē sene alterī saeculō
prōspiciente quam illud īdem: 5

> Edepól, senectūs, sí nīl quicquam aliúd vitī
> Appórtēs tēcum, quom ádvenīs, ūnum íd sat est,
> Quod díū vīvendō múlta, quae nōn vólt, videt.

Et multa fortasse, quae volt! Atque in ea, quae nōn
volt, saepe etiam adulēscentia incurrit. Illud vērō 10
īdem Caecilius vitiōsius:

> Tum equidem ín senectā hōc dēputō misérrimum,
> Sentíre eā aetāte śumpse esse odiōsum álterī.

Jūcundum potius quam odiōsum. **26.** Ut enim adulēscentibus bonā indole praeditīs sapientēs senēs dē- 15
lectantur leviorque fit senectūs eōrum, quī ā juventūte
coluntur et dīliguntur, sīc adulēscentēs senum prae-
ceptīs gaudent, quibus ad virtūtum studia dūcuntur;
nec minus intellegō mē vōbīs quam mihi vōs esse jū-
cundōs. Sed vidētis, ut senectūs nōn modo languida 20
atque iners nōn sit, vērum etiam sit operōsa et semper
agēns aliquid et mōliēns, tāle scīlicet, quāle cūjusque
studium in superiōre vītā fuit.

Many even continue the pursuit of knowledge in old age. — Solon

Quid, quī etiam addiscunt aliquid? ut et Solōnem
versibus glōriantem vidēmus, quī sē cottīdiē aliquid addis- 25
centem dīcit senem fierī, et ego fēcī, quī litterās Graecās
senex didicī; quās quidem sīc avidē arripuī, — quasi
diūturnam sitim explēre cupiēns, — ut ea ipsa mihi nōta
ɛssent, quibus mē nunc exemplīs ūtī vidētis. Quod cum

fēcisse Sōcratem in fidibus audīrem, vellem equidem
etiam illud (discēbant enim fidibus antīquī), sed in
litterīs certē ēlabōrāvī.

The second charge; lack of physical strength. Strength not neces-
sary in old age

IX. 27. Nec nunc quidem vīrēs dēsīderō adulēs-
5 centis (is enim erat locus alter de vitiīs senectūtis),
nōn plūs, quam adulēscēns taurī aut elephantī dēsī-
derābam. Quod est, eō decet ūtī et, quicquid agās,
agere prō vīribus. Quae enim vōx potest esse contemptior quam Milōnis Crotōniātae? Quī cum jam
10 senex esset athlētāsque sē exercentēs in curriculō
vidēret, aspexisse lacertōs suōs dīcitur illacrimānsque
dīxisse: '*At hī quidem mortuī jam sunt.*' Nōn vērō
tam istī quam tū ipse, nūgātor! Neque enim ex tē
umquam es nōbilitātus, sed ex lateribus et lacertīs
15 tuīs. Nihil Sex. Aelius tāle, nihil multīs annīs ante
Ti. Coruncānius, nihil modo P. Crassus, ā quibus jūra
cīvibus praescrībēbantur; quōrum ūsque ad extrēmum
spīritum est prōvecta prūdentia. 28. Ōrātor metuō
nē languēscat senectūte; est enim mūnus ejus nōn
20 ingenī sōlum, sed laterum etiam et vīrium. Omnīnō
canōrum illud in vōce splendēscit etiam nesciŏ quō
pactō in senectūte, quod equidem adhūc nŏn āmīsī.
et vidētis annōs; sed tamen est decōrus senis sermō
quiētus et remissus, facitque per sē ipsa sibi audien-
25 tiam disertī senis cōmpta et mītis ōrātiō. Quam sī
ipse exsequī nequeās, possīs tamen Scīpiōnī praecipere
et Laeliō. Quid enim est jūcundius senectūte stīpātā
studiīs juventūtis? 29. An nē illās quidem vīrēs

senectūtī relinquimus, ut adulēscentēs doceat, īnsti-
tuat, ad omne officī mūnus īnstruat? Quō quidem
opere quid potest esse praeclārius? Mihi vērō et Cn.
et P. Scīpiōnēs et avī tuī duo, L. Aemilius et P. Āfri-
cānus, comitātū nōbilium juvenum fortūnātī vidēban- 5
tur, nec ūllī bonārum artium magistrī nōn beātī
putandī, quamvīs cōnsenuerint vīrēs atque dēfēcerint.
Etsī ista ipsa dēfectiō vīrium adulēscentiae vitiīs efficitur saepius quam senectūtis; libīdinōsa enim et intemperāns adulēscentia effētum corpus trādit senectūtī. 10
30. Cȳrus quidem apud Xenophōntem eō sermōne,
quem moriēns habuit, cum admodum senex esset, negat
sē umquam sēnsisse senectūtem suam imbēcilliōrem
factam, quam adulēscentia fuisset. Ego L. Metellum
meminī puer, quī cum quadrienniō post alterum cōn- 15
sulātum pontifex maximus factus esset, vīgintī et duōs
annōs eī sacerdōtiō praefuit, ita bonīs esse vīribus
extrēmō tempore aetātis, ut adulēscentiam nōn requī-
reret. Nihil necesse est mihi dē mē ipsō dīcere,
quamquam est id quidem senīle aetātīque nostrae 20
concēditur.

Nestor as an example; others

X. 31. Vidētisne, ut apud Homērum saepissimē
Nestor dē virtūtibus suīs praedicet? Tertiam jam
enim aetātem hominum vidēbat, nec erat eī verendum, ne vēra praedicāns dē sē nimis vidērētur aut 25
īnsolēns aut loquāx. Etenim, ut ait Homērus, '*ex
ejus linguā melle dulcior fluēbat ōrātiō,*' quam ad suāvitātem nūllīs egēbat corporis vīribus. Et tamen dux
ille Graeciae nūsquam optat, ut Ajācis similēs habeat

decem, sed ut Nestoris; quod sī sibi acciderit, nōn
dubitat, quīn brevī sit Trōja peritūra. 32. Sed
redeō ad mē. Quārtum agō annum et octōgēsimum;
vellem equidem idem possem glōriārī, quod Cȳrus, sed
5 tamen hōc queō dīcere, nōn mē quidem eīs esse vīribus,
quibus aut mīles bellō Pūnicō aut quaestor eōdem
bellō aut cōnsul in Hispāniā fuerim aut quadrienniō
post, cum tribūnus mīlitāris dēpugnāvī apud Ther-
mopylās M'. Glabriōne cōnsule, sed tamen, ut vōs
10 vidētis, nōn plānē mē ēnervāvit, nōn afflīxit senectūs,
nōn Cūria vīrēs meās dēsīderat, nōn Rōstra, nōn amīcī,
nōn clientēs, nōn hospitēs. Nec enim umquam sum
assēnsus veterī illī laudātōque prōverbiō, quod monet
mātūrē fierī senem, sī diū velīs senex esse. Ego vērō
15 mē minus diū senem esse māllem quam esse senem,
ante quam essem. Itaque nēmō adhūc convenīre mē
voluit, cui fuerim occupātus. 33. At minus habeō
vīrium quam vestrum utervīs. Nē vōs quidem T.
Pontī centuriōnis vīrēs habētis; num idcircō est ille
20 praestantior? Moderātiō modo vīrium adsit, et tantum, quantum potest quisque, nītātur; nē ille nōn
magnō dēsīderiō tenēbitur vīrium. Olympiae per stadium ingressus esse Milō dīcitur, cum umerīs susti-
nēret bovem. Utrum igitur hās corporis an Pȳthagorae
25 tibi mālīs vīrēs ingenī darī? Dēnique istō bonō ūtāre,
dum adsit; cum absit, nē requīrās; nisi forte adulēscentēs pueritiam, paululum aetāte prōgressī adulēscentiam dēbent requīrere. Cursus est certus aetātis
et ūna via nātūrae, eaque simplex, suaque cuique
30 partī aetātis tempestīvitās est data, ut et īnfīrmitās
puerōrum et ferōcitās juvenum et gravitās jam cōn-

stantis aetātis et senectūtis mātūritās nātūrāle quiddam habeat, quod suō tempore percipī dēbeat. **34.**
Audīre tē arbitror, Scīpiō, hospes tuus avītus Masinissa
quae faciat hodiē nōnāgintā nātus annōs; cum ingressus iter pedibus sit, in equum omnīnō nōn ascen- 5
dere, cum autem equō, ex equō nōn dēscendere, nūllō
imbrī, nūllō frīgore addūcī, ut capite opertō sit, summam esse in eō siccitātem corporis, itaque omnia exsequī
rēgis officia et mūnera. Potest igitur exercitātiō et
temperantia etiam in senectūte cōnservāre aliquid prīs- 10
tinī rōboris.

XI. Nē sint in senectūte vīrēs. Nē postulantur
quidem vīrēs ā senectūte. Ergō et lēgibus et īnstitūtīs
vacat aetās nostra mūneribus eīs, quae nōn possunt
sine vīribus sustinērī. Itaque nōn modo, quod nōn 15
possumus, sed nē quantum possumus quidem cōgimur.
35. At multī ita sunt imbēcillī senēs, ut nūllum officī
aut omnīnō vītae mūnus exsequī possint. At id quidem nōn proprium senectūtis vitium est, sed commūne
valētūdinis. Quam fuit imbēcillus P. Āfricānī fīlius, 20
is quī tē adoptāvit, quam tenuī aut nūllā potius valē-
tūdine! Quod nī ita fuisset, alterum illud exstitisset
lūmen cīvitātis; ad paternam enim magnitūdinem
animī doctrīna ūberior accesserat. Quid mīrum igitur
in senibus, sī īnfirmī sunt aliquandō, cum id nē adu- 25
lēscentēs quidem effugere possint? Resistendum,
Laelī et Scīpiō, senectūtī est, ejusque vitia dīligentiā
compēnsanda sunt; pugnandum, tamquam contrā mor-
bum, sīc contrā senectūtem. **36.** Habenda ratiō valētūdinis; ūtendum exercitātiōnibus modicīs; tantum cibī 30
et pōtiōnis adhibendum, ut reficiantur vīrēs, nōn oppri-

mantur. Nec vērō corporī sōlum subveniendum est,
sed mentī atque animō multō magis; nam haec quoque, nisi tamquam lūminī oleum īnstīllēs, exstinguuntur
senectūte. Et corpora quidem exercitātiōnum dēfatī-
5 gātiōne ingravēscunt, animī autem exercendō levantur.
Nam quōs ait Caecilius cōmicōs stultōs senēs, hōs significat crēdulōs, oblīviōsōs, dissolūtōs, quae vitia sunt
nōn senectūtis, sed inertis, ignāvae, somniculōsae senectūtis. Ut petulantia, ut libīdō magis est adulē-
10 scentium quam senum, nec tamen omnium adulēscen-
tium, sed nōn probōrum, sīc ista senīlis stultitia, quae
dēlīrātiō appellārī solet, senum levium est, nōn omnium. **37.** Quattuor rōbustōs fīliōs, quīnque fīliās,
tantam domum, tantās clientēlās Appius regēbat et
15 caecus et senex; intentum enim animum tamquam
arcum habēbat nec languēscēns succumbēbat senectūtī;
tenēbat nōn modo auctōritātem, sed etiam imperium
in suōs, metuēbant servī, verēbantur līberī, cārum
omnēs habēbant; vigēbat in illā domō patrius mōs et
20 disciplīna. **38.** Ita enim senectūs honesta est, sī sē
ipsa dēfendit, sī jūs suum retinet, sī nēminī ēmanci-
pāta est, sī ūsque ad ultimum spīritum dominātur in
suōs. Ut enim adulēscentem, in quō est senīle aliquid,
sīc senem, in quō est aliquid adulēscentis, probō;
25 quod quī sequitur, corpore senex esse poterit, animō
numquam erit. Septimus mihi liber Orīginum est in
manibus, omnia antīquitātis monumenta colligō, causārum illūstrium, quāscumque dēfendī, nunc cum
maximē cōnficiō ōrātiōnēs, jūs augurium, pontificium,
30 cīvīle trāctō, multum etiam Graecīs litterīs ūtor Pȳ-
thagorēōrumque mōre, exercendae memoriae grātiā,

quid quōque diē dīxerim, audierim, ēgerim, commemorō vesperī. Haec sunt exercitātiōnēs ingenī, haec
curricula mentis, in hīs dēsūdāns atque ēlabōrāns corporis vīrēs nōn magnō opere dēsīderō. Adsum amīcīs,
veniō in senātum frequēns ultrōque afferō rēs multum 5
et diū cōgitātās eāsque tueor animī, nōn corporis vīribus. Quas sī exsequī nequīrem, tamen mē lectulus
meus oblectāret ea ipsa cōgitantem, quae jam agere
nōn possem; sed ut possim, facit ācta vīta. Semper
enim in hīs studiīs labōribusque vīventī nōn intellegi- 10
tur quandō obrēpat senectūs. Ita sēnsim sine sēnsū
aetās senēscit nec subitō frangitur, sed diūturnitāte
exstinguitur.

The third charge: old age deprived of pleasure

XII. **39.** Sequitur tertia vituperātiō senectūtis,
quod eam carēre dīcunt voluptātibus. Ō praeclārum 15
mūnus aetātis, siquidem id aufert ā nōbīs, quod est
in adulēscentiā vitiōsissimum! Accipite enim, optimī
adulēscentēs, veterem ōrātiōnem Archȳtae Tarentīnī,
magnī in prīmīs et praeclārī virī, quae mihi trādita
est, cum essem adulēscēns Tarentī cum Q. Maximō. 20

Pleasure the greatest bane that afflicts mankind

Nūllam capitāliōrem pestem quam voluptātem corporis
hominibus dīcēbat ā nātūrā datam, cūjus voluptātis
avidae libīdinēs temere et effrēnātē ad potiendum in-
citārentur. **40.** Hinc patriae prōditiōnēs, hinc rērum
pūblicārum ēversiōnēs, hinc cum hostibus clandestīna 25
colloquia nāscī, nūllum dēnique scelus, nūllum malum
facinus esse, ad quod suscipiendum nōn libīdō voluptā-

tis impelleret, stupra vērō et adulteria et omne tāle
flāgitium nūllīs excitārī aliīs illecebrīs nisi voluptātis;
cumque hominī sīve Nātūra sīve quis deus nihil mente
praestābilius dedisset, huic dīvīnō mūnerī ac dōnō nihil
5 tam esse inimīcum quam voluptātem. **41.** Nec enim
libīdine dominante temperantiae locum esse, neque omnīnō in voluptātis rēgnō virtūtem posse cōnsistere.
Quod quō magis intellegī posset, fingere animō jubē-
bat tantā incitātum aliquem voluptāte corporis, quanta
10 percipi posset maxima. Nēminī cēnsēbat fore dubium,
quīn tam diū, dum ita gaudēret, nihil agitāre mente,
nihil ratiōne, nihil cōgitātiōne cōnsequī posset. Quōcircā nihil esse tam dētestābile tamque pestiferum
quam voluptātem, siquidem ea, cum major esset atque
15 longinquior, omne animī lūmen exstingueret. Haec
cum C. Pontiō Samnīte, patre ejus, ā quō Caudīnō
proeliō Sp. Postumius, T. Veturius cōnsulēs superātī
sunt, locūtum Archȳtam Nearchus Tarentīnus hospes
noster, quī in amīcitiā populī Rōmānī permānserat, sē
20 ā majōribus nātū accēpisse dīcēbat, cum quidem eī
sermōnī interfuisset Platō Athēniēnsis, quem Tarentum vēnisse L. Camillō, Ap. Claudiō cōnsulibus reperiō.

We should be grateful that old age saves us from the temptation of
youth

42. Quōrsus hōc? Ut intellegerētis, sī voluptātem
aspernārī ratiōne et sapientiā nōn possēmus, magnam
25 habendam esse senectūtī grātiam, quae efficeret, ut id
nōn lībēret, quod nōn oportēret. Impedit enim cōnsilium voluptās, ratiōnī inimīca est, mentis, ut ita
dīcam, praestringit oculōs nec habet ūllum cum virtūte

commercium. Invītus fēcī, ut fortissimī virī T. Flā-
minīnī frātrem, L. Flāminīnum, ē senātū ēicerem
septem annīs post quam cōnsul fuisset, sed notandam
putāvī libīdinem. Ille enim, cum esset cōnsul in
Galliā, exōrātus in convīviō ā scortō est, ut secūrī 5
ferīret aliquem eōrum, quī in vinculīs essent damnātī
reī capitālis. Hīc Titō frātre suō cēnsōre, quī proximus ante mē fuerat, ēlāpsus est; mihi vērō et Flaccō
neutiquam probārī potuit tam flāgitiōsa et tam perdita
libīdō, quae cum probrō prīvātō conjungeret imperī 10
dēdecus.

XIII. **43.** Saepe audīvī ex majōribus nātū, quī sē
porrō puerōs ā senibus audīsse dīcēbant, mīrārī solitum
C. Fabricium, quod, cum apud rēgem Pyrrhum lēgātus
esset, audīsset ā Thessalō Cīneā esse quendam Athēnīs, 15
quī sē sapientem profitērētur, eumque dīcere omnia,
quae facerēmus, ad voluptātem esse referenda. Quod
ex eō audientēs M'. Cūrium et Ti. Coruncānium optāre
solitōs, ut id Samnītibus ipsīque Pyrrhō persuādērētur,
quō facilius vincī possent, cum sē voluptātibus dedis- 20
sent. Vīxerat M'. Cūrius cum P. Deciō, quī quīn-
quenniō ante eum cōnsulem sē prō rē pūblicā quārtō
cōnsulātū dēvōverat; nōrat eundem Fabricius, nōrat
Coruncānius; quī cum ex suā vītā, tum ex ejus, quem
dīcō, Decī, factō jūdicābant esse profectō aliquid nātūrā 25
pulchrum atque praeclārum, quod suā sponte peterētur,
quodque sprētā et contemptā voluptāte optimus quisque sequerētur. **44.** Quōrsus igitur tam multa dē
voluptāte? Quia nōn modo vituperātiō nūlla, sed
etiam summa laus senectūtis est, quod ea voluptātēs 30
nūllās magnopere dēsīderat.

Many simple pleasures remain for old men

Caret epulīs exstrūctīsque mēnsīs et frequentibus
pōculīs, caret ergō etiam vīnulentiā et crūditāte
et īnsomniīs. Sed sī aliquid dandum est voluptātī,
quoniam ejus blanditiīs nōn facile obsistimus (dī-
5 vīnē enim Platō ēscam malōrum appellat voluptātem, quod eā vidēlicet hominēs capiantur ut piscēs),
quamquam immoderātīs epulīs caret senectūs, modicīs tamen convīviīs dēlectārī potest. C. Duellium
M. F., quī Poenōs classe prīmus dēvīcerat, redeun-
10 tem ā cēnā senem saepe vidēbam puer; dēlectābā-
tur cēreō fūnālī et tībīcine, quae sibi nūllō
exemplō prīvātus sūmpserat; tantum licentiae dabat
glōria. 45. Sed quid ego aliōs? Ad mē ipsum jam
revertar. Prīmum habuī semper sodālēs. Sodālitātēs
15 autem Magnae Mātris mē quaestōre cōnstitūtae sunt
sacrīs Īdaeīs acceptīs. Epulābar igitur cum sodāli-
bus omnīnō modicē, sed erat quīdam fervor aetātis;
quā prōgrediente omnia fīunt in diēs mītiōra. Neque
enim ipsōrum convīviōrum dēlectātiōnem voluptātibus
20 corporis magis quam coetū amīcōrum et sermōnibus
mētiēbar. Bene enim majōrēs accubitiōnem epulārem
amīcōrum, quia vītae conjūnctiōnem habēret, convīvium nōmināvērunt, melius quam Graecī, quī hōc
idem tum compōtātiōnem, tum concēnātiōnem vocant,
25 ut, quod in eō genere minimum est, id maximē probāre
videantur.

Pleasures of conversation

XIV. 46. Ego vērō propter sermōnis dēlectātiōnem
tempestīvīs quoque convīviīs dēlector, nec cum aequā-

íibus sōlum, quī paucī admodum restant, sed cum vestrā
etiam aetāte atque vōbīscum, habeōque senectūtī magnam grātiam, quae mihi sermōnis aviditātem auxit,
pōtiōnis et cibī sustulit. Quodsī quem etiam ista dēlectant (nē omnīnō bellum indīxisse videar voluptātī, 5
cūjus est fortasse quīdam nātūrālis modus), nōn intellegō nē in istīs quidem ipsīs voluptātibus carēre sēnsū
senectūtem. Mē vērō et magisteria dēlectant ā majō-
ríbus īnstitūta et is sermō, quī mōre majōrum ā summō
adhibētur in pōculō, et pōcula, sīcut in Symposiō Xe- 10
nophōntis est, minūta atque rōrantia, et refrīgerātiō
aestāte et vicissim aut sōl aut īgnis hībernus ; quae
quidem etiam in Sabīnīs persequī soleō convīviumque
vīcīnōrum cottīdiē compleō, quod ad multam noctem,
quam maximē possumus, variō sermōne prōdūcimus. 15
47. At nōn est voluptātum tanta quasi tītillātiō in
senibus. Crēdō, sed nē dēsīderātiō quidem; nihil
autem est molestum, quod nōn dēsīderēs. Bene Sophoclēs, cum ex eō quīdam jam affectō aetāte quaere-
ret, ūterēturne rēbus veneriīs: '*Dī meliōra!*' inquit ; 20
'*libenter vērō istinc sīcut ab dominō agrestī ac furiōsō
profūgī.*' Cupidīs enim rērum tālium odiōsum fortasse
et molestum est carēre, satiātīs vērō et explētīs jūcundius est carēre quam fruī. Quamquam nōn caret is
quī nōn dēsīderat; ergō hōc nōn dēsīderāre dīcō esse 25
jūcundius. **48.** Quodsī istīs ipsīs voluptātibus bona
aetās fruitur libentius, prīmum parvulīs fruitur rēbus,
ut dīximus, deinde eīs, quibus senectūs, etiamsī nōn
abundē potītur, nōn omnīnō caret. Ut Turpiōne Am-
biviō magis dēlectātur, quī in prīmā caveā spectat, dē- 30
lectātur tamen etiam, quī in ultimā, sīc adulēscentia

voluptātēs propter intuēns magis fortasse laetātur, sed
dēlectātur etiam senectūs, procul eās spectāns, tantum
quantum sat est.

Pleasures of study

49. At illa quantī sunt, animum tamquam ēmeri-
5 tīs stippendiīs libīdinis, ambitiōnis, contentiōnis, in-
imīcitiārum, cupiditātum omnium sēcum esse sēcum-
que, ut dīcitur, vīvere! Sī vērō habet aliquod
tamquam pābulum studī atque doctrīnae, nihil est
ōtiōsā senectūte jūcundius. Exercērī vidēbāmus in
10 studiō dīmētiendī paene caelī atque terrae C. Gallum,
familiārem patris tuī, Scīpiō. Quotiēns illum lūx noctū
aliquid dēscrībere ingressum, quotiēns nox oppressit,
cum māne coepisset! Quam dēlectābat eum dēfectiō-
nes sōlis et lūnae multō ante nōbīs praedīcere!
15 **50**. Quid in leviōribus studiīs, sed tamen acūtīs?
Quam gaudēbat bellō suō Pūnicō Naevius! Quam Tru-
culentō Plautus, quam Pseudolō! Vīdī etiam senem
Līvium; quī cum sex annīs ante quam ego nātus sum,
fābulam docuisset Centōne Tuditānōque cōnsulibus,
20 ūsque ad adulēscentiam meam prōcessit aetāte. Quid
dē P. Licinī Crassī et pontificiī et cīvīlis jūris studiō
loquar aut dē hūjus P. Scīpiōnis, quī hīs paucīs diēbus pontifex maximus factus est? Atque eōs omnēs,
quōs commemorāvī, hīs studiīs flagrantēs senēs vīdi-
25 mus. M. vērō Cethēgum, quem rēctē 'Suādae medullam' dīxit Ennius, quantō studiō exercērī in dīcendō
vidēbāmus etiam senem! Quae sunt igitur epulārum
aut lūdōrum aut scortōrum voluptātēs cum hīs voluptātibus comparandae? Atque haec quidem studia

doctrīnae; quae quidem prūdentibus et bene īnstitūtīs
pariter cum aetāte crēscunt, ut honestum illud Solōnis
sit, quod ait versiculō quōdam, ut ante dīxī, senēscere
sē multa in diēs addiscentem, quā voluptāte animī
nūlla certē potest esse major.   5

The pleasures of farming

XV. 51. Veniō nunc ad voluptātēs agricolārum,
quibus ego incrēdibiliter dēlector; quae nec ūllā im-
pediuntur senectūte et mihi ad sapientis vītam proximē
videntur accēdere.   Habent enim ratiōnem cum terrā,
quae numquam recūsat imperium nec umquam sine 10
ūsūrā reddit, quod accēpit, sed aliās minōre, plērumque
majōre cum fēnore.   Quamquam mē quidem nōn
frūctus modo, sed etiam ipsīus terrae vīs ac nātūra
dēlectat.   Quae cum gremiō mollītō ac subāctō spar-
sum sēmen excēpit, prīmum id occaecātum cohibet, 15
ex quō occātiō, quae hōc efficit, nōminātā est, deinde
tepefactum vapōre et compressū suō diffundit et ēlicit
herbēscentem ex eō viriditātem, quae nīxa fibrīs stirpium sēnsim adulēscit culmōque ērēcta geniculātō
vāgīnīs jam quasi pūbēscēns inclūditur; ē quibus 20
cum ēmersit, fundit frūgem spīcī ōrdine strūctam et
contrā avium minōrum morsūs mūnītur vāllō aristā-
rum. 52. Quid ego vītium ortūs, satūs, incrēmenta
commemorem? Satiārī dēlectātiōne nōn possum, ut
meae senectūtis requiētem oblectāmentumque nōscātis. 24
Omittō enim vim ipsam omnium, quae generantur ē
terrā; quae ex fīcī tantulō grānō aut ex acinī vīnāceō
aut ex cēterārum frūgum aut stirpium minūtissimīs
sēminibus tantōs truncōs rāmōsque prōcreet.   Malleolī,

plantae, sarmenta, vīvirādīcēs, prōpāginēs nōnne efficiunt, ut quemvīs cum admīrātiōne dēlectent? Vītis
quidem, quae nātūrā cadūca est et, nisi fulta est, fertur
ad terram, eadem, ut sē ērigat, clāviculīs suīs quasi
5 manibus, quicquid est nacta, complectitur; quam serpentem multiplicī lāpsū et errāticō ferrō amputāns
coërcet ars agricolārum, nē silvēscat sarmentīs et in
omnēs partēs nimia fundātur. 53. Itaque ineunte
vēre in eīs, quae relīcta sunt, exsistit tamquam ad
10 articulōs sarmentōrum ea, quae gemma dīcitur, ā quā
oriēns ūva sē ostendit, quae et sūcō terrae et calōre
sōlis augēscēns prīmō est peracerba gustātū, dein
mātūrāta dulcēscit vestītaque pampinīs nec modicō
tepōre caret et nimiōs sōlis dēfendit ārdōrēs. Quā
15 quid potest esse cum frūctū laetius, tum aspectū pulchrius? Cūjus quidem nōn ūtilitās mē sōlum, ut ante
dīxī, sed etiam cultūra et nātūra ipsa dēlectat, admini-
culōrum ōrdinēs, capitum jugātiō, religātiō et prōpā-
gātiō vītium, sarmentōrum ea, quam dīxī, aliōrum
20 amputātiō, aliōrum immissiō. Quid ego irrigātiōnēs,
quid fossiōnēs agrī repastinātiōnēsque prōferam, quibus fit multō terra fēcundior? Quid dē ūtilitāte loquar
stercorandī? 54. Dīxī in eō librō, quem dē rēbus rūs-
ticīs scrīpsī; dē quā doctus Hēsiodus nē verbum qui-
25 dem fēcit, cum dē cultūrā agrī scrīberet. At Homērus,
qui multīs, ut mihi vidētur, ante saeculīs fuit, Lāërtam
lēnientem dēsīderium, quod capiēbat ē fīliō, colentem
agrum et eum stercorantem facit. Nec vērō segetibus
sōlum et prātīs et vīneīs et arbustīs rēs rūsticae laetae
30 sunt, sed hortīs etiam et pōmāriīs, tum pecudum pāstū,
apium exāminibus, flōrum omnium varietāte. Nec

cōnsitiōnēs modo dēlectant, sed etiam īnsitiōnēs, quibus nihil invēnit agrī cultūra sollertius. **XVI. 55.** Possum persequī permulta oblectāmenta rērum rūsticārum, sed ea ipsa, quae dīxī, sentiō fuisse longiōra. Ignōscētis autem; nam et studiō rūsticārum 5 rērum prōvectus sum, et senectūs est nātūra loquācior, nē ab omnibus eam vitiīs videar vindicāre. Ergō in hāc vītā M'. Cūrius, cum dē Samnītibus, dē Sabīnīs, dē Pyrrhō triumphāsset, cōnsūmpsit extrēmum tempus aetātis. Cūjus quidem ego vīllam contemplāns (abest 10 enim nōn longē ā meā) admīrārī satis nōn possum vel hominis ipsīus continentiam vel temporum disciplīnam. Nam Cūriō ad focum sedentī magnum aurī pondus Samnītēs cum attulissent, repudiātī sunt; nōn enim aurum habēre praeclārum sibi vidērī dīxit, sed eīs, quī 15 habērent aurum, imperāre. **56.** Poteratne tantus animus efficere nōn jūcundam senectūtem? Sed veniō ad agricolās, nē ā mē ipsō recēdam. In agrīs erant tum senātōrēs, id est senēs, siquidem arantī L. Quīnctiō Cincinnātō nūntiātum est eum dictātōrem esse factum; 20 cūjus dictātōris jussū magister equitum C. Servīlius Ahāla Sp. Maelium rēgnum appetentem occupātum interēmit. Ā vīllā in senātum arcessēbātur et Cūrius et cēterī senēs, ex quō, quī eōs arcessēbant, viātōrēs nōminātī sunt. Num igitur hōrum senectūs miserā- 25 bilis fuit, quī sē agrī cultiōne oblectābant? Meā quidem sententiā haud sciō an nūlla beātior possit esse, neque sōlum officiō, quod hominum generī ūniversō cultūra agrōrum est salūtāris, sed et dēlectātiōne, quam dīxī, et saturitāte cōpiāque rērum omnium, quae ad 30 vīctum hominum, ad cultum etiam deōrum pertinent,

ut, quoniam haec quīdam dēsīderant, in grātiam jam
cum voluptāte redeāmus. Semper enim bonī assiduī-
que dominī referta cella vīnāria, oleāria, etiam penāria
est, vīllaque tōta locuplēs est, abundat porcō, haedō,
5 agnō, gallīnā, lacte, cāseō, melle. Jam hortum ipsī
agricolae succīdiam alteram appellant. Condītiōra
facit haec supervacāneīs etiam operīs aucupium atque
vēnātiō. **57.** Quid dē prātōrum viriditāte aut arborum ōrdinibus aut vīneārum olīvētōrumve speciē plūra
10 dīcam? Brevī praecīdam: Agrō bene cultō nihil potest
esse nec ūsū ūberius nec speciē ōrnātius; ad quem
fruendum nōn modo nōn retardat, vērum etiam invītat
atque allectat senectūs. Ubi enim potest illa aetās
aut calēscere vel aprīcātiōne melius vel īgnī aut vicis-
15 sim umbrīs aquīsve refrīgerārī salūbrius? **58.** Sibi
habeant igitur arma, sibi equōs, sibi hastās, sibi clā-
vam et pīlam, sibi natātiōnēs atque cursūs; nōbīs senibus ex lūsiōnibus multīs tālōs relinquant et tesserās,
— id ipsum ut lubēbit, quoniam sine eīs beāta esse
20 senectūs potest.

Xenophon's description of Cyrus, the Younger

XVII. **59.** Multās ad rēs perūtilēs Xenophōntis
librī sunt; quōs legite, quaesō, studiōsē, ut facitis.
Quam cōpiōsē ab eō agrī cultūra laudātur in eō librō,
quī est dē tuendā rē familiārī, quī Oeconomicus īnscrī-
25 bitur! Atque ut intellegātis nihil eī tam rēgāle vidērī
quam studium agrī colendī, Sōcratēs in eō librō loquitur cum Crītobūlō Cȳrum minōrem, Persārum rēgem,
praestantem ingeniō atque imperī glōriā, cum Lysander Lacedaemonius, vir summae virtūtis, vēnisset ad

eum Sardīs eīque lōna ā sociīs attulisset, et cēteris in
rēbus cōn:em ergā Lysandrum atque hūmānum fuisse
et eī quendam consaeptum agrum dīligenter cōnsitum
ostendisse. Cum autem admīrārētur Lysander et prō-
cēritātēs arborum et dīrēctōs in quīncūncem ōrdinēs et 5
humum subāctam atque pūram et suāvitātem odōrum,
quī afflārentur ex flōribus, tum eum dīxisse mīrārī sē
nōn modo dīligentiam, sed etiam sollertiam ejus, ā quō
essent illa dīmēnsa atque discrīpta; et Cȳrum respondisse: ' *Atquī ego ista sum omnia dīmēnsus; meī sunt* 10
ōrdinēs, mea discrīptiō, multae etiam istārum arborum
meā manū sunt satae.' Tum Lysandrum intuentem
purpuram ejus et nitōrem corporis ōrnātumque Persi-
cum multō aurō multīsque gemmīs dīxisse: ' *Rīte vērō*
tē, Cȳre, beātum ferunt, quoniam virtūtī tuae fortūna con- 15
jūncta est.' **60.** Hāc igitur fortūnā fruī licet senibus,
nec aetās impedit, quō minus et cēterārum rērum et
iu prīmīs agrī colendī studia teneāmus ūsque ad ultimum
tempus senectūtis. M. quidem Valerium Corvīnum
accēpimus ad centēsimum annum perdūxisse, cum esset, 20
āctā jam aetāte, in agrīs eōsque coleret; cūjus inter
prīmum et sextum cōnsulātum sex et quadrāgintā annī
interfuērunt. Ita, quantum spatium aetātis majōrēs
ad senectūtis initium esse voluērunt, tantus illī cursus
honōrum fuit; atque hūjus extrēma aetās hōc beātior 25
quam media, quod auctōritātis habēbat plūs, labōris
minus; apex est autem senectūtis auctōritās. **61.** Quanta
fuit in L. Caeciliō Metellō, quanta in A. Atīliō Cālātīnō!
in quem illud ēlogium :

Hunc ūnum plūrimae cōnsentiunt gentēs   **30**
Populī prīmārium fuisse virum.

Nōtum est tōtum carmen incīsum in sepulcrō. Jūre
igitur gravis, cūjus dē laudibus omnium esset fāma cōn-
sentiēns. Quem virum nūper P. Crassum, pontificem
maximum, quem posteā M. Lepidum, eōdem sacerdō-
5 tiō praeditum, vīdimus! Quid dē Paulō aut Āfricānō
loquar aut, ut jam ante, dē Maximō? quōrum nōn in
sententiā sōlum, sed etiam in nūtū residēbat auctōritās.
Habet senectūs, honōrāta praesertim, tantam auctōritātem, ut ea plūris sit quam omnēs adulēscentiae
10 voluptātēs.

Only high character can deserve praise

XVIII. 62. Sed in omnī ōrātiōne mementōte eam
mē senectūtem laudāre, quae fundāmentīs adulēscentiae cōnstitūta sit. Ex quō efficitur, id quod ego
magnō quondam cum assēnsū omnium dīxī, miseram
15 esse senectūtem, quae sē ōrātiōne dēfenderet. Nōn
cānī nec rūgae repente auctōritātem arripere possunt,
sed honestē ācta superior aetās frūctūs capit auctōritātis extrēmōs. 63. Haec enim ipsa sunt honōrābilia,
quae videntur levia atque commūnia, salūtārī, appetī,
20 dēcēdī, assurgī, dēdūcī, redūcī, cōnsulī; quae et apud
nōs et in aliīs cīvitātibus, ut quaeque optimē mōrāta
est, ita dīligentissimē observantur. Lysandrum Lace-
daemonium, cūjus modo fēcī mentiōnem, dīcere ajunt
solitum Lacedaemonem esse honestissimum domicilium
25 senectūtis; nūsquam enim tantum tribuitur aetātī, nūsquam est senectūs honōrātior. Quīn etiam memoriae
prōditum est, cum Athēnīs lūdīs quīdam in theātrum
grandis nātū vēnisset, magnō cōnsessū locum nūsquam
eī datum ā suīs cīvibus; cum autem ad Lacedaemoniōs

accessisset, quī lēgātī cum essent, certō in locō cōnsē-
derant, cōnsurrēxisse omnēs illī dīcuntur et senem
sessum recēpisse. **64.** Quibus cum ā cūnctō cōnsessū
plausus esset multiplex datus, dīxisse ex eīs quendam
Athēniēnsēs scīre, quae rēcta essent, sed facere nōlle. 5
Multa in vestrō collēgiō praeclāra, sed hōc, dē quō
agimus, in prīmīs, quod, ut quisque aetāte antecēdit,
ita sententiae prīncipātum tenet, neque sōlum honōre
antecēdentibus, sed eīs etiam, quī cum imperiō sunt,
majōrēs nātū augurēs antepōnuntur. Quae sunt igitur 10
voluptātēs corporis cum auctōritātis praemiīs comparandae? Quibus quī splendidē ūsī sunt, eī mihi videntur fābulam aetātis perēgisse nec tamquam inexercitātī
histriōnēs in extrēmō āctū corruisse.

65. At sunt mōrōsī et anxiī et īrācundī et difficilēs 15
senēs. Sī quaerimus, etiam avārī; sed haec mōrum
vitia sunt, nōn senectūtis. Ac mōrōsitās tamen et ea
vitia, quae dīxī, habent aliquid excūsātiōnis nōn illīus
quidem jūstae, sed quae probārī posse videātur; con-
temnī sē putant, dēspicī, illūdī; praetereā in fragilī 20
corpore odiōsa omnis offēnsiō est. Quae tamen omnia
dulciōra fiunt et mōribus bonīs et artibus, idque cum
in vītā, tum in scaenā intellegī potest ex eīs frātribus,
quī in Adelphīs sunt. Quanta in alterō dīritās, in
alterō cōmitās! Sīc sē rēs habet: ut enim nōn omne 25
vīnum, sic nōn omnis nātūra vetustāte coacēscit. Se-
vēritātem in senectūte probō, sed eam, sīcut alia, modi
cam, acerbitātem nūllō modō. **66.** Avāritia vērō
senīlis quid sibi velit, nōn intellegō; potest enim quicquam esse absurdius quam, quō viae minus restet, eō 30
plūs viāticī quaerere?

The fourth charge: nearness of death

XIX. Quārta restat causa, quae maximē angere
atque sollicitam habēre nostram aetātem vidētur,
appropinquātiō mortis, quae certē ā senectūte nōn
potest esse longē. Ō miserum senem, quī mortem
5 contemnendam esse in tam longā aetāte nōn vīderit!
quae aut plānē neglegenda est, sī omnīnō exstinguit
animum, aut etiam optanda, sī aliquō eum dēdūcit,
ubi sit futūrus aeternus. **67.** Atquī tertium certē nihil
invenīrī potest; quid igitur timeam, sī aut nōn miser
10 post mortem aut beātus etiam futūrus sum? Quamquam quis est tam stultus, quamvīs sit adulēscēns, cui
sit explōrātum sē ad vesperum esse vīctūrum? Quīn
etiam aetās illa multō plūrēs quam nostra cāsūs mortis
habet; facilius in morbōs incidunt adulēscentēs, gra-
15 vius aegrōtant, trīstius cūrantur. Itaque paucī veni-
unt ad senectūtem; quod nī ita accideret, melius et
prūdentius vīverētur. Mēns enim et ratiō et cōnsilium
in senibus est; quī sī nūllī fuissent, nūllae omnīnō
cīvītātēs fuissent. Sed redeō ad mortem impendentem.

Death comes to all periods of life. The old man has achieved what
the young merely hope

20 Quod est istud crīmen senectūtis, cum id eī videātiⁿ
cum adulēscentiā esse commūne? **68.** Sēnsī ego in
optimō fīliō, tū in exspectātīs ad amplissimam dignitātem frātribus, Scīpiō, mortem omnī aetātī esse com-
mūnem. At spērat adulēscēns diū sē vīctūrum, quod
25 spērāre idem senex nōn potest. Īnsipienter spērat.
Quid enim stultius quam incerta prō certīs habēre, falsa
prō vērīs? At senex nē quod spēret quidem habet.

At est eō meliōre condiciōne quam adulēscēns, quoniam id, quod ille spērat, hīc cōnsecūtus est; ille vult
diū vīvere, hic diū vīxit. 69. Quamquam, o dī bonī!
quid est in hominis nātūrā diū? Dā enim summum
tempus, exspectēmus Tartessiōrum rēgis aetātem (fuit 5
enim, ut scrīptum videō, Arganthōnius quīdam Gādi-
bus, qui octōgintā rēgnāvit annōs, centum vīgintī
vīxit) — sed mihi nē diūturnum quidem quicquam
vidētur, in quō est aliquid extrēmum. Cum enim id
advēnit, tum illud, quod praeteriit, efflūxit; tantum 10
remanet, quod virtūte et rēctē factīs cōnsecūtus sīs;
hōrae quidem cēdunt et diēs et mēnsēs et annī, nec
praeteritum tempus umquam revertitur, nec, quid se-
quātur, scīrī potest; quod cuique temporis ad vīvendum datur, eō dēbet esse contentus.   15

"Act well thy part; there all the honor lies"

70. Neque enim histriōnī, ut placeat, peragenda fābula
est, modo, in quōcumque fuerit āctū, probētur, neque sapientī ūsque ad 'Plaudite' veniendum est. Breve enim
tempus aetātis satis longum est ad bene honestēque
vīvendum; sīn prōcesserit longius, nōn magis dolendum 20
est, quam agricolae dolent, praeteritā vērnī temporis suā-
vitāte, aestātem autumnumque vēnisse. Vēr enim tamquam adulēscentiam significat ostenditque frūctūs fu-
tūrōs, reliqua autem tempora dēmetendis frūctibus et
percipiendīs accommodāta sunt. 71. Frūctus autem se- 25
nectūtis est, ut saepe dīxī, ante partōrum bonōrum
memoria et cōpia. Omnia autem, quae secundum
nātūram fīunt, sunt habenda in bonīs. Quid est autem
tam secundum nātūram quam senibus ēmorī? Quod

idem contingit adulēscentĭbus adversante et repugnante nātūrā.

The naturalness of death in case of the old

Itaque adulēscentēs mihi morī sīc videntur, ut
cum aquae multitūdine flammae vīs opprimitur, senēs
5 autem sīc, ut cum suā sponte, nūlla adhibitā vī, cōn-
sūmptus īgnis exstinguitur; et quasi pōma ex arbori-
bus, crūda sī sunt, vī āvelluntur, sī mātūra et cocta,
dēcidunt, sīc vītam adulēscentibus vīs aufert, ser.ibus
mātūritās; quae quidem mihi tam jūcunda est, ut,
10 quō propius ad mortem accēdam, quasi terram vidēre
videar aliquandōque in portum ex longā nāvigātiōne
esse ventūrus.

XX. **72.** Senectūtis autem nūllus est certus terminus, rēctēque in eā vīvitur, quoad mūnus officī exsequī
15 et tuērī possīs mortemque contemnere; ex quō fit, ut
animōsior etiam senectūs sit quam adulēscentia et fortior. Hōc illud est, quod Pīsistratō tyrannō ā Solōne
respōnsum est, cum illī quaerentī, quā tandem rē frētus sibi tam audāciter obsisteret, respondisse dīcitur;
20 '*Senectūte.*' Sed vīvendī est fīnis optimus, cum inte-
grā mente certīsque sēnsibus opus ipsa suum eadem,
quae coagmentāvit, nātūra dissolvit. Ut nāvem, ut
aedificium īdem dēstruit facillimē, quī cōnstrūxit, sīc
hominem eadem optimē, quae conglūtināvit, nātūra
25 dissolvit. Jam omnis conglūtinātiō recēns aegrē, in-
veterāta facile dīvellitur. Ita fit, ut illud breve vītae
reliquum nec avidē appetendum senibus nec sine causā
dēserendum sit. **73.** Vetatque Pȳthagorās injussū im-
perātōris, id est deī, dē praesidiō et statiōne vītae dē-

cedere. Solōnis quidem sapientis ēlogium est, quō sē
negat velle suam mortem dolōre amīcōrum et lāmentīs
vacāre. Vult, crēdō, sē esse cārum suīs; sed haud
sciō an melius Ennius:

> Nēmō mē dacrumīs decoret neque fūnera flētū   5
> Faxit.

Nōn cēnset lūgendam esse mortem, quam immortālitās
cōnsequātur. **74.** Jam sēnsus moriendī aliquis esse
potest, isque ad exiguum tempus, praesertim senī; post
mortem quidem sēnsus aut optandus aut nūllus est. 10

*One should cultivate a disregard of death. Famous examples of
this spirit*

Sed hōc meditātum ab adulēscentiā dēbet esse, mortem
ut neglegāmus, sine quā meditātiōne tranquillō animō
esse nēmō potest. Moriendum enim certē est, et incertum an hōc ipsō diē. Mortem igitur omnibus hōrīs
impendentem timēns quī poterit animō cōnsistere? 15
De quā nōn ita longā disputātiōne opus esse vidētur,
cum recorder nōn L. Brūtum, quī in līberandā patriā
est interfectus, **75.** nōn duōs Deciōs, quī ad voluntā-
riam mortem cursum equōrum incitāvērunt, nōn M.
Atīlium, quī ad supplicium est profectus, ut fidem 20
hostī datam cōnservāret, nōn duōs Scīpiōnēs, quī iter
Poenīs vel corporibus suīs obstruere voluērunt, nōn
avum tuum L. Paulum, quī morte luit collēgae in Can-
nēnsī ignōminiā temeritātem, nōn M. Marcellum, cūjus
interitum nē crūdēlissimus quidem hostis honōre se- 25
pultūrae carēre passus est, sed legiōnēs nostrās. quod
scrīpsī in Orīginibus, in eum locum saepe profectās
alacrī animō et ērēctō, unde sē reditūrās numquam

arbiträrentur. Quod igitur adulēscentēs, et eī quidem
nōn sōlum indoctī, sed etiam rūsticī, contemnunt, id
doctī senēs extimēscent? **76.** Omnīnō, ut mihi quidem vidētur, studiōrum omnium satietās vītae facit
5 satietātem. Sunt pueritiae studia certa; num igitur
ea dēsīderant adulēscentēs? Sunt ineuntis adulēscentiae; num ea cōnstāns jam requīrit aetās, quae media
dīcitur? Sunt etiam ejus aetātis; ne ea quidem quae-
runtur in senectūte. Sunt extrēma quaedam studia
10 senectūtis; ergō, ut superiōrum aetātum studia occidunt, sīc occidunt etiam senectūtis; quod cum ēvenit,
satietās vītae tempus mātūrum mortis affert.

Cato's personal convictions: foundations of his belief

XXI. 77. Equidem nōn videō, cūr, quid ipse sentiam de morte, nōn audeam vōbīs dīcere, quod eō
15 cernere mihi melius videor, quō ab eā propius absum.
Ego vestrōs patrēs, tuum, Scīpiō tuumque, Laelī, virōs
clārissimōs mihique amīcissimōs, vīvere arbitror, et
eam quidem vītam, quae est sōla vīta nōminanda.
Nam, dum sumus inclūsī in hīs compāgibus corporis,
20 mūnere quōdam necessitātis et gravī opere perfungi-
mur; est enim animus caelestis ex altissimō domiciliō
dēpressus et quasi dēmersus in terram, locum dīvīnae
nātūrae aeternitātīque contrārium. Sed crēdō deōs
immortālēs sparsisse animōs in corpora hūmāna, ut
25 essent, quī terrās tuērentur, quīque caelestium ōrdi-
nem contemplantēs imitārentur eum vītae modō atque
cōnstantiā. Nec mē sōlum ratiō ac disputātiō impulit,
ut ita crēderem, sed nōbilitās etiam summōrum philosophōrum et auctōritās. **78.** Audiēbam Pythagoram

Pȳthagoreōsque, incolās paene nostrōs, quī essent
Italicī philosophī quondam nōminātī, numquam dubi-
tāsse, quīn ūniversā mente dīvīnā dēlībātōs animōs
habērēmus. Dēmōnstrābantur mihi praetereā, quae
Sōcratēs suprēmō vītae diē dē immortālitāte animōrum 5
disseruisset, is quī esset omnium sapientissimus ōrā-
culō Apollinis jūdicātus. Quid multa? Sic persuāsī
mihi, sīc sentiō, cum tanta celeritās animōrum sit,
tanta memoria praeteritōrum futūrōrumque prūdentia,
tot artēs, tantae scientiae, tot inventa, nōn posse eam 10
nātūram, quae rēs eās contineat, esse mortālem; cumque semper agitētur animus nec prīncipium mōtūs
habeat, quia sē ipse moveat, nē fīnem quidem habi-
tūrum esse mōtūs, quia numquam sē ipse sit relictū-
rus; et, cum simplex animī esset nātūra neque habēret 15
in sē quicquam admixtum dispār suī atque dissimile,
nōn posse eum dīvidī; quod sī nōn posset, nōn posse
interīre; magnōque esse argūmentō hominēs scīre plē-
raque ante quam nātī sint, quod jam puerī, cum artēs
difficilēs discant, ita celeriter rēs innumerābilēs arripi- 20
ant, ut eās nōn tum prīmum accipere videantur, sed
reminīscī et recordārī.   Haec Platōnis ferē.

Testimony of Cyrus the Elder

XXII. **79.** Apud Xenophōntem autem moriēns
Cȳrus Major haec dīcit: '*Nōlīte arbitrārī, ō mihi*
cārissimī fīliī, mē, cum ā vōbīs discesserō, nūsquam 25
aut nūllum fore. Nec enim, dum eram vōbīscum, ani-
mum meum vidēbātis, sed eum esse in hōc corpore ex cis
rēbus, quās gerēbam, intellegēbātis. Eundem igitur esse
crēditōte, etiamsī nūllum vidēbitis. **80.** *Nec vērō clārō-*

*rum virōrum post mortem honōrēs permanērent, sī nihil
eōrum ipsōrum animī efficerent, quo diūtius memoriam
suī tenērēmus.   Mihi quidem numquam persuādērī potuit
animōs, dum in corporibus essent mortālibus, vīvere, cum*
5 *excessissent ex eīs, ēmorī, nec vērō tum animum esse īn-
sipientem, cum ex īnsipientī corpore ēvāsisset, sed cum
omnī admixtiōne corporis līberātus pūrus et integer esse
coepisset, tum esse sapientem.   Atque etiam cum hominis
nātūra morte dissolvitur, cēterārum rērum perspicuum est*
10 *quō quaeque discēdat;   abeunt enim illūc omnia, unde
orta sunt, animus autem sōlus, nec cum adest nec cum
discēdit, appāret.   Jam vērō vidētis nihil esse mortī tam
simile quam somnum.* **81.** *Atquī dormientium animī
maximē dēclārant dīvīnitātem suam;   multa enim, cum*
15 *remissī et līberī sunt, futūra prōspiciunt.   Ex quō intellegitur, quālēs futūrī sint, cum sē plānē corporis vinculīs
relaxāverint.   Quārē, sī haec ita sunt, sīc mē colitōte,'*
inquit, *'ut deum;   sīn ūnā est interitūrus animus cum
corpore, vōs tamen deōs verentēs, quī hanc omnem pul-*
20 *chritūdinem   tuentur   et   regunt,   memoriam   nostrī   piē
inviolātēque servābitis.'* Cȳrus quidem haec moriēns;
nōs, si placet, nostra videāmus.

XXIII. **82.** Nēmō umquam mihi, Scīpiō, persuādē-
bit aut patrem tuum Paulum aut duōs avōs, Paulum
25 et Āfricānum, aut Āfricānī patrem aut patruum aut
multōs praestantēs virōs, quōs ēnumerāre nōn est
necesse, tanta esse conātōs, quae ad posteritātis memoriam pertinērent, nisi animō cernerent posteritātem
ad sē ipsōs pertinēre.

Hope in immortality affords an impulse for right-doing

An cēnsēs, ut dē mē ipse aliquid mōre senum glōrier,
mē tantōs labōrēs diurnōs nocturnōsque domī mīlitiaeque
susceptūrum fuisse, sī īsdem fīnibus glōriam meam,
quibus vītam, essem terminātūrus? Nōnne multō
melius fuisset ōtiōsam aetātem et quiētam sine ūllō aut 5
labōre aut contentiōne trādūcere? Sed nesciō quō
modō animus ērigēns sē posteritātem ita semper prō-
spiciēbat, quasi, cum excessisset ē vītā, tum dēnique victūrus esset. Quod quidem nī ita sē habēret,
ut animī immortālēs essent, haud optimī cūjusque ani- 10
mus maximē ad immortālitātem et glōriam nīterētur.

Significance of the difference in men's attitude toward death

83. Quid, quod sapientissimus quisque aequissimō
animō moritur, stultissimus inīquissimō? Nōnne vōbīs
vidētur is animus, quī plūs cernat et longius, vidēre
sē ad meliōra proficīscī, ille autem, cūjus obtūsior sit 15
aciēs, nōn vidēre? Equidem efferor studiō patrēs
vestrōs, quōs coluī et dīlēxī, videndī, neque vērō eōs
sōlōs convenīre aveō, quōs ipse cognōvī, sed illōs
etiam, dē quibus audīvī et lēgī et ipse cōnscrīpsī.

Strength of Cato's hope for the future

Quō quidem mē proficīscentem haud sānē quis facile 20
retrāxerit nec tamquam Peliam recoxerit. Et sī quis
deus mihi largiātur, ut ex hāc aetāte repuerāscam et
in cūnīs vāgiam, valdē recūsem nec vērō velim quasi
dēcursō spatiō ad carcerēs ā calce revocārī. **84.** Quid
habet enim vīta commodī? Quid nōn potius labōris? 25

Sed habeat sānē; habet certē tamen aut satietātem
aut modum. Nōu lubet enim mihi dēplōrāre vītam,
quod multī, et eī doctī, saepe fēcērunt, neque mē
vīxisse paenitet, quoniam ita vīxī, ut nōn frūstrā mē
5 nātum exīstimem, et ex vītā ita discēdō tamquam
ex hospitiō, nōn tamquam ē domō. Commorandī
enim nātūra dēvorsōrium nōbīs, nōn habitandī dedit.
Ō praeclārum diem, cum in illud dīvīnum animōrum
concilium coetumque proficīscar cumque ex hāc turbā
10 et colluviōne discēdam! Proficīscar enim nōn ad eōs
sōlum virōs, dē quibus ante dīxī, vērum etiam ad
Catōnem meum, quō nēmō vir melior nātus est,
nēmō pietāte praestantior; cūjus ā mē corpus est
cremātum, quod contrā decuit ab illō meum, animus
15 vērō nōn mē dēserēns, sed respectāns in ea profectō loca discessit, quō mihi ipsī cernēbat esse veniendum. Quem ego meum cāsum fortiter ferre vīcus
sum, nōn quō aequō animō ferrem, sed mē ipse cōn-
sōlābar exīstimāns nōn longinquum inter nōs dīgres-
20 sum et discessum fore.

85. Hīs mihi rēbus, Scīpiō (id enim tē cum Laeliō admīrārī solēre dīxistī), levis est senectūs, nec sōlum nōn molesta, sed etiam jūcunda. Quodsī in hōc errō, quī animōs
hominum immortālēs esse crēdam, libenter errō nec mihi
25 hunc errōrem, quō dēlector, dum vīvō, extorquērī volō; sīn
mortuus, ut quīdam minūtī philosophī cēnsent, nihil sentiam, nōn vereor, nē hunc errōrem meum philosophī mortuī
irrīdeant. Quodsī nōn sumus immortālēs futūrī, tamen
exstinguī hominī suō tempore optābile est. Nam habet
30 nātūra ut aliārum omnium rērum, sīc vīvendī modum.
Senectūs autem aetātis est perāctiō tamquam fābulae,

cūjus dēfatīgātiōnem fugere dēbēmus, praesertim ad-
jūnctā satietāte.

Haec habuī, dē senectūte quae dīcerem; ad quam
utinam perveniātis! ut ea, quae ex mē audīstis, rē
expertī probāre possītis. 5

NOTES

DE SENECTUTE

Time of Composition of the de Senectute. — With the over-throw of Pompey at Pharsalus in 48 B.C. and the consequent ascendancy of Julius Caesar, Cicero had retired completely from the arena of political life. Resigning himself of necessity to the centralizing policy of Caesar, he sought consolation in his ever favorite pursuit of philosophy, and it is to these closing years of his life that his chief philosophical works belong. It is still a disputed question whether the de Senectute was written shortly before or shortly after the assassination of Caesar (March 15, 44 B.C.). Conservative opinion at present tends to recognize the earlier date as the more probable, and to refer the composition of the work either to the last months of 45 B.C. or to the very earliest part (January or February) of 44.

Atticus. — The essay is dedicated to Cicero's intimate friend Titus Pomponius Atticus. Atticus was born in 109 B.C., of an old and wealthy equestrian family. From 88 to 65 B.C. he had resided at Athens, devoting his time to literary and philosophical studies. Returning to Rome in 65, he lived on terms of intimacy with the first men of his day. His friendship with Cicero had begun early in life, when the two were students together, and is well attested by the sixteen books of letters (Epistulae ad Atticum) which have come down to us. This correspondence begins in 68 B.C. and continues for twenty-five years, ending only a few months before Cicero's death (Dec. 7, 43 B.C.). Atticus never entered public life. His death occurred eleven years after that of Cicero, in 32 B.C.

Occasion of the Dialogue; its Dramatic Date. — Scipio and Laelius meeting at the house of the elder Cato express their wonder at the cheerfulness with which he bears the burden of age. Cato's answer leads the young men to request that he will set forth to them the means whereby old age may be made easy and happy. In compliance Cato proceeds to consider in detail the various accusations brought against old age, and to show how groundless these are. The greater part of the work is taken up by Cato's remarks. The participation of Scipio and Laelius in the conversation is so slight that the composition is practically an essay, not a dialogue.

The dramatic date of the conversation is 150 B.C., the year before Cato's death.

The Interlocutors:

(a) *Cato.* " M. Porcius Cato was a Sabine farmer who rose from the plough to the highest honors of the Republic. Born in 234 B.C., a soldier at seventeen, praetor in 198 B.C., and consul in 195 B.C., a veteran in the fields of war and oratory, he was the last representative of old-fashioned, middle-class conservatism, a bitter foe to new men and new manners, a latter-day Cincinnatus. He had served from the Trasimene to Zama, in Sardinia, Spain, Macedon, with skill, courage, success. Accused forty-four times, accuser as often, the grey-eyed, red-haired man had literally fought his way up with his rough-and-ready wit, his nervous oratory, his practical ability and business habits. For thirty-five years the most influential man in Rome, he had acted in every capacity, as general, administrator, and envoy. He was a man whose virtues served his own ends, whose real but well-trumpeted austerity was a stalking-horse for his personal acrimony and ambition. Narrow, reactionary, and self-righteous, as he was honest, active, and well-meaning, a good hater and a persistent critic, at once a bully and a moralist, he took up his text daily against the backslidings and iniquities of the time, against Hellenism, luxury, immorality, and corruption, especially as personified in the Scipios and Flaminini of his day. At bottom he was a genuine man, but it was unlucky that the strongest reforming force should have taken shape in this political gladiator and typical Roman, this hard-hitting, sharp-witted, keenly commercial, upright, vulgar Philistine." (How and Leigh, History of Rome to the Death of Caesar, p. 303.)

Cato lived to an advanced old age, dying in 149 B.C., the year after the date of the conversation represented in the de Senectute. Much has been made of the tradition that in his last years he was an assiduous student of Greek. But it is not likely that his study extended to the imaginative works of Greek literature, the masterpieces of Greek poets and philosophers. His interest in Greek was probably solely a practical one, and limited to the use of Greek sources in the composition of his historical work, the Origines. Appreciation for the ideal in literature and art he never possessed; in fact he cherished the intensest conviction that the indulgence of these sentiments involved a distinct menace to the welfare of the state. Hence it is not credible that in his old age he should have renounced the convictions of a lifetime and have turned with enthusiasm to the models of the creative genius of the Greeks. Only six years before his death, besides giving other evidences of his anti-Hellenic spirit, he had been a prime mover in expediting the departure from Rome of three Greek philosophers, Diogenes, Critolaus, and Carneades, who having come to the city on a diplomatic errand were using their leisure to set forth to the Romans the tenets of their respective schools.

It is, then, an ideal Cato that meets us in the de Senectute, not the real Cato of flesh and blood who opposed so stoutly throughout his whole career the tendencies and sentiments for which he is represented by Cicero as cherishing so lofty an enthusiasm.

(b) *Scipio*. The Scipio of the de Senectute (the younger Africanus) was a son of Lucius Aemilius Paulus, the conqueror of Macedonia. The name Scipio he took from his adoptive father, P. Cornelius Scipio (son of the great Africanus), adding the surname Aemilianus in token of his actual descent. Scipio was born about 185 B.C., and was therefore about thirty-five years of age at the time of the alleged dialogue. Though he early began to devote himself to the profession of arms, he possessed also decided literary tastes, and cultivated friendly relations with the contemporary poets Lucilius and Terence. Rumor had it that he even assisted Terence in the composition of his plays. For Cato, Scipio entertained a profound admiration, despite the old hostility between the two families, and is said to have taken that sturdy exemplar of the homely virtues as his own model.

(c) *Laelius*. Gaius Laelius, surnamed Sapiens, was of about the same age as Scipio, and was attached to him by ties of the closest friendship, as his father had been attached to the elder Africanus. Hence Laelius is appropriately made the chief speaker in Cicero's essay on friendship (the Laelius or de Amicitia). Laelius held various public offices, but was chiefly distinguished for his enlightened interest in literature and philosophy.

Ennius. — Ennius, from whose Annals Cato so often quotes in the de Senectute, was born at Rudiae in Calabria in 239 B.C., and died in 169. He was serving as a soldier in the Second Punic War when he attracted the attention and won the friendship of Cato, who brought him to Rome in 204 B.C. Here for a time he gained a livelihood by teaching; later his poetic gifts secured him the powerful support of the elder Africanus and others. Ennius's chief work is his Annales, of which, unfortunately, only fragments have come down to us. This was an historical poem, and dealt with the story of Roman achievement from the earliest times down to and including the stirring events of Ennius's own day.

Page 120, 1. O Tite, *etc.*: these three lines, like the two below, are quoted from the Annals of the poet Ennius (see Introd. p. 332). In their original context they are addressed by an Epirote shepherd to the Roman general, Titus Quinctius Flamininus; Cicero here applies them to his friend, Titus Pomponius Atticus (see Introd. p. 330). **si quid te adjŭero**: *if I help you at all.* Flamininus in 198 b.c. had undertaken the direction of the campaign against Philip V. of Macedon. After landing in Epirus he was much embarrassed in his operations by the mountainous character of the country, until Charŏpus, a friendly Epirote chief, sent to him the shepherd already mentioned, to act as guide. The shepherd inquires whether he is to receive any reward in case he extricates the general from his present embarrassment; *quid* is Accusative of 'Result Produced' (Internal Object), — *render any help.* B. 176, 2, *a*; A. 390, *c*; G. 333, 1; H. 409, 1. *adjŭero* is for the regular *adjŭvero*, with shortening of the *ŭ* (before a vowel) after the disappearance of the *v.* **levasso**: an old future-perfect, equivalent in meaning to the customary form, *levavero.*

2. **coquit**: in the figurative sense of 'vex,' 'harass.' **versāt**: note the length of the *a.* This was the original quantity of this termination, though it was already tending to become shortened in Ennius's day.

4. **licet enim**, *etc.*: *for I may address you.* **versibus eisdem**: *in the identical lines; eisdem* is here especially emphatic, as shown by its unusual position after its substantive.

6. **ille vir**: *i.e.* the herdsman. **haud magna cum re**: *poor; re* is here used in the sense of *re familiari*, 'property,' 'possessions.' **plenus fidĕi**: *i.e. loyal;* in early Latin final *s* was so lightly sounded that, as in the present instance, it often failed to 'make position.' **fidei**: *fides, res, spes* regularly formed the genitive and dative in *-ĕī.* Here, however, the *e* is long, *fidēī.* This seems to have been the original quantity, and appears often in Early Latin.

7. **quamquam certo scio**: *and yet I know for certain, quamquam* is here corrective.

8. **noctesque diesque**: *que . . . que* are correlative.

9. **novi**: *I am acquainted with*, as contrasted with *intellego* (in the following line), *I am aware of the fact.* **moderationem et aequitatem**: *self-control and evenness.*

10. **cognomen**: *viz. Atticus*, given in consequence of his long residence at Athens and his intimate acquaintance with Greek literature. **humanitatem et prudentiam**: *culture and good sense.*

12. **eisdem rebus**: the allusion is to the existing political situ-

ation. According as we place the composition of the de Senectute before or after Caesar's death, the reference will be to Caesar's threatened usurpation of regal power or to Antony's policy of self-aggrandizement.   **me ipsum**: the thought is inaccurately expressed. We should have expected *ego ipse* (*sc. commoveor*), ' by which I myself am disturbed.'   **gravius**: *rather seriously.*

13. quarum: *for which*, an extension of the ordinary force of the Objective Genitive.   **major**: *i.e.* a larger theme.

14. nunc: as opposed to the ' later occasion ' just alluded to. **visum est mihi**: *I have decided.*

15. ad te conscribere: *i.e.* to write and send to you; hence *ad* with the accusative.

17. senectutis: Cicero was now sixty-two years old, Atticus sixty-four. *Senectus* seems to have been an elastic term among the Romans, as ' old age ' is with us; *senectutis* depends on *onere.*

18. etsi: corrective, like *quamquam* above, in line 7. **te quidem**: *quidem* serves to emphasize *te*, and to suggest a possible contrast between Atticus and Cicero. Cicero is sure that Atticus at any rate will bear old age philosophically, whatever his own attitude may prove to be.

PAGE **121**, 1. **sed occurrebas**: *i.e.* Cicero feels that Atticus, despite his natural equanimity and good sense, may nevertheless appreciate the tribute he offers.

3. eo munere: *of that tribute, viz.* my essay on old age; *eo* here is not correlative with *quo*, but refers back to the thought involved in *scribere.*   **quo uteretur**: a relative clause of purpose. **uterque nostrum**: *i.e.* Cicero in the writing and Atticus in the reading.

4. mihi quidem: *to me at any rate; cf. te quidem,* p. 120, line 18.

6. effecerit mollem etiam et jucundam senectutem: *has made old age actually easy and pleasant.*

7. satis digne = adequately.

8. cui qui pareat, *etc.*: *since he who obeys it* (philosophy) *can pass every period of life without annoyance.,* lit. *he who obeys which can pass.* The peculiarity of the passage lies in the fact that *cui*, while serving to introduce *possit*, is itself governed by *pareat*, which is subordinate to *possit; possit* is a Subjunctive of Characteristic with the accessory notion of cause. B. 283, 3; A. 535, *e; pareat* is attracted to the mood of *possit.*

9. de ceteris: *on other subjects.* Outside of the nominative and accusative Cicero regularly uses an adjective in agreement with *res*, to denote ' other things,' ' many things,' etc. So here *de ceteris rebus* would have been the regular form of expression.

10. **hunc librum**: emphatic and contrasted with the writings suggested by *de ceteris*.

11. **tribuimus**: *I have put in the mouth of*. Note the editorial ' we.'

12. **Tithono**: the son of Laomedon. In response to the prayers of Aurora, who loved him, the gods had made Tithonus immortal; but they did not confer upon him the boon of perpetual youth. Hence he is said to have shrivelled away and finally to have been changed into a grasshopper. **Aristo Ceus**: *Aristo of Ceos*. Aristo was an unimportant Peripatetic philosopher who flourished about 225 b.c. As we gather from this passage, he was the author of a dialogue on old age, in which he had made Tithonus the chief speaker. Aristo's works have not come down to us.

13. **in fabula**: *in a myth, i.e.* in putting my sentiments in the mouth of a mythical character like Tithonus. **M. Catoni seni**: *Marcus Cato the Elder* (234–149 b.c. See Introd. p. 331, *a*). Cicero adds *seni* to distinguish this Cato from his own contemporary, M. Cato, called *Uticensis*, a great-grandson of the elder Cato.

14. **apud quem**: *in whose presence*, or *at whose house*. **Laelium et Scipionem**: see Introd. p. 332, *b, c*. The participation of Laelius and Scipio in the conversation is extremely slight; the de Senectute is in no proper sense a dialogue.

15. **facimus**: *I represent*. **admirantes**: *i.e. expressing their admiration*.

17. **eruditius**: *with greater elegance*, or *greater polish*.

18. **in suis libris**: of Cato's works the only one that has come down to us is the treatise on farming, de Agri Cultura. This work shows almost a total absence of literary skill, and makes it clear why Cicero should have thought it necessary to apologize for the elaborate form in which Cato is made to set forth his views on old age. **quarum constat eum perstudiosum fuisse**: it is doubtful whether Cato's interest ever extended to the finer literary masterpieces of the Greeks. More likely such attention as he is reported to have given to Greek in his old age was confined to historical works in the Greek language; these probably served as important sources in the composition of his Origines; see Introd. p. 331.

20. **plura**: supply in sense some such word as *dicere*.

22. **saepe numero**: *often;* sometimes written *saepenumero*.

23. **cum . . . tum**: *not only . . . but also*. **ceterarum rerum**: *in other things*. Objective Genitive. See note on *quarum*, p. 120, l. 13.

24. **vel maxime**: *vel* is simply intensive.

25. **quod senserim**: the indicative is ordinarily used in causal clauses introduced by *quod* denoting the reason of the speaker,

but the subjunctive may be used to indicate the reason of the speaker when the main verb refers to a past state of mind. That is the case here, — *saepe numero admirari soleo* being equivalent to ' I have often wondered.'

26. Aetna gravius: Cicero regularly confines his use of the Ablative of Comparison to negative expressions, interrogative expressions implying a negative, and a few proverbial phrases such as *melle dulcius, vita carius, Aetna gravius.*

28. rem haud sane difficilem admirari videmini: the thought is inaccurately expressed. Cicero really means: ' What you wonder at, Scipio and Laelius, does not seem to me a really difficult thing.' Cato does not mean to say that the young men seem to admire, — for their admiration was beyond question, — but simply that the thing which they admire does not seem remarkable to him.

PAGE **122,** 1. **quibus enim,** *etc.: for to those who have no resources, etc.; quibus* is Dative of Possession.

3. a se ipsi: as usual, the intensive is joined with the subject instead of agreeing with the reflexive.

5. est: *belongs.* **in primis:** *especially;* sometimes written *imprimis.*

6. adeptam: here used passively.

8. putassent: this represents a pluperfect indicative of direct discourse (*putaveramus*). *Putaveram* is frequently used in Latin, corresponding to the English ' I thought.' **primum:** elliptical, — *in the first place* (let us inquire).

9. falsum putare: *to think what was false; falsum* is here used as a substantive. **qui:** *how; qui* was originally an ablative or instrumental, but it early acquired the adverbial force of ' how.' Traces of its original case function may still be seen in *quicum.* **adulescentiae senectus,** *etc.:* as here used, *adulescentia* is the period from boyhood to old age, *i.e.* the period of growing powers.

12. quam si: *quam si* here has the force of *instead of.*

13. praeterita aetas . . . cum effluxisset, *etc.:* the most natural interpretation of this sentence seems to be this: ' even an unlimited period of past time would not be able, when once it was gone, to comfort the foolish age of these men I am talking about ' ; *posset* is the apodosis of a contrary-to-fact conditional sentence, the protasis of which is implied in *quamvis longa* (' were it never so long '). The subjunctive in *cum effluxisset* is due to attraction.

16. opinione vestra: *the notion you have.* By employing this word Cato affects modesty, implying that the compliment paid him by the young man was the result of a mere notion or fancy.

17. nostro cognomine: *viz. Sapiens;* see note on *cognomen.*

p. 120, line 10.   in hoc sumus sapientes : the emphasis rests upon the words *in hoc:* the apodosis corresponding to the protasis *si . . . soletis* is to be supplied in thought ; we may understand some such thought as, ' I will say,' ' Let me point out.' Such ellipses are frequent in Latin.

18.   naturam, optimam ducem, sequimur : this was a cardinal doctrine of the Stoics, — ' to live according to Nature,' *i.e.* Nature's plan.

19.   cum . . . discriptae sint : *cum* has causal force.   In view of Nature's wise allotment of the other parts of life, it is not likely that she has neglected old age.

21.   inerti poëta : *an unskilful poet.*

22.   necesse fuit esse aliquid extremum : *there had to be something final.*   **tamquam :** here, *just as.*

24.   quasi vietum et caducum, *etc.:* we have here an instance of what may be called the ' apologetic ' *quasi.*   Both *tamquam* and *quasi* are often thus used when the author employs a word or phrase in some unusual figurative sense, where an English writer might have added, ' so to speak,' ' if I may employ that term,' or something of the sort.   Thus here the writer apologizes for his bold use of *vietus,* which properly meant ' bent,' ' twisted,' ' shrivelled,' but which is here figuratively applied to the conditions of old age.   Translate ; *something shrivelled, so to speak, and ready to fall with the fulness of time.   Aliquid* is to be supplied with *vietum* and *caducum.*

25.   molliter : *calmly, patiently.*   **quid est enim,** *etc.:* ' for what does the battle of the giants with the gods signify but rebellion against Nature ? '   Cato's last remarks had been devoted to emphasizing the importance of living in accordance with Nature's plan.   We must do this, he says ; otherwise we shall be rebelling against Nature, and against this the legend of the contest of the giants should warn us.   For that legend typifies rebellion against Nature.

27.   atqui : *and yet; i.e.* despite their agreement with what Cato has said, the young men wish to learn how old age may be made tolerable.   **gratissimum :** used substantively, — *a thing most welcome to us.*   **ut . . . pollicear :** *to speak* (lit. *promise*) for *Scipio too, i.e.* as well as for himself.

29.   volumus quidem certe : Laelius has just said that they both hoped (*speramus*) to become old, but realizing that this is asserting too much, he at once hastens to qualify this *speramus* by saying that at least they *wished* to become old men.   **fieri :** had the infinitive depended directly upon *speramus,* it would regularly have taken the form *nos futuros esse;* but its construction is determined by *volumus.*

PAGE **123, 4. futurum est**: different in force from *erit; erit* would have referred the matter distinctly to the future; *futurum est* indicates rather a present prospect, — 'is likely to prove agreeable.'

5. volumus sane: *we really do wish.*

6. qua nobis quoque ingrediendum sit: *where we too must travel.*

7. istuc . . . quale sit: *to see the nature of the goal at which you have arrived,* lit. *to see that thing . . . of what sort it is.* (Prolepsis or Anticipation. B. 374, 5; A. 576; G. 468).

10. pares cum paribus congregantur: note the reflexive meaning of the passive *congregantur.* For the thought, *cf.* the English 'Birds of a feather flock together.'

12. quae . . . deplorare solebant: owing to the interruption caused by the parenthesis, the writer here repeats the thought already expressed in *querelis aequalium,* — *complaints which they used to make,* lit. *which things they used to complain; quae* is accusative of 'Result Produced' (Internal Object). See note on *quid,* p. 120, line 1.   **C. Salinator**: naval commander in the war against Antiochus, 191 B.C.   **Sp. Albinus**: consul in 186 B.C.

13. tum . . . tum: *partly . . . partly.*

14. sine quibus . . . putarent: *without which (they said) they thought life was not life;* subjunctive in implied indirect discourse.

15. spernerentur: not as strong in meaning as our 'spurn,' 'despise,' but more nearly equivalent to our 'neglect,' 'slight.'

16. essent soliti: subjunctive by attraction.   **qui,** *etc.*: note the adversative force of this sentence, — *but these men did not seem to me to blame, etc.*   **id quod esset accusandum**: practically a subordinate clause in indirect discourse, *non id accusare videbantur* being equivalent to *non eos id accusare putabam;* hence the subjunctive.

18. usu venirent: *would happen,* lit. *would come by experience.*

20. cognovi: here, *I have known.*   **sine querela**: the prepositional phrase is used as an adjective modifier of *senectutem.* **qui . . . non moleste ferrent**: *who by no means regretted,* lit. *who bore it not ill.* The object of *ferrent* is *se laxatos esse.* Note the litotes in *non moleste;* except for this we should have had *nec* (correlative with *nec* following) instead of *et . . . non.*

23. non in aetate: *not in the time of life.*   **moderati**: *of self-control; moderati homines* are those *qui sibi moderantur.*

24. difficiles: *churlish;* hard to deal with or hard to please. **inhumani**: *i.e. devoid of culture (humanitas).*

25. importunitas, inhumanitas: these words convey in substantive form the ideas contained in *difficiles* and *inhumani* respectively, — *boorishness, lack of culture.* **omni aetati**: *to every period of life.*

27. **dixerit quispiam**: *some one may say;* potential subjunctive.

28. **opes**: *resources,* and so *influence.* **copias**: *wealth.* **dignitatem**: *high standing,* both political and social.

31. **sed nequaquam in isto sunt omnia**: *i.e.* the whole case is by no means comprised in that.

PAGE 124, 1. Themistocles: the famous Athenian statesman, commander of the Greeks at Salamis.

2. **Seriphio cuidam**: *a certain Seriphian.* Seriphos, one of the Cyclades, was so small and rocky that it became proverbial in antiquity for its insignificance and barrenness. **ille**: *i.e.* the Seriphian.

4. **nec hercule**: supply in sense *clarus fuissem.*

6. **quod**: referring loosely to the point of the story just narrated.

7. **levis**: *i.e.* easy to bear. **ne . . . quidem**: *ne . . . quidem,* as frequently, merely repeats the negative idea. B. 347, 2; A. 327; G. 445; H. 656, 2.

8. **nec insipienti**, *etc.: nor to a fool can it fail to be burdensome, even in the midst of the greatest plenty.* Note the chiastic arrangement in *nec levis ne sapienti quidem* on the one hand, and *nec insipienti non gravis* on the other.

9. **aptissima omnino . . . arma**: *altogether the most suitable weapons; senectutis* is a Possessive Genitive, *i.e.* weapons for old age to use.

10. **artes exercitationesque virtutum**: *liberal arts and the practice of the virtues; artes* is here used in the sense of *artes liberales.* Notice the use of the plural in *exercitationes;* repeated instances are thought of.

11. **quae**: referring to *virtutes.* **cum diu multumque vixeris**: *when you have had a long and eventful life; vixeris* is in the perfect subjunctive. Note the indefinite second singular. B. 356, 3. Subordinate clauses containing this indefinite second person singular stand regularly in the subjunctive. *Cf.* p. 132, line 7.

13. **deserunt**: used absolutely.

14. **id quidem**: *that, of course.*

15. **bene factorum**: *good deeds; bene facta* is often used as a substantive.

17. **Q. Maximum**: *Quintus Fabius Maximus,* surnamed Cunctator 'Delayer,' from his policy of avoiding a pitched battle with Hannibal. **Tarentum recepit**: Tarentum had been captured by Hannibal in 212 B.C., but Fabius recovered it three years later.

18. senem adulescens: in Latin contrasted words are often put in juxtaposition.   **erat enim**: *for there was.*

19. condita: *tempered*, lit. *seasoned* (*condio*).

20. quamquam: corrective, as p. 120, line 7.

21. non admodum grandem, *etc.*: *when not so very old, yet well along in life.*

22. anno post . . . quam ego natus sum: *a year after I was born, i.e.* in 233 B.C.; *post . . . quam* for *postquam*, as often. Cato's point had been merely to cite Fabius as an illustration of how ' liberal arts and the practice of the virtues ' make old age pleasant and easy to bear; but, with an old man's tendency to indulge in digression, he begins to recount his own experiences as a soldier under Maximus, although the recital of these incidents does not in the least serve to illuminate the question at issue. Such digressions, especially in the way of personal reminiscences on Cato's part, meet us frequently in the de Senectute, and constitute a striking feature of the art with which Cicero has depicted the character of the aged Cato.

23. quartum consule: *consul for the fourth time.*   This was in 214 B.C.

24. adulescentulus: *when a young man;* Cato was twenty years old at the time.   **ad Capuam**: *to the neighborhood of Capua.*

26. quem magistratum: in English, *an office which.*

27. cum . . . fuit: the indicative is used to denote *the point of time at which.*

28. suasor: *a supporter.*   **legis Cinciae**: so called from the name of the tribune who introduced it, M. Cincius Alimentus. The chief feature of this law was that it forbade advocates to receive fees for professional service.   This provision remained a principle of Roman law until the reign of the Emperor Claudius, when it was slightly modified.

PAGE **125**, 1. **plane grandis**: *quite old*, implying less, however, than *admodum senex*.   The time referred to is that previous to Fabius's support of the *lex Cincia*, which was in 204 B.C., the year before his death.   **juveniliter exsultantem**: *i.e.* exulting in the enthusiasm of young manhood, as opposed to Fabius, who was *plane grandis.*   Hannibal was only thirty-two years old at the time (215 B.C.).

2. patientia: *endurance, persistence.*

3. familiaris noster: *my intimate friend; noster* for *meus*, as *nos* for *ego*.   **Ennius**: as verb of the sentence, supply *ait*, or some such word.

4. unus homo nobis: the quotation is from the Annals. Virgil imitates this line in Aeneid, VI, 846:

Tu Maximus ille es
Unus qui nobis cunctando restituis rem.

restituit: implying that when Fabius took the field the Roman fortunes were at a low ebb. This was particularly the case on the occasion of Fabius's second command, in 215 B.C., the year after the disastrous defeat at Cannae.

5. **noenum**: *not*, an archaic form. **rumores**: *i.e.* the popular report that Fabius's avoidance of a direct engagement with Hannibal was prompted by cowardice. **ponebāt**: note the preservation of the original quantity of the final *a*; *cf.* note on *versat*, p. 120, line 2.

6. **plusque magisque**: with adjectives and verbs *plus* denotes a *higher degree of intensity*, *magis*, a *wider extent* of application; thus here, *plus claret* = 'has a greater brilliancy'; *magis claret*, = 'diffuses a wider radiance': *-que . . . -que* are correlatives.

7. **Tarentum**: made emphatic by its position, — *in case of Tarentum, now*.

8. **Salinatori**: Cicero's memory is probably inaccurate in this reference to Salinator. It was Titus Livius Macatus who lost Tarentum.

10. **mea opera**: *through my instrumentality;* the chief emphasis rests upon *mea*.

12. **praestantior**: supply *erat*. **in toga**: *i.e.* in peace, civil life.

13. **qui consul iterum**: *for he, when consul a second time* (228 B.C.); the relative clause begins a justification of the statement just made. **quiescente**: *i.e.* taking no side in the matter.

14. **C. Flaminio**: in 232 B.C., in opposition to the expressed policy (*auctoritas*) of the senate, Flaminius had secured the passage of an agrarian law providing for the distribution of certain lands in northern Italy among the citizens of Rome. Cicero seems to be in error in making Fabius and Carvilius colleagues in 232 B.C. Their consulship was in 228 B.C., but the fact of Fabius's sturdy opposition to Flaminius's law is beyond question.

15. **agrum Picentem et Gallicum**: the Picene lands lay near the Adriatic, east of Umbria and north of the Sabine territory; the *ager Gallicus* was slightly further north. **contra senatus auctoritatem**: an *auctoritas senatus* was simply an expression of opinion by way of formal resolution; it had no binding force.

16. **dividenti**: *i.e.* trying to secure the division; the participle has a conative force.

17. **optimis auspiciis**: *under most favorable auspices;* Ablative of Attendant Circumstance. B. 221.

18. **ferrentur**: *were proposed; legem ferre* is the technical phrase for introducing a bill for enactment.

19. multa: emphatic, — *many are the excellent qualities which I came to know in that hero.*

20. nihil admirabilius: *nothing worthier of admiration;* supply *cognovi.* **quam quo modo**: *than the way in which; cf. quem magistratum gessi,* ' an office which I held,' p. 124, line 26.

21. mortem fili: this son, who also bore the name Q. Fabius Maximus, had been consul in 213 B.C., and died about 205, shortly before his aged father.

22. in manibus: *in circulation, i.e.* may still be read. **laudatio**: *i.e. laudatio funebris,* the funeral eulogy. **quam cum legimus**: *and when we read it.*

23. contemnimus: *regard as insignificant (in comparison); contemno* is usually less strong than the English ' despise.' **in luce atque in oculis civium**: *in the public view and before the eyes of his fellow-citizens; lux* in the sense of ' publicity' is a frequent figure in Latin.

24. magnus: supply *erat; cf. praestantior,* above, line 12. **intus domique**: *in the privacy of his home;* hendiadys.

25. quae praecepta: *what good advice!*

26. notitia: *familiarity.* **scientia**: *theoretical knowledge, knowledge of the principles.*

27. multae litterae: *i.e.* much knowledge of books or literature. **ut in homine Romano**: *for a Roman; ut* is here restrictive. In such cases the expression is elliptical. Thus here we might supply *litterae inveniuntur,* — ' so far as literary knowledge is found in a Roman.' Cicero evidently recognizes that as a class his countrymen were not conspicuous for a profound knowledge of books. Such preëminence was never a prevalent ideal with the Romans. **omnia**: with *bella.*

28. domestica: *i.e.* wars in which Romans were engaged.

29. externa: wars which other nations waged. **cujus** = *et eius.* **ita**: *ita* does not modify *cupide,* but *fruebar,* and simply serves to anticipate the *quasi*-clause.

30. illo extincto: Fabius died in 203 B.C. **fore, unde discerem, neminem**: *I should have nobody to learn from; unde,* by a common idiom, is here equivalent to *a quo;* the clause *unde discerem* is a relative clause of purpose. Special emphasis rests upon *neminem,* as is shown by its unusual position at the end of the sentence.

PAGE 126, 1. **quorsus**: *why?* **igitur**: *now,* — a mere particle of transition, as frequently. **haec tam multa**: object of *dixi* or some similar verb to be supplied.

2. **quia profecto**: *because, of course.* **nefas dictu**: *an outrageous thing to say.*

3. **nec** = *et . . . non.*

4. **Scipiones aut Maximi**: *i.e.* men like Scipio or Maximus. This generic use of the plural of proper names is common.   **ut, ut, ut, ut**: notice the emphasis gained by the repetition of the particle, — anaphora.

5. **pedestres**: *on land;* for *terrestres*, as often.

6. **est etiam**: *there is also, i.e.* as well as the old age of men who, like Fabius, have been active in the field, there is also the peaceful old age of those who have passed a life of devotion to literature or philosophy.   **quiete et pure atque eleganter actae**: *quiete* is opposed to the stir and activity of a public life ; *pure* refers to the refined character of the pursuits alluded to ; while *eleganter* implies that they call for the exercise of taste and discrimination.

7. **placida ac lenis senectus**: *a tranquil and peaceful old age.* The thought of this sentence is somewhat condensed.   Two ideas are combined in a single expression : (1) There is also the old age of a life spent in retired pursuits.   (2) Such an old age is peaceful and tranquil.   **qualem accepimus Platonis**: abbreviated for *qualem accepimus fuisse senectutem Platonis.*   Plato, pupil of Socrates and founder of the Athenian Academy, lived from 429 to 347 B.C.

8. **uno et octogesimo**: *unus* for *primus* as often in such combinations.

9. **scribens est mortuus**: best taken literally.   Another account reports him to have died at a wedding feast.   Petrarch and Leibnitz also are said to have died pen in hand.   **Isocratis**: Greek orator and rhetorician (436–338 B.C.).   He is said to have trained more famous orators than any other rhetorician of antiquity.

10. **librum**: *speech*, as often.   **Panathenaicus**: this oration delivered at the Panathenaic festival, was a defence and eulogy of Athens as the great civilizing force of Hellas.

12. **Leontinus Gorgias**: *Gorgias of Leontini* (in Sicily), 480–373 B.C.   He was a famous sophist and rhetorician.   **centum et septem complevit annos**: *i.e.* rounded out the sum of one hundred and seven years.

13. **studio atque opere**: *zeal for his profession;* hendiadys.

14. **cur tam diu vellet esse in vita**: implying that he might have terminated life by suicide, a step which was held by the Stoics and Epicureans to be justifiable under certain circumstances.

15. **nihil habeo quod accusem**: *I have no reason to blame.* The exact nature of the subjunctive after *nihil habeo quod* and *nihil est quod* is uncertain.

16. **praeclarum responsum**: in apposition with the previous sentence.

17. **docto homine**: *a scholar*. **sua enim vitia**, *etc.*: the emphasis rests upon *sua* and *suam*, — *for 'tis their own defects and their own faults that fools lay to the charge of old age.*

18. **quod**: *i.e.* he did not lay his own defects to old age.

20. **sicut fortis equos**, *etc.*: cited from the Annals. **fortis equos**: *a gallant steed; equos* was the spelling of Ennius, and continued regularly in vogue till about the time of Cicero's death. Cicero, accordingly, probably wrote *equos, equom* (not *equus, equum*), although editors hesitate to introduce this spelling into our text. See B. L. L.[1] § 57. **spatio supremo**: *in the final lap.* In the Greek hippodrome the chariots raced twelve times around the course.

21. **vicit Olumpia**: *has won an Olympic victory;* Cognate Accusative. B. 176, 4, *a*; A. 390; G. 333, 2; H. 409. **confectus quiescit**: the final *s* does not 'make position.' See note on *plenus*, p. 120, line 6.

22. **victoris**: here used as an adjective. **suam**: *sc. senectutem.*

23. **quem meminisse**: when used of persons in the sense of 'recall,' *memini* regularly takes the accusative. **probe** = *bene*.

24. **hi consules**: *the present consuls, i.e.* those for the year 150 B.C., when the conversation is represented to have taken place. **T. Flamininus**: not the Titus Flamininus mentioned p. 120, line 1.

25. **M'**: the apostrophe is probably a relic of an early *M* made with five strokes which occasionally appears in archaic inscriptions (𐌌).

26. **iterum**: this applies to *Philippo* only. Caepio and Philippus were colleagues in 169 B.C.

27. **legem Voconiam**: so called from the tribune Quintus Voconius Saxa, who introduced it. The purpose of the law was to restrict the amount of money bequeathed to women, and so to check their extravagance, as well as to prevent the growing tendency toward the alienation of property from the great families.

28. **bonis lateribus**: *lusty lungs.*

PAGE 127, 3. **etenim**: grammatically *etenim* introduces *reperio*, — *for, when I think it over, I find four reasons why old age seems wretched.* Logically, however, it anticipates the clause *Earum . . . videamus*, which practically means 'No one of these four reasons is sound'; so that the paragraph as a whole might be loosely paraphrased thus: 'For of the four reasons which, upon consideration, I find advanced in support of the wretchedness of old age, — of these four reasons not one is sound'.

---

[1] Bennett's *Latin Language.*

This brings the thought into close connection with the assertion that Ennius actually seemed to enjoy old age, and furnishes the transition from the introductory portion of the essay to the discussion proper.   **complector**: in this figurative sense the phrases *complector animo, complector mente* are regularly combined with a direct object; here we may supply in sense *rem*, 'the subject.'

4. quod avocet, quod faciat, *etc.*: the subjunctive indicates that the reason is not the speaker's, but exists in the mind of others, *viz.* of those who think old age wretched.

5. alteram = *secundam*, as often.

8. quamque justa: *quamque* = *et quam*.

10. a rebus gerendis senectus abstrahit: merely a statement of the first objection brought against old age.   **quibus**: with omission of the preposition, which has just been expressed with *rebus*. With relatives and interrogatives, such omission is frequent.

11. an eis: *is it not merely from those?*   *An* not infrequently occurs with the force of *-ne, nonne*.   **juventute et viribus**: *the strength of youth*, — hendiadys.

12. igitur: merely inferential, — *are there, then, no pursuits, etc.?*   **quae . . . administrentur**: *which are performed*, — not *may be* or *can be*. The Subjunctive is one of Characteristic. **vel infirmis corporibus**: *even though the body is feeble; vel* is intensive.

13. tamen: *i.e.* in spite of feeble bodies.   But to us the thought seems sufficiently clear without this particle.   **nihil ergo agebat,** *etc.*: *was it nothing, then, that Maximus did?*   Notice the anaphora in *nihil, nihil, nihil.*

14. L. Paulus, pater tuus: Lucius Aemilius Paulus, conqueror of the Macedonian king Perseus at Pydna in 168 B.C. Scipio was the son of this Paulus, and received the name of Scipio as a result of his adoption by L. Cornelius Scipio, son of the conqueror of Hannibal.   To the name of his adoptive father, Scipio added the *cognomen* Aemilianus, taken from the gentile name (Aemilius) of his actual father, Paulus.

15. fili mei: Cato's son, Marcus Porcius Cato, married Aemilia, Paulus's daughter. He died when praetor elect in 152 B.C., and is touchingly alluded to again near the close of this dialogue, p. 158, line 11 ff.   **ceteri senes**: *i.e.* the other old men whom every one at once recalls.   **Fabricii, Curii, Coruncanii** the generic plural, as *Scipiones, Maximi*, p. 126, line 4, *i.e.* Fabricius, Curius, Coruncanius, and men of that stamp. Fabricius, famous for the simplicity and integrity of his character, was especially conspicuous in the war against Pyrrhus (281–275

B.C.). Curius was a contemporary of Fabricius, and like him served with distinction in the war against Pyrrhus. Coruncanius, though the least famous of the three men here mentioned, was accounted one of the most remarkable characters of his day (consul 280 B.C.), and achieved success in war with the Etruscans, as well as against Pyrrhus.

16. cum . . . defendebant: the *cum*-clause here seems to be ' explicative,' like Cicero's *cum tacent, clamant*, ' their silence is a shout'; so here, *was their defence of the state inactivity (nihil agebant)*!

17. ad Appi Claudi, *etc.: Appius Claudius, besides being old, was also blind;* lit. *to the old age of Appius it was added that he was blind*. Appius was censor in 312 B.C., and consul in 306 and 295. The Appia Via was constructed under his supervision.

19. ad pacem . . . faciendum: *faciendum* is to be taken with *pacem* as well as with *foedus*.

21. persecutus est: *has set forth.*

22. quo vobis, *etc.:* the citation is from the Annals; *vobis* is the so-called Ethical Dative. **rectae quae stare solebant**: *rectae* seems here used figuratively for *sound, sane*, and to be contrasted with *dementes* in the next line.

23. antehac: here dissyllabic by synizesis. **dementes**: with adverbial force, — *senselessly; mentes dementes* illustrates the figure called oxymoron (' contradiction'), *senseless senses*. **viai**: archaic genitive, dependent upon *quo*, — lit. *whither of the way*.

24. ceteraque: *i.e.* the other points of Appius's speech. **gravissime**: *most impressively*. **carmen**: *the poem, passage*.

25. et tamen: *and apart from that, i.e.* apart from Ennius's account, Appius's own speech is also preserved. It was still extant a hundred years later in Cicero's day.

27. cum . . . interfuissent censorque . . . fuisset: we have here an illustration of the most extreme development of the *cum*-clause of situation or circumstance. All temporal notion has vanished, and only the circumstantial force is left. The nearest English equivalent is the awkward nominative absolute, — *ten years having intervened between the two consulships, and the censorship having preceded his first consulship*.

PAGE **128**, 1. **ex quo intellegitur**: *from which it is (readily) understood*.

2. **Pyrrhi bello**: Ablative of Time. **grandem sane**: *quite an old man;* he had been elected to the censorship in 312 B.C. As the office of censor was one of great dignity, it is unlikely that Appius was less than forty years of age at the time he filled it.

This would make him over seventy years old at the time referred to.

3. sic : *viz.* that he was able to determine the public policy at this advanced age.   **nihil afferunt :** *adduce no argument, i.e.* no argument that proves old age wretched.

4. similesque sunt ut si qui . . . dicant : the diction is clumsy and unusual.

6. scandant, cursent, exhauriant, sedeat : the subjunctives are due to the indirect discourse.

8. quietus : *without moving (from his place).*   **non facit :** *sc. senectus.*

9. non viribus aut velocitate, *etc.:* these phrases are made emphatic by their position, — *'tis not by strength of body, or by speed of movement or swiftness, that great matters are accomplished; corporum* limits *viribus* as well as *velocitate* and *celeritate.*

11. consilio, auctoritate, sententia : *deliberation, influence, judgment.*   **quibus,** *etc.:* an illustration of the construction called ἀπὸ κοινοῦ (' in common'), by which a single word or phrase is made to limit two different words, but in a different construction with each.   Thus here *quibus* is Ablative of Separation with *orbari,* but Ablative of Specification with *augeri,* lit. (*qualities*) *of which old age is not only not wont to be deprived, but in respect to which it is even wont to be increased* (*i.e.* more liberally endowed).

13. nisi forte : this phrase regularly, as here, implies that the supposition is absurd.   **miles et tribunus et legatus et consul :** note the emphasis gained by the polysyndeton, *et . . . et . . . et . . . et.*   There were six *tribuni militum* in a legion ; they commanded in turn, each for two months.   The *legatus* stood next to the commander-in-chief, and was under his immediate supervision ; the *consul,* when he took the field, was the commanding general.

14. vario genere : the English idiom is *various kinds.*

15. nunc videor, *etc.:* join *nunc* closely with *cum,* — *now that.*

17. male jam diu cogitanti : *which has long been plotting mischief.*   **bellum multo ante denuntio :** Cato means that he declares war against Carthage long before the actual commencement of hostilities.   He saw the approaching conflict, and did his best to precipitate it, regularly ending his speeches in the Senate with the declaration : *censeo Karthaginem esse delendam.*

19. quam palmam : *this glory, i.e.* of destroying Carthage. Cicero cleverly utilizes the subsequent overthrow and destruction of Carthage by Scipio in 146 B.C. (four years after the date of this dialogue).

20. ut . . . persequare: explanatory of *palmam*, — *of completing what your grandfather left undone;* the reference in *avi* is to the elder Scipio, the hero of the Second Punic War.

21. tertius et tricesimus annus: this is inaccurate. Scipio died in 185 B.C., *thirty-five* years before the date of the dialogue.

22. excipient: lit. *take up, i.e.* one after another, and so *transmit, perpetuate.*

24. cum . . . creatus esset: *having been chosen consul a second time in my consulship.* The *cum*-clause is like *cum . . . interfuissent*, p. 127, line 27.

25. num igitur, *etc.*: *igitur* like *ergo* at p. 127, line 12.

26. paeniteret: referring to present time, — *would he now be regretting?* Had Scipio lived to his hundredth year, he would have been eighty-four at the time of the dialogue; hence the use of the imperfect tense.

27. nec enim . . . uteretur: *no! for he would not be making use.* **excursione, saltu**: *i.e.* in military operations.

28. consilio, ratione, sententia: see note on line 11, *consilio, auctoritate, sententia; ratio* is *reason, i.e.* the exercise of the reasoning faculties.

29. quae nisi essent, *etc.*: *unless these qualities were in old men.*

30. summum consilium: *the highest deliberative body.*

31. quidem: *in fact.*

PAGE 129. **1. ut sunt**: *just as they are* (*old men*). The reference is to the γέροντες or councillors (lit. *old men*), who formed the so-called γερουσία. Cicero's point is that, while the Romans called their councillors *senatores* (a word suggesting *senex*), the Lacedaemonians called their councillors *senes* outright.

2. quodsi voletis: *if you will* (*only*), — not so strong as *wish* in this instance.

3. externa: *foreign history.*

5. cedo: *tell me.* **qui**: *how.*

6. in Naevi poetae Lupo: *in ' The Wolf' of the poet Naevius.* Naevius was one of the very earliest Latin writers (270–199 B.C.). Of his numerous works, Bellum Punicum (a poem in Saturnian measure on the First Punic War), tragedies and comedies, only a few brief fragments have come down to us. It has been conjectured that the words above cited were addressed by Amulius to the ambassadors whom the Veientian king Vibe had dispatched to the Alban court. The answer to the question is given in the words: *Proveniebant oratores, etc.* **respondentur et alia et hoc in primis**: *other replies are given, but this in particular.*

8. stulti, adulescentuli: *fools, boys.* The point is not that these particular youths were fools, but that youths who undertake to wrest the control of government from older men, are fools as a class.

9. temeritas est videlicet, *etc.:* *rashness, it is plain to see, is a characteristic of youth (florentis aetatis).*

11. at memoria minuitur : *but, it is alleged, memory is impaired.* This use of *at* to introduce the view of an opponent is very common in argumentation. **credo :** *I suppose so;* not ironical. **nisi eam exerceas :** *unless you exercise it;* the second singular is used of an indefinite subject precisely like our English ' you.' For the subjunctive, see the note on p. 124, line 11.

12. natura tardior : *naturally rather dull.*

13. perceperat : *knew,* lit. *had acquired.*

14. qui Aristides esset, *etc.: to greet Aristides as Lysimachus.* As object of *salutare* understand *eum,* to which *Lysimachum* stands in the relation of predicate accusative. There is a certain dry humor in the illustration chosen by Cato. The rivalry between Themistocles and Aristides had been so keen that Themistocles was hardly likely to forget his old opponent or to confuse him with another man. Lysimachus was Aristides's father.

15. equidem : while not etymologically connected with *ego,* this word in Cicero is regularly equivalent to *ego quidem,* ' I for my part,' ' I at least,' *etc.*

16. qui sunt : *who are still living.*

17. nec sepulcra legens, *etc.: nor am I afraid of losing my memory by reading epitaphs, as they say.* **quod ajunt :** *quod* refers loosely for its antecedent to the idea suggested by the context, *viz.:* Those who read epitaphs, lose their memory. Doubtless this saying was largely true, in so far, at least, as those who were found engaged in studying the tombstones were already old men of waning faculties.

18. his ipsis legendis : *by reading these very tombstones.*

19. quemquam senem : *any old man.* Note the use of *quisquam* for *ullus.*

20. omnia quae curant : *all things in which they take interest.*

21. vadimonia constituta : *the bail they have given,* lit. *the bail fixed, viz.* by the court.

22. quid juris consulti, *etc.: senes* belongs with all these nominatives, — *how is it in case of aged lawyers, aged pontiffs, aged augurs, aged philosophers,* lit. *jurists as old men, augurs as old men, etc.* Some verb is to be supplied in sense with these words, *fecerunt,* for example.

23. quam multa meminerunt : *how many things they (are obliged to) remember;* i.e. the very nature of their profession obliges them to possess retentive memories.

24. manent : emphatic by position. **ingenia :** *faculties.*

modo permaneat, *etc.: provided only interest and industry continue.*

26. honoratis: this word does not here mean *honored,* but designates men distinguished by holding public offices, *honores.*

PAGE **130, 1. Sophocles:** the greatest of the Greek tragedians. He lived from 496–406 B.C. Seven of his tragedies have come down to us.

2. quod propter studium cum . . . videretur: *and when in consequence of this pursuit he seemed.*

3. a filiis: the common account attributes this action to a single son, Iophon; but the whole story is apocryphal.

4. quem ad modum male rem gerentibus, *etc.: just as fathers who mismanage their estates are wont to be removed from (control of) their property,* lit. *it is wont to be interdicted to fathers from their property;* **patribus** is Dative of Reference; **bonis,** Ablative of Separation. B. 188, 1, *a*; A. 364, N. 1; G. 390, 2, N. 3. **nostro more:** this Roman custom was legally recognized in the Laws of the Twelve Tables (about 450 B.C.).

5. quasi desipientem: *as being in his dotage.*

7. eam fabulam: *the play.* **quam in manibus habebat:** *which he had in hand, on which he was engaged.* For another sense of *in manibus,* see p. 125, line 22, note. **et proxime scripserat:** *and upon which he had just been writing.*

8. Oedipum Coloneum: *the Oedipus at Colónus. Coloneus* is an adjective. The play has come down to us, and represents the aged Oedipus arriving in his wanderings at the Attic deme of Colonus. The tradition is that the passage chosen by the poet for recitation on the occasion referred to was the magnificent choral ode in praise of Athens (verses 668–719), a part of which runs as follows:

> Of all the lands far famed for goodly steeds,
> Thou com'st, O stranger, to the noblest spot,
> Colonos, glistening bright,
> Where, evermore, in thickets freshly green,
> The clear-voiced nightingale
> Still haunts, and pours her song,
> By purpling ivy hid,
> And the thick leafage sacred to the God.
>
> — PLUMPTRE's Translation.

9. num illud carmen, *etc.: whether that poem seemed (the work) of a dotard.*

10. sententiis: *votes.* **liberatus:** in the iudicial sense,—*acquitted.*

11. **Homerum, Hesiodum,** *etc.:* the enumeration of distinguished names embraces three classes: poets (Homer, Hesiod, Simonides, Stesichorus), rhetoricians (Isocrates, Gorgias), philosophers (Pythagoras, Democritus, *etc.*). It should be borne in mind that Cato here mentions only those poets, rhetoricians, and philosophers who lived to an advanced age. **Homerum**: said by Herodotus to have flourished about 850 B.C. **Hesiodum**: *Hesiod,* a native of Ascra in Boeotia, flourished about 750 B.C. His greatest work, the Works and Days ("Εργα καί 'Ημέραι) suggested much to Virgil in the composition of the Georgics.

12. **Simonidem**: *Simónides.* There were two poets of this name, — Simonides of Amorgos and Simonides of Ceos. The latter was the more famous of the two; he flourished at the time of the Persian wars (490–480 B.C.), and composed the extant epigram in honor of the Spartans who fell at Thermopylae. **Stesichorum**: *Stesíchorus,* a famous lyric poet of Himera in Sicily. He flourished about 600 B.C. All his works are lost barring a few fragments. It is said that a nightingale sang upon his lips at his birth. **Isocraten, Gorgian**: see notes on p. 126, lines 9, 12. *Isocrates,* though of the 3d declension, forms its accusative after the analogy of Greek nouns in -*ēs* of the 1st declension. Similarly *Xenocraten* below.

13. **Pythagoram**: *Pythágoras* of Samos, founder of the Pythagorean school. He flourished in the latter half of the sixth century B.C. Mysticism was a pronounced feature in his system; his most famous doctrine was the theory of transmigration of souls (Metempsychosis).

14. **Democritum**: *Demócritus,* of Abdera in Thrace, 460–361 B.C., one of the earliest representatives of the atomic theory. **Xenocraten**: *Xenócrates,* of Chalcédon, 396–314 B.C., a pupil of Plato, and one of his successors in the presidency of the Academy, — a post which he occupied for twenty-five years.

15. **Zenonem**: *Zeno,* of Citium in Cyprus, about 350–250 B.C. He was founder of the Stoic school, of which he was for nearly sixty years the president. **Cleanthem**: *Cleanthes,* of Assos in Asia Minor, 300–220 B.C., a Stoic and a disciple of Zeno.

16. **Diogenem Stoicum**: *Diógenes, the Stoic,* not to be confounded with Diogenes, the Cynic. He had visited Rome in 155 B.C., five years previous to the time of this dialogue, and was evidently an old man at that time, though the years of his birth and death are unknown. He had come to Rome in company with Carneades and Critolaus as an ambassador, and during his stay had begun to expound his philosophical views. Cato's opposition to Greek ideas was so deeply rooted that he took the lead in

securing Diogenes's departure from the city. The enthusiasm, therefore, with which Cicero makes Cato refer to Diogenes is not in keeping with the facts.

18. age: *come!*

19. ista divina studia: *viz.* poetry, philosophy, *etc.* **ex agro Sabino rusticos**: *farmers in the Sabine territory.*

21. numquam fere: *scarcely ever.*

22. majora: *important,* lit. *greater* (than ordinary). **non serendis**, *etc.*: *not in the way of planting, gathering, or storing the crops.* Notice the zeugma in *serendis fructibus;* accuracy would call for some such word as *seminibus.* The use of the ablative here without *in* is extremely peculiar; most scholars explain the construction as an ablative absolute. Observe that *non* here does not counteract the negative force of *numquam,* but repeats it. B. 347, 2; A. 327, 2; G. 445; H. 656, 2.

23. in aliis: *in other things; aliis* is here contrasted with the following *quae sciunt nihil ad se omnino pertinere,* and hence practically means: *in matters that concern them.*

24. senex: here with adjectival force.

25. idem: nominative plural, — *they also.*

26. pertinere: in the sense of *vitally concern.*

27. quae . . . prosint: *to benefit,* — relative clause of purpose. **alteri saeclo**: *the next* (lit. *the other*) *generation.* Note that *saeclum* is the original form of this word, whence *saeculum* by the development of a parasitic vowel.

28. Statius: Caecilius Statius, by birth an Insubrian Gaul. He was a comic poet, and lived about 220–166 B.C. Only fragments of his works remain. **in Synephebis**: *in his Synephébi,* the title of a play. The original was by the Greek poet Menander; Caecilius translated and adapted it for Roman audiences.

29. quamvis sit senex: *however old he may be.* **quaerenti**: *to (the person) inquiring.*

PAGE **131**, 4. **melius**: supply some such verb as *dicit,* — *Caecilius gives us a better sentiment* (lit. *says better*) *with regard to the old man,* etc. The passage from *et melius* to *sed videtis,* sixteen lines below, is really a digression from the point at present under discussion. Cato is endeavoring to show that old men even superintend the work on their own farms. In developing this point he quotes two passages from Statius in support of his contention. These two citations lead to others, which, though they are concerned with the general subject of old age, are nevertheless not germane to the present topic, *viz.* the allegation that old age withdraws men from active occupation. See the note on p. 124, line 22.

5. **quam illud idem**: *than he does in what follows*, lit. *than the same (Caecilius says) the following.*

6. **edepol, senectus**, *etc.*: these lines are quoted from Statius's Plocium (The Necklace). **nil . . . viti**: *no other evil; quicquam* is redundant.

7. **apportes**: *should bring.*   **quom**: the earlier form of *cum*, and possibly still in common use when Cicero wrote the de Senectute.   **sat**: *sat* for *satis* is common in archaic Latin.

8. **quae non volt, videt**: the subject is general, — *one sees many things that one does not wish; volt*, the early form of *vult*, may have been still the prevailing form in Cicero's day.   In the next two lines *volt* is written by most editors, on the assumption that Cicero intentionally reproduces the diction of Caecilius.

10. **illud vero**, *etc.*: *but the following utterance of the same Caecilius is still worse*, lit. *the same Caecilius (says) the following worse.*

12. **tum equidem**, *etc.*: quoted from Caecilius's Ephesio. **senecta**: poetical for *senectus.*

13. **ea aetate**: *at that time of life;* the phrase limits *sentire.* **eumpse**: *i.e. eum+pse* (B. L. L. § 196), archaic for *ipsum; cf. ipse* for **is-pse; eumpse* is the subject of *esse*, and is equivalent to *se ipsum*, 'oneself.'   **odiosum**: *a bore.*   **alteri**: *sc. aetati, i.e.* to the young, lit. *to the other period of life.*

14. **jucundum potius quam odiosum**: preserve the ellipsis in translation.

19. **nec minus intellego**: the inaccuracy of expression is identical with that noted p. 120, line 11, *te suspicor eisdem rebus quibus me ipsum commoveri.*   What Cato really means is: *I see that I am no less agreeable to you than you actually are to me.* Strictly the Latin should be: *nec minus intellego me vobis esse jucundum quam mihi vos estis.*

20. **sed videtis**: Cato here returns from his somewhat lengthy digression (see above on line 4), and resumes the point under discussion, *viz.* the activity of old men.   **ut senectus**, *etc.*: *how old age, etc.;* indirect question.

21. **verum etiam**: *but even.*

22. **agens et moliens**: *doing and undertaking;* this predicate use of the present participle is rare.   **tale scilicet**, *etc.*: *some such thing, of course, as, etc.*   The occupation of the old man will depend upon his earlier pursuits.

24. **quid?** *etc.*: *what of those who, etc.?*   **ut et Solonem versibus gloriantem videmus**: *et* before *Solonem* is correlative with the *et* before *ego* below, but should not be rendered in English translation.   Solon is the famous Athenian lawgiver, 638–558 B.C. He was a poet as well as a statesman, and numerous fragments of his works have come down to us.

26. **et ego feci**: *and (just as) I have done.*
27. **senex**: *when an old man.*   **sic avide**: *so eagerly.*
28. **nota essent**: *became known, familiar.*
29. **quibus me nunc exemplis uti videtis**: *which you now see me using as examples; exemplis* stands in predicate relation to *quibus*, which depends directly upon *uti*. The passage is somewhat apologetic. Cicero evidently feels that his picture of Cato attributes to the old Roman a greater familiarity with Greek thought and letters than he actually possessed; hence the attempt to account for the origin of the alleged learning. See Introd. p. 331.   **quod cum . . . audirem**: *quod* refers to the idea of constantly adding to one's knowledge or accomplishments; *cum* here is causal. We should naturally expect the present (*audiam*). The imperfect is the result of attraction to the tense of *vellem*.

PAGE **132**, 1. **in fidibus**: *in case of the lyre.*   **vellem**: apodosis of a conditional sentence contrary-to-fact, with omitted protasis.
2. **discebant fidibus**: *used to learn the lyre,* lit. *learn with the lyre.* B. 218, 7.   **in litteris certe**: *on literature at any rate, i.e.* if not on anything else.
4. **desidero**: *feel the need of, the lack of.*
5. **locus alter**: *the second point.*
6. **non plus**: the negative as p. 124, line 7.
7. **quod est**: *what you have;* the antecedent of *quod* is *eo.* **quicquid agas**: clauses introduced by indefinite relatives (*quisquis quicumque, etc.*) ordinarily stand in the indicative; but all subordinate clauses expressed in the indefinite second singular regularly take the subjunctive.
8. **quae vóx**: *what utterance?*
9. **Milonis Crotoniatae**: *Milo of Crotóna,* in southern Italy, a famous athlete of the sixth century B.C. He won repeated victories in the Olympic and Pythian games.   **qui cum,** *etc.: for when he was, etc.*
12. **hi quidem**: almost *these, alas!*
13. **isti**: *sc. sunt mortui.*
14. **ex lateribus**: *is consequence of your wind; latera* is used as above, p. 126, line 28.
15. **nihil, nihil, nihil**: note the anaphora.   **Sex. Aelius**: *Sextus Aelius,* consul 198 B.C., famous as a jurist and an orator.
16. **Ti. Coruncanius**: see note on p. 127, line 15.   **modo**: *recently.*   **P. Crassus**: the use of *modo* would suggest that the reference is to some one nearer the present time than either Coruncanius or Aelius. Publius Licinius Crassus, consul in 171 B.C., naturally suggests himself as the person Cicero has in mind. That Crassus, however, was not eminent as a jurist, and Cicero

has probably confused him with P. Licinius Crassus Dives, pontifex maximus in 212 B.C. and consul in 205, a man famed for his knowledge of pontifical law. **jura praescribebantur**: *laws were interpreted.*

18. **est provecta**: *continued.* **prudentia**: *wisdom.* **orator metuo ne languescat**: as the order of the words shows, *orator* is here emphatic, — *as regards the orator, I fear he may become feeble.*

19. **senectute**: causal. **munus ejus**: *his function.*

20. **omnino canorum** illud, *etc.: to be sure that melodious quality in the voice somehow even improves in old age.* Note the mixed metaphor in *canorum . . . splendescit; splendesco* properly applies only to what presents itself to the eye. *Omnino* is contrasted with *sed tamen*, — 'to be sure the voice improves; yet apart from that an old man's talk is often engaging.'

23. **et videtis annos**: though grammatically co-ordinate with what precedes, this clause is logically subordinate, being equivalent to 'old though I am' or 'in spite of my years.' **sed tamen est**, *etc.: but yet the quiet and unimpassioned conversation of an old man has a grace about it.*

24. **quietus et remissus**: *quietus* = 'without movement,' as contrasted with the lively gesticulation of the orator; *remissus* = 'without passion,' *i.e.* without the mental and moral excitement of the orator. **facit sibi audientiam**: *gains itself a hearing.*

25. **compta et mitis**: *smooth and easy.* **quam si . . . nequeas**: *if you should be unable to practise this; quam* refers to *oratio.*

26. **Scipioni et Laelio**: *a Scipio and a Laelius.*

27. **senectute stipata studiis juventutis**: *an old age thronged with eager youths,* lit. *with the eagerness of youth;* the abstract for the concrete. Notice the alliteration in *senectute stipata studiis.*

28. **an ne illas quidem vires**, *etc.: or do we leave to old age not even the strength to teach young men?* illas vires is explained by the following *ut*-clauses.

PAGE **133**, 1. **instituat**: *instruct.*

2. **ad omne offici munus**: *for the performance of every duty,* lit. *for all performance of duty.* **instruat**: *prepare, equip; cf. instrumentum,* 'outfit,' 'equipment,' *instructus,* 'fitted out,' 'equipped.' **quo quidem**, *etc.: than this task what can be more glorious?*

3. **Cn. et P. Scipiones**: these were respectively the uncle and father of the elder Africanus. They both rendered important services in the earlier half of the Second Punic War, and fell in Spain in 212 B.C. Note the plural in *Scipiones;* this is usual

when the names of two persons of the same family are combined
by a copulative conjunction.

4. **avi tui duo, L. Aemilius et P. Africanus**: Lucius Aemilius
(Paulus), the father of Lucius Aemilius Paulus Macedonicus, the
conqueror of Perseus, was the actual grandfather of the younger
Scipio; Publius Africanus was his adoptive grandfather.

6. **bonarum artium**: *liberal arts.*   **non beati putandi**: *are
to be thought other than happy; cf.* p. 124, line 8, *non gravis; sunt*
is to be supplied with *putandi.*

7. **quamvis consenuerint vires**, *etc.: however much their
strength may have waned and failed.*

8. **etsi**: corrective.

10. **effetum**: best taken as in predicate relation to *corpus*, —
hands the body over to old age all worn out, i.e. in a state of ex-
haustion.

11. **Cyrus**: Cyrus the Elder, king of Persia, the hero of Xenophon's Cyropaedía. He lived from 599 to 529 B.C.   **apud
Xenophontem**: *in Xenophon, i.e.* in his writings, — a common
use of *apud.*

14. **Metellum**: consul in 251 B.C., in the First Punic War; he
died in 221.

15. **memini puer**: the expression is inexact.   Cicero has evidently combined two ideas:

(1) ' As a boy, I noticed that Metellus was strong.'

(2) ' I now remember that Metellus was strong.'

English admits the same form of expression, however.   **cum
factus esset**: the *cum*-clause is purely circumstantial, — *having
been made pontifex maximus;* see note on p. 127, line 27.

17. **esse**: the present infinitive occurs repeatedly with *memini*
where in English we should expect the perfect.

19. **nihil necesse est**: *it is not at all necessary.*

20. **id quidem**: *i.e.* to speak of one's self.   **senile**: *characteristic of old men.*

22. **videtisne**: *don't you see?* when appended to the verb, *-ne*
frequently has the force of *nonne.*   B. 162, 2, *c*; A. 332, *c.*

23. **praedicet**: here, *boasts.*

24. **nec erat ei verendum**: *nor did he have occasion to fear.*

25. **vera praedicans**: *in telling the truth.*

26. **insolens aut loquax**: *arrogant or garrulous.*

27. **quam ad suavitatem**: *for which eloquence.*

28. **et tamen**: *i.e.* in spite of his lack of bodily strength.   **dux
ille Graeciae**: the reference is to Agamemnon; *ille* when following a substantive regularly means, as here, *that famous, that well-
known.*

29. **nusquam**: *i.e. nowhere* in Homer.   **ut . . . habeat**: the

clause is the object of *optat*.   **Ajacis similes**: in Cicero *similis*, when governing words designating persons, is regularly followed by the genitive.

PAGE 134, 1. **sed ut Nestoris**: elliptical for *sed ut decem Nestoris similes habeat*.   **quod si sibi acciderit**: *if this fortune should be his; acciderit* is in the subjunctive by attraction to *sit peritura*.

4. **vellem equidem idem possem gloriari**: *would that I could make the same boast; vellem* is in the subjunctive as expressing the apodosis of a contrary-to-fact conditional sentence, the protasis of which is omitted, — *I would wish* (were it possible); *possem* is logically the object of *vellem*, being developed from an original optative subjunctive, — *would I were able; ut* is regularly absent in this idiom. B. 296, 1, *a*.   **idem**: B. 176, 2, *a*; A. 390, *c*; G. 333, 1; H. 409, 1.   **sed tamen hoc queo dicere**, *etc.*: the thought is inaccurately expressed ; what Cato means is : ' Though I am not as strong as I once was, yet I can say that old age has not entirely shattered me.' Instead of this, the clause *me . . . esse* is made principal instead of subordinate, while *afflixit* and *desiderat* are put in the indicative instead of in the infinitive. Logically the thought demanded: *hoc queo dicere, cum eis viribus non sim quibus fuerim, tamen me non afflixisse senectutem, non curiam desiderare*.   Note that *queo* unaccompanied by a negative is rare.

5. **eis viribus**: Ablative of Quality.

6. **miles bello Punico**: in 217 B.C.   **quaestor eodem bello**: in 204 B.C.

7. **consul in Hispania**: *in Spain in my consulship;* in 195 B.C. In honor of Cato's successes in Spain, the Senate decreed a three days' thanksgiving. Cato declared that he had captured more cities in Spain than he had spent days in the province.

8. **tribunus militaris**: this was in 191 B.C., in the war against Antiochus.   **cum depugnavi**: *cum* with the indicative to denote the point of time at which; *depugno* is ' to fight it out,' ' fight to the end.'

10. **non, non**, *etc.*: observe the emphasis produced by the repetition of the *non*.

12. **clientes**: including not only his political followers at Rome, but also those foreign nations or cities whose protector he was.   **hospites**: *guest-friends;* strangers at Rome who had relations of hospitality with Cato.   **nec enim**: *nor indeed.*

13. **laudato** = ' oft-quoted.'

14. **mature fieri senem**, *etc.*: the saying obviously means Begin early to exercise the discretion of age, if you would live to

a good old age.' Cato's criticism of the proverb is based upon a misinterpretation of its real significance. He takes it as though it were intended to mean : ' Begin early to cultivate the inactivity of age, if you would remain an old man long.' The infinitive with *moneo* is less common than a subjunctive clause, but is admissible when *moneo* lacks a personal object.

15. me senem esse mallem: *volo, nolo, malo* more commonly take the infinitive without subject accusative to denote another action of the same subject; *mallem* here represents the apodosis of a contrary-to-fact conditional sentence, the protasis of which is omitted, — *I should prefer (were I bold enough to express a preference)*. Cf. the use of *vellem*, above, line 4.

16. ante quam essem: subjunctive by attraction. **convenire me** = *to have an interview with me.*

17. cui fuerim occupatus: lit. *to whom I have been engaged, i.e.* whom I have refused to see. The subjunctive is one of Characteristic. **at minus habeo :** *at*, as above, p. 129, line 11, introduces the view of an opponent, — *but, you may urge, etc.*

18. T. Ponti centurionis: the centurions were usually men of great strength and stature. Nothing further is known of the Pontius here referred to.

20. praestantior: *a better man.* **moderatio modo virium adsit:** *let there only be a control over one's strength.* The subjunctive is Jussive, with the accessory force of a Proviso.

21. ne ille: *such a man, I assure you;* this is the asseverative *ne.* In its use it is restricted to combination with pronouns, — personal, demonstrative, and possessive. It regularly precedes the word which it emphasizes. **non desiderio tenebitur:** *will not be possessed with longing for, i.e.* will not feel the lack of. *Cf. desidero*, above, p. 132, line 4.

22. Olympiae per stadium, *etc.:* according to the story Milo had carried the animal daily as it grew.

23. cum sustineret bovem: *carrying an ox;* another circumstantial *cum*-clause; see note on p. 127, line 27.

24. igitur: merely transitional. **has corporis:** *sc. vires.* **Pythagorae :** Pythagoras was a townsman of Milo, a fact which lends additional force to the comparison.

25. utare: the command is general; hence the indefinite second singular. B. 356, 3 ; A. 439, *a* ; G. 263, 2, *a.*

26. dum adsit, cum absit: the subjunctive is the result of attraction. Notice the chiastic arrangement in :

utare, dum adsit :: cum absit, ne requiras.

ne requiras: this form of prohibition is unusual in prose; *noli* with the infinitive is the rule. The subject of *requiras* is general just as was the case with *utare*.   **nisi forte**: see note on p. 128, line 13.

27. pueritiam, adulescentiam: *boyhood, young manhood.* **paululum aetate progressi**: referring to those in middle life.

28. cursus est certus aetatis: *there is a regular course of life.*

29. suaque . . . tempestivitas: *and to each part of life its own proper character* (lit. *seasonableness) is allotted.*

30. infirmitas puerorum: *the helplessness of children.*

31. ferocitas: *impetuosity.* **gravitas**: *steadiness.* **jam constantis**: *already settled, i.e.* middle (life).

PAGE 135, 1. **naturale quiddam**: *a certain natural (product),* as shown by *percipi,* ' to be reaped.'

2. quod debeat: Subjunctive of Characteristic.

3. hospes tuus avitus: *the guest-friend of your grandfather, i.e.* of the elder Africanus, between whom and Masinissa there existed a strong friendship.   **Masinissa**: king of the Numidians.   In the Second Punic War he was at the outset an ally of the Carthaginians, but later became a supporter of the Romans.

4. hodie: *i.e.* still.

5. pedibus: *on foot.*   **omnino non ascendere**: *does not mount at all.*

7. imbri: *imber* is not properly an *i*-stem, but has taken on the *i*-stem inflection in the ablative singular.   **capite operto**: Ablative of Quality.

8. siccitatem: *soundness; siccitas,* lit. ' dryness,' is opposed to that physical state in which the body is affected with unwholesome humors.

9. officia et munera: *functions and duties;* a favorite phrase with Cicero.   **potest**, *etc.*: as the position indicates, *potest* is specially emphatic, — *it is possible, therefore, for exercise and self-control to preserve, etc.*

12. ne sint, *etc.*: *granting that there is not strength in old age,* lit. *let there not be strength.*   Concessive Subjunctive.

13. a senectute: *of old age.*

14. muneribus eis quae, *etc.*: military service is particularly meant.

15. non modo: here used for *non modo non.*   This occurs regularly when the idea modified by *non modo (non)* is reserved for a second member introduced by *ne . . . quidem.*   **quod non possumus**: as antecedent of *quod,* understand *id,* Accusative of Result with *cogimur.* B. 176, 2, *b*; A. 390, *c*; G. 333, 1; H. 409, 1.

17. at multi: *at* is here again used to introduce the view of an imaginary opponent; but below in *at id quidem, at* introduces

Cato's own reply. **nullum offici aut omnino vitae munus exsequi**: *no obligation nor any function of life at all.* Under *offici munera* would fall obligations to the state, to one's family. or friends; under *vitae munera*, the ordinary care of one's person and attention to one's personal wants.

20. **valetudinis**: primarily *health*, but unless accompanied by some such word as *bona*, it ordinarily means *poor health;* so here. **P. Africani filius**: son of the elder Africanus; his feeble health prevented his entering public life.

22. **quod ni ita fuisset**: *unless this had been so.* **alterum lumen**: *the second light;* the elder Africanus was the first. **illud**: *he (i.e. Africani filius),* attracted from *ille* by the neuter predicate noun, *lumen.* **exstitisset**: lit. *would have stood forth.* The metaphor is " mixed."

23. **paternam**: *his father's.*

25. **in senibus**: *in case of old men.*

26. **resistendum**: emphatic, as shown by the position, — *the thing to do, Laelius and Scipio, is to resist old age.*

28. **pugnandum**: *sc. est.* **tamquam, sic**: *just as, so.*

30. **utendum**: *one must use.* **tantum cibi**: *(only) so much food.*

31. **ut reficiantur vires, non opprimantur**: Subjunctive of Result.

PAGE 136, 1. **subveniendum est**: *we must come to the relief of.*

2. **menti atque animo**: when used with precision *mens* refers to the intellect, *animus* to the feelings and will; together the two words embrace all the mental and moral faculties. **haec quoque**: *i.e. mens* and *animus.*

3. **nisi tamquam, etc.**: *tamquam* (' apologetic '; see note on p. 122, line 24) modifies the entire phrase *lumini oleum instilles,* — 'unless, so to speak, one keeps pouring oil into the lamp,' *i.e.* the oil of study and reflection into the lamp of the mind; for the subjunctive in *instilles,* see note on p. 124, line 11.

4. **corpora quidem**: *quidem* serves merely to emphasize *corpora,* and so to heighten the antithesis between *corpora ingravescunt* and *animi levantur.*

5. **exercendo**: *by exercising them.*

6. **quos ait, etc.**: *(those) whom Caecilius characterizes as the foolish old men of the comic stage; ait* here takes the construction (unusual for this verb) of two accusatives, direct object and predicate accusative. For Caecilius, see note on p. 130, line 28. **comico stultos senes**: the quotation is from Caecilius's Epiclērus (' The Heiress'). **hos significat, etc.** *by these he means, etc.*: lit. *he means these (as being) credulous, etc.;* here again we

have two accusatives, direct object and predicate accusative, a construction not elsewhere found with *significo*.

7. **credulos**: the credulous father is a stock figure of Latin comedy.   **dissolutos**: *shattered, broken down.*   **quae vitia**. *faults which; cf. quem magistratum,* p. 124, line 26.

8. **inertis, ignavae**: *iners* implies merely a lack of activity, *ignavus* refers rather to the disinclination to be active.

9. **petulantia, libido**: *wantonness, lust.*

11. **sed non proborum**: *but (merely) of those who are not upright; non proborum* is less abrupt than *improborum* would have been.   **senilis** = *senum*, — the adjective for the genitive of the substantive, as often in Latin.

12. **deliratio**: *dotage.*

14. **tantam, tantas**: *i.e.* so great, as is well known, hence nearly equivalent to *magnam, permagnam.*   **Appius**: Appius Claudius Caecus; see p. 127, line 17.

15. **intentum**: *stretched.*

16. **languescens**: the participle has the force of an adverb. — *feebly.*

17. **auctoritatem**: referring possibly to the *patria potestas,* which gave the father absolute control over his children.   **imperium**: stronger than *auctoritas;* technically *imperium* designated the absolute power with which the higher Roman magistrates (*consul* and *praetor*) were formally invested by the *Comitia Curiata.* The word is here figuratively applied to a private individual.

18. **verebantur**: *reverenced.*

19. **patrius**: *inherited from the fathers, i.e.* 'the good old.' **mos**: in English we should employ the plural.

20. **ita enim**: *for on this condition; ita* is explained by the following *si*-clauses.   **honesta**: *honorable, held in honor.*

21. **emancipata est**: *is in bondage,* lit. *is sold; emancipare* primarily meant ' to transfer,' and was used not only of property and slaves, but also of freemen.   Later it came to be used of the formal act of sale by which slaves were liberated, and so acquired the meaning *set free,* — the exact opposite of the meaning in our passage.

23. **senile aliquid**: *a touch of the old man.*

25. **quod qui sequitur**: *he who makes this his object.*

26. **septimus liber Originum**: Cato's Origines was an historical work.   The second and third books treated of the origin and settlement of the Italian towns, whence the title of the work. **est in manibus**: *i.e. is under way; cf. habebat in manibus,* p. 130, line 7.

28. **nunc cum maxime**: *now especially, just now.* This ex-

pression, which is fairly frequent, results from an ellipsis; thus here the full thought would have been expressed by *nunc conficio cum maxime conficio,* ' I am now preparing, at a time when I am especially preparing,' *i.e.* ' I am preparing now especially.' Sometimes *cum maxime* alone stands in the same sense.

29. **conficio**: *i.e.* prepare for publication. One hundred and fifty of Cato's speeches were known to Cicero, as he himself elsewhere tells us. **jus augurium, pontificium, civile**: *jus augurium* was the code of the augurs; the *jus pontificium* emanated from the *pontifices*, who had the oversight and direction of the religious observances of the state; *jus civile* seems here to be contrasted with *jus augurium* and *jus pontificium, i.e.* the secular jurisprudence is opposed to the religious.

30. **multum utor**: *make much use.* On this adverbial use of *multum*, originally an Accusative of Result, see B. 176, 3; A. 390, *d*, N. 2.

31. **exercendae memoriae gratia**: to be taken only with *commemoro*, not with *Pythagoreorum more.*

PAGE 137, 2. **haec**: unusual form for *hae*, but found occasionally elsewhere in Cicero. **exercitationes ingeni**: intellectual pursuits are contrasted with athletic training. **haec curricula mentis**: as contrasted with the wrestling- or boxing-ground.

3. **desudans**: *de-* is intensive, as in *depugnavi,* p. 134, line 8.

4. **adsum amicis**: *I assist my friends; adesse* is used especially in the sense of rendering legal assistance.

5. **ultroque**: *of my own motion.* The Roman senators in debate were not held closely to the question before the house. Cato, therefore, simply means that when he addressed the senate he exercised his parliamentary privilege, and brought up such matters as he saw fit.

6. **easque tueor**: *I maintain them, defend them, i.e.* in debate.

7. **quas exsequi nequirem**: see note on p. 132, line 25, *quam si exsequi nequeas.* **lectulus**: a sort of reading-couch or sofa.

8. **ea ipsa cogitantem**: *planning those very things.* **quae jam agere non possem**: *even though I could not carry them into execution; quae possem* is a relative clause denoting a condition contrary to fact.

9. **ut possim**: emphatic by position, — *that I can do so, is the result of my past life.*

10. **viventi**: agreeing with *ei* understood, which is Dative of Agent with *intellegitur,* — *for by a man living constantly in these pursuits and toils, it is not noticed, etc.*

11. **ita sensim**, *etc.: so gradually does life wane;* this is the

' retrospective ' *ita; i.e.* the particle looks back to the preceding sentence, of which it furnishes a justification ; observe the alliteration in *sensim sine sensu senescit.*

15. **quod . . . dicunt,** *etc.: the fact that they say it is devoid of pleasures;* explanatory of *tertia vituperatio.* **voluptatibus :** *i.e.* bodily pleasures.

16. **aetatis :** here, *old age.*

17. **accipite enim . . . veterem orationem :** *for listen to the words uttered long ago.*

18. **Archytae :** *Archytas,* of Tarentum, a famous Pythagorean philosopher who flourished about 400 B.C. He was eminent also as a mathematician, statesman, and general.

20. **adulescens :** *as a young man;* in apposition with the subject of *essem.* **Tarenti cum Q. Maximo :** see p. 124, line 25.

22. **a natura :** nature is here personified ; hence the employment of the preposition. **cujus voluptatis avidae :** *through eagerness for which,* lit. *eager for which pleasure;* but the repetition of the antecedent in the relative clause cannot be reproduced in English.

23. **temere :** *blindly; temere* was originally the locative of a lost nominative *temus,* meaning ' darkness ' ; hence ' in the dark,' ' blindly,' later ' rashly,' ' heedlessly.' **ad potiendum :** *for attaining it; i.e.* pleasure.

26. **malum facinus :** *evil deed; facinus* here has its original force of ' act,' ' deed,' which is regular in early Latin. Cicero usually employs it in the sense of ' crime.'

PAGE **138**, 1. **impelleret :** *sc. homines.*

2. **nisi :** *than, except.*

3. **cumque :** *and while, though.* **homini :** *i.e.* mankind. **sive Natura sive quis deus :** *be it nature or some god;* Cato does not attempt to determine which it was.

4. **muneri ac dono :** *boon and gift.* The two words are here closely synonymous. When used with precision, *donum* is the general term, *munus* is more specific, being restricted to gracious gifts, or gifts bestowed for a special purpose.

6. **libidine dominante :** the ablative absolute here denotes both time and circumstance, — ' while lust is master ' or ' under the rule of lust.' **temperantiae :** Dative of Possession, — *self-control has no place.* **neque omnino,** *etc.: nor can virtue gain a footing at all in the realm of pleasure.*

8. **fingere animo :** *to imagine, conceive of; animo* is ablative.

9. **tanta, quanta,** *etc.: just as much pleasure as could possibly be enjoyed;* observe the emphasis secured by the position of *maxima* at the end of its clause.

11. **tam diu dum**: *so long as;* an unusual form of expression for *quam diu.* **ita gauderet**: *took enjoyment in this way, i.e.* in unrestrained self-indulgence. **agitare**: *pursue.*

12. **ratione**: to be joined with *consequi.*

14. **siquidem**: here in the secondary meaning of *since;* it is used differently above, p. 137, line 16. **major atque longinquior**: *more intense and longer continued.*

16. **C. Pontio**: his full name was Gaius Pontius Herennius. His son, Gaius Pontius Telesinus, defeated the Romans at the battle of the Caudine Forks. **Caudino proelio**: this disastrous defeat of the Roman arms occurred in the Second Samnite War, 321 B.C. The Roman army was forced to go 'under the yoke.'

18. **locutum Archytam**: supply *esse;* the infinitive depends upon *accepisse.* **Nearchus**: a philosopher of the Pythagorean school. **hospes noster**: *noster* for *meus,* as frequently.

19. **qui . . . permanserat**: *who had remained loyal to the Roman people.* Many of the Tarentines, through jealousy of Rome, had sympathized with the Carthaginians, and the city had been handed over to Hannibal in 212 B.C.

20. **cum . . . interfuisset**: *Plato the Athenian having been present at that conversation;* here again *cum* is entirely devoid of temporal force, and the clause is purely circumstantial; see note on p. 127, line 27. The *cum*-clause is to be taken, of course, only with *locutum* (*esse*).

22. **L. Camillo, Ap. Claudio consulibus**: this was in the year 349 B.C. Plato's last visit to Italy is said to hav occurred in 361 B.C. Cicero, therefore, is probably in error here.

23. **quorsus hoc**: supply *dixi* or some such word. **ut intellegeretis**: the imperfect is used because the *ut*-clause is felt as depending upon *dixi* or some other verb of saying to be supplied, — *I said this in order that you might understand.* Hence also the other subordinate subjunctives in this passage are in the imperfect. In English we should use the present.

24. **magnam . . . gratiam**: *great gratitude ought to be entertained toward old age.*

25. **quae efficeret, etc.**: the relative clause has causal force, — lit. *since it brings it about that that is not pleasant, which ought not* (*to be*).

26. **liberet**: from *libet.*

27. **ut ita dicam**: *so to speak;* the phrase is introduced as an apology for the unusual metaphor *mentis oculos.*

PAGE 139, 1. **invitus feci ut eicerem**: a periphrasis for *invitus ejeci.* Special emphasis rests upon *invitus,* — *it was unwillingly that I removed.* **T. Flaminini**: already mentioned, p. 120, line 1.

2. L. Flamininum: he had served under his brother in the Macedonian War. **e senatu eicerem**: this was in 184 B.C. The censors possessed the right of degrading any citizen whose conduct in their opinion merited punishment.

3. post quam consul fuisset: the subjunctive here is due entirely to attraction, the clause being felt as an integral part of the thought begun in *ut eicerem*. Flamininus had been consul in 192 B.C. Hence the interval was really eight years, not seven, as stated by Cicero. **notandam**: *notare* was the technical term for designating the official action of the censors in rebuking the conduct of a citizen, just as *nota* was used of the ' mark ' or ' brand ' put upon him.

4. libidinem: *profligacy.* **cum esset consul in Gallia** *when he was in Gaul in his consulship. Gallia* in Cato's time applied only to cis-Alpine Gaul, *i.e.* northern Italy.

5. a scorto: a young lad of whom Flamininus was very fond. Livy tells us that the man executed was a noble Bojan who had fled to Flamininus for protection. **securi feriret**: *behead*, lit. *strike with the axe.* Livy says Flamininus stabbed the Bojan with his own hand.

7. Tito censore: in 189 B.C. The censors were chosen every five years, but held office for eighteen months only.

8. elapsus est: *i.e.* escaped punishment. **mihi et Flacco**: Cato and Flaccus were censors in 184 B.C. In 195 they had been colleagues in the consulship.

10. quae conjungeret: Clause of Characteristic with accessory notion of cause, *since it joined.* **imperi dedecus**: *disgrace to the imperium*, with which the consul had been formally invested. See note on p. 136, line 17.

13. porro: *in turn*, lit. *further on.* More commonly *porro* looks forward to the future. **mirari**. *i.e* express his wonder.

14. Fabricium: see note on p. 127, line 15. **apud Pyrrhum**: *i.e.* at Pyrrhus's headquarters. In 281 B.C. Pyrrhus had crossed over from Epirus to Italy to assist the Tarentines in war against the Romans.

15. Cinea: *Cineas*, a valued adviser of Pyrrhus. He had been a pupil of Demosthenes, and was distinguished as an orator. **queridam**: the reference is to Epicurus, founder of the philosophical school that bears his name. Epicurus was born at Samos 342 B.C., and taught at Athens from 306 till his death in 270 B.C. He did not, however, as here intimated, make sensual pleasure the chief end of life. It was happiness in the sense of the highest bodily, mental, and spiritual tranquillity that he declared to be the *summum bonum.* Yet his doctrines easily came to be misunderstood and perverted, so that ultimately Epicureanism became synonymous with physical self-indulgence.

16. **se sapientem profiteretur**: *set up for a philosopher.*

17. **ad voluptatem**: *i.e.* to pleasure as a standard or ideal.

18. **Curium, Coruncanium**: see p. 127, line 15.. **optare**: *i.e.* to express the wish.

19. **ut id Samnitibus** . . . **persuaderetur**: *that the Samnites and Pyrrhus himself might be convinced of this; id* is the Accusative of Result retained in the passive.

21. **vixerat**: *i.e.* had been intimate. **P. Decio**: his full name was Publius Decius Mus.

22. **eum**: *i.e.* Curius.

23. **devoverat**: this was in 295 B.C. at the Battle of Sentinum, in which the Romans defeated the combined forces of the Gauls and Samnites. Decius's father, also, P. Decius Mus, had previously offered his life in the same way at the Battle of Veseris, 340 B.C. The act of *devotio* was a formal one, and was accompanied by a regular ceremonial. The citizen who thus ' devoted himself ' mounted a charger, and rode to death in the midst of the enemy. The sacrifice was believed to propitiate the gods of the lower world, and thus to ensure victory.

24. **cum** . . . **tum**: *not only . . . but also.* **ex ejus, quem dico. Deci facto**: *from the act of him whom I mention, viz. Decius.*

25. **natura pulchrum atque praeclarum**: *naturally noble and glorious.*

26. **quod sua sponte peteretur**, *etc.*: *to be sought for its own sake, and for all the best men to pursue, scorning and despising pleasure;* the subjunctives are not merely subordinate clauses in indirect discourse, but are relative clauses of purpose as well, and would be in the subjunctive even in direct statement.

28. **quorsus**: elliptical, as p. 126, line 1.

29. **vituperatio nulla**: *i.e.* constitutes no ground of blame.

PAGE **140**, 1. **caret** . . . **caret**: in the first *caret* the idea of deprivation is prominent, in the second the idea of avoiding. **frequentibus poculis**: *round after round of cups.*

3. **si aliquid dandum est**: *if some concession must be made.*

4. **divine**: hardly stronger than the English *finely* or *admirably.*

5. **escam malorum**: *the bait of bad men, i.e.* the lure which traps them.

6. **quod videlicet**: *evidently because.*

8. **C. Duellium**: he had defeated the Carthaginian fleet off Mylae, a town on the north coast of Sicily, in 260 B.C.

9. **M. F.** = *Marci filium.*

10. **senem**: Duellius was probably seventy-five years old when Cato was a lad of ten.   **delectabatur**: Cato began by citing Duellius as an illustration of his assertion that old men can enjoy moderate banquets, but having once mentioned Duellius he goes on after the rambling fashion of an old man to relate other circumstances which have no connection whatever with the point at issue. *Cf.* the similar digressions, p. 124, line 22; p. 131, line 4; p. 145, line 21.

11. **nullo exemplo**: *without precedent*, lit. *in accordance with no example.*

12. **privatus**: *as a private citizen.*

13. **alios**: supply *commemorem*, or some such word.   **iam**: *straightway.*

14. **primum**: *in the first place; primum* leads us to expect *deinde* later on, instead of which the second point is introduced by *ego vero*, below, line 27.   **sodales**: this corresponds approximately to our ' club-friends '; a *sodalis* was a member of a *sodalitas*, a club organized sometimes for social purposes only, at other times, as here, for the maintenance of a special ritual. In either case banqueting seems to have been a recognized feature of the organization.

15. **Magnae Matris**: *i.e.* in honor of the Great Mother of the gods, Cybĕle. Her Greek designation of μεγάλη μήτηρ suggested the name of the Megalesian Games (*Ludi Megalenses*).   **me quaestore**: 204 B.C.

16. **sacris Idaeis acceptis**: the ablative absolute here denotes time, — *at the time the Idaean worship was introduced.* The worship of Cybele is called Idaean because one of her chief sanctuaries was situated on Mount Ida in the Troad.   The cult of Cybele was introduced in accordance with the directions of an oracle, which had bidden the Romans to bring to the city a meteoric stone worshipped as the image of Cybele at Pessïnus in Galatia.

17. **omnino modice**: *moderately withal.*   **aetatis**: here, *of youth.*

18. **qua progrediente**: *and as life advances; qua*, though referring to *aetatis*, does not refer to it in the sense of *youth*, — the meaning which *aetatis* has in connection with *fervor*, — but in the general sense of *life*.   **omnia fiunt mitiora**: *i.e.* all pleasures grow less keen, lose their edge.

20. **coetu amicorum et sermonibus**: the logical contrast is not so much between *voluptatibus* and *coetu et sermonibus*, as between *corporis* and *coetu et sermonibus*. Cato means to say that he gauged his enjoyments not so much by pleasures of the body as by those derived from meeting his friends and talking with them.

21. bene enim, *etc.: for our fathers did well in calling the reclining of friends at table a 'convivium,' because it involved a living together.*

24. tum compotationem, tum concenationem: *now a drinking together, now an eating together.*

25. quod in eo genere minimum est: *what is of least consequence in that sort (of thing), i.e.* the mere satisfaction of the appetite as opposed to the delights of social intercourse.

28. tempestivis conviviis: *protracted banquets;* a *convivium tempestivum* was one that began early, before the usual time (2 or 3 P.M.), and so lasted long.

PAGE **141, 1. qui pauci admodum:** *very few of whom;* for *quorum pauci admodum.* **cum vestra aetate:** *i.e.* with those of your time of life.

3. quae auxit: the relative clause here has causal force, — *since it has increased.* **auxit, sustulit:** note the adversative asyndeton, — *has increased, . . . but has removed.* B. 346, *b.*

5. ne videar: explaining the purpose of the assertion. **omnino:** *i.e.* war to the knife, lit. *altogether.*

6. cujus est . . . naturalis modus: *a certain measure of which, perhaps, is justified by nature.*

7. ne in istis quidem ipsis voluptatibus: *even in those very pleasures; ne . . . quidem* after a negative, as p. 124, line 7. **sensu:** *feeling.*

8. magisteria: lit. *presidencies, i.e.* the custom of having a presiding officer (*magister bibendi*) at a banquet to direct the drinking and the talk. The *magister bibendi* was usually chosen by a throw of the dice.

9. qui a summo adhibetur in poculo: *which is held over the wine, beginning at the head of the table,* lit. *from the top.*

11. minuta atque rorantia: *rorantia* defies translation. Literally *roro* means ' to bedew,' ' moisten '; here it suggests the few drops (as of dew) which the cups contained. **refrigeratio aestate:** *a cool apartment in summer;* the temporal ablative *aestate* serves (quite irregularly) as an attributive modifier of *refrigeratio,* corresponding to *hibernus* with *sol* and *ignis.*

12. sol aut ignis hibernus: *sun or fire in winter.* **quae quidem:** *a programme which, in fact.*

13. in Sabinis: *on my Sabine farm. Sabinis* is masculine. By a peculiar idiom the Romans used the name of a people dwelling in a district to designate an estate situated there ; hence *mei Sabini, mei Tusci,* lit. *my Sabines, my Tuscans,* in the sense of ' my Sabine estate,' ' my Tuscan estate.' **convivium vicinorum compleo:** *fill up the feast with my neighbors.* Verbs of filling are

more commonly construed with the ablative, but occasionally
take the genitive.

14. **ad multam noctem quam maxime possumus**: *as far into
the night as possible.*

16. **quasi titillatio**: *titillatio* properly means 'tickling';
here it is transferred to denote keenness of sensation; hence the
'apologetic' *quasi;* see note on p. 122, line 24.

17. **desideratio**: *longing;* the word does not occur elsewhere
in this sense. **nihil autem est molestum**, *etc.:* the thought is
inaccurately expressed. Cicero really means: 'the lack of a
thing that you do not want, is not annoying.'

18. **bene Sophocles**: *sc. dixit.*

20. **utereturne rebus veneriis**: *enjoyed the delights of love.*
di meliora: elliptical for *di meliora duint* (= *dent*), — *Heaven
forbid!*

21. **istinc**: *i.e. ab istis rebus veneriis.*

23. **satiatis et expletis**: the two words are closely synonymous;
see note on p. 135, line 9.

24. **quamquam**: corrective; see p. 120, line 7.

25. **hoc non desiderare**: *this absence of longing;* hoc limits
the substantive idea represented by the infinitive.

26. **bona aetas**: *i.e.* youth.

27. **libentius**: *with greater zest.* **primum**: *in the first place*
(I will say).

29. **potitur**: apparently used to avoid the repetition of *fruitur,*
which has already occurred twice in the sentence. **Turpione
Ambivio**: *Ambivius Turpio,* an actor and theatrical manager
of the time of Terence, in whose plays he often appeared.
When the *praenomen* is omitted, the two other names are occasionally transposed as here.

30. **in prima cavea**: *in the front part of the theatre;* the name
cavea, lit. *hollow space,* was applied to the sloping rows of seats
in a theatre. **spectat**: used absolutely, — *looks on.* **delectatur tamen**, *etc.: yet he also is pleased who looks on from the
back part (of the theatre)* ; supply *cavea* with *ultima,* and *spectat*
with *qui.*

PAGE 142, 1. **propter**: adverbial, — *(from) near at hand.*

2. **tantum quantum sat est**: modifying *delectatur;* the expression is periphrastic for the simple *satis,* 'sufficiently'; *sat,*
for *satis,* is archaic.

4. **at illa quanti sunt animum . . . secum esse**, *etc.: but
what a precious thing it is for the mind to be with itself, etc. Illa*
is explained by the following appositional infinitives *esse* and
vivere. The singular, *illud,* might have been used instead of *illa·*

quanti is Genitive of Value.   **tamquam emeritis stippendiis libidinis**: *having finished the service of lust, so to speak; stippendia emereri* lit. means *to serve out one's campaigns, i.e.* to serve the number prescribed by law.   The boldness of the figure calls forth the 'apologetic' particle *tamquam*.   Roman writers are particularly fond of military figures.

6. **secumque, ut dicitur, vivere**: *ut dicitur* indicates that the expression was a current or proverbial one.

7. **aliquod tamquam pabulum**, *etc.: some food for study, so to speak; pabulum* is properly *fodder* for animals; hence the 'apologetic' *tamquam*.

9. **otiosa**: *i.e.* free from public service or responsibility. **exerceri**: *engaged.*

10. **paene**: limiting *caeli et terrae.*   C. **Gallum**: Gaius Sulpicius Gallus, a man eminent as an astronomer.   He served under L. Aemilius in the campaign against Perseus, and by his prediction of an eclipse saved the army from panic.   In 166 B.C. he filled the office of consul.

11. **patris tui**: *i.e.* Aemilius Paulus.

12. **describere**: *i.e.* to draw some chart, astronomical or geographical.   **oppressit**: *surprised.*

13. **quam delectabat eum**: *how it delighted him!*   The subject of *delectabat* is *praedicere.*

14. **multo ante**: *i.e.* long before the actual eclipse.

15. **levioribus**: *less severe.*   **acutis**: *i.e.* demanding *keenness, acumen.*

16. **bello Punico Naevius**: the allusion is to Naevius's celebrated epic poem in Saturnian verse on the First Punic War, in which Naevius had taken an active part.   Only a few fragments of this work have come down to us.   **quam Truculento Plautus, quam Pseudolo**: T. Maccius Plautus, the greatest Roman writer of comedy, lived from about 250 to 184 B.C.   Among the twenty plays of Plautus that have been preserved, the Truculentus takes low rank; the Pseudolus, on the other hand, is one of the best.

17. **vidi etiam senem Livium**: *I saw Livius too when he was an old man.*   The reference is to Livius Andronīcus (about 283–204 B.C.), not to be confounded with the historian Livy (Titus Livius Patavīnus), who lived more than two centuries later. Livius Andronīcus, though not the first Latin writer, was the real pioneer of Roman literature.   He had come to Rome as a slave after the capture of Tarentum (272 B.C.), and in 240 B.C., six years before the birth of Cato, had brought out the first play at Rome.   One of his most celebrated works was the translation of the Odyssey into Saturnians.

18. **cum fabulam docuisset**: *having brought out a play;* an-

other circumstantial *cum*-clause; see ρ. 127, line 27; *fabulam docere*, lit. ' teach a play,' *i.e.* teach the actors their parts, is the regular phrase for ' bringing out a play.'

20. quid: *why ?*

21. P. Licini Crassi: see note on p. 132, line 16.

22. hujus P. Scipionis: *the Publius Scipio now living;* the reference is to P. Cornelius Scipio Nasica Corculum. his **paucis diebus**: *a few days ago*, lit. in the *course of these few days.*

24. senes: *when old men.*

25. M. Cethegum: mentioned p. 124, line 27, as a colleague of Tuditanus in the consulship (204 B.C.). **Suadae medullam**: *the quintessence* (lit. *marrow*) *of Persuasion, i.e.* of eloquence.

29. comparandae: *sc. sunt, deserve to be compared.*

PAGE 143, 1. prudentibus et bene institutis: *in case of wise and well-trained men;* Dative of Reference.

2. honestum: *i.e.* does its author credit: *honestus* when applied to things often means ' conferring honor.' **illud Solonis quod ait**: *that observation of Solon, which he makes.*

3. versiculo quodam · see note on p. 131, line 25. The verse was a dactylic pentameter; hence the diminutive *versiculus*, as denoting a verse shorter than the hexameter.

7. nec: correlative with *et* after *senectute.*

8. ad sapientis vitam: *i.e. to the (ideal) life of a philosopher* **proxime accedere**: *to make the nearest approach.*

9. habent rationem, *etc.*: the whole passage abounds in mercantile figures: *habent rationem*, ' keep account '; *numquam recusat imperium*, ' never refuses their draft '; *nec umquam sine usura reddit*, ' never passes a dividend.' **cum Terra**: *with Mother Earth; terra* is here personified, being conceived as the banker with whom account is kept.

11. alias: here = *sometimes*, correlative with the following *plerumque.*

13. vis ac natura: *power and nature.*

14. quae cum, *etc.*: explanatory of the foregoing sentence, — *for when she, etc.* **gremio**: *on her bosom:* the ablative is strictly instrumental, though doubtless possessing, even to the Roman mind, a slight locative force. **mollito ac subacto**: *broken up and made mellow, i.e.* by ploughing; Hysteron Proteron, B. 374, 7.

15. primum occaecatum, *etc.*: *first she holds it in hiding, from which (circumstance) the (process) which accomplishes that is called ' occatio ' (harrowing).* Cicero means that the Romans applied the name *occatio* to harrowing because that operation hid (*occaecavit*) the seed under the surface of the soil; but this etymology, like so many others suggested by ancient writers, is purely fanciful.

16. **quae hoc efficit, nominata est**: both the relative *quae* and the subject of *nominata est* have been attracted into the gender of the predicate noun *occatio*. Logically we should have expected *quod* and *nominatum est*, but attraction is practically the rule in cases like this.   **deinde tepefactum vapore**, *etc.*: *then when she has warmed it (the seed) with the heat of her embrace, she makes it expand;* note the hendiadys in *vapore et compressu*.

17. **elicit**: *brings forth.*

18. **herbescentem viriditatem**: *the green-growing plant*, lit. *the bladed greenness.*   **stirpium**: we should have expected *stirpis.*

19. **erecta**: with reflexive force, — *raising itself.*

20. **vaginis**: *i.e.* each new joint is protected by a sheath or bract.   **jam quasi pubescens**: *with the down of youth, so to speak, already upon it; pubesco* strictly applies to boys whose cheeks are just beginning to show the down of youth.   Cicero here applies the word to a growing plant, but with an apology (*quasi*) for the boldness of the figure.   **e quibus**: *i.e.* from the *vaginae.*

21. **fundit**: *brings forth;* suggesting abundance.   **spici ordine structam**: *arranged in regular ears*, lit. *in the orderliness of the ear.*   Note that Cicero here uses *spicum, i;* the usual word is *spica, ae.*

23. **quid**: *why?*   **ortus, satus**: *ortus* seems to refer to the springing up of vines, *satus* to their planting.   Observe the use of the plural to denote repeated instances.

24. **ut noscatis**: not the purpose of *satiari*, but of Cato's statement — 'this I say that you may know.'

26. **vim ipsam**: *i.e. the natural capacity.*   **omnium**: neuter; =*omnium rerum;* see note on p. 121, line 9.   **quae generantur e terra**: a circumlocution for *plants*, for which Latin has no single word.

27. **tantulo**: *i.e. so tiny* as we know them.   **acini vinaceo**: *the stone of a grape.*

29. **procreet**: Subjunctive of Characteristic, with accessory notion of cause, — *since it brings forth.*   **malleoli, plantae, sarmenta, viviradices, propagines**: *mallets, sprouts, cuttings, divisions, layers.*   A "layer" (*propago*) is a shoot whose tip, either naturally or artificially, has become embedded in the earth and has taken root.   Our black raspberry propagates itself naturally in this way.   A "division" (*viviradix*) is the name technically applied to a vertical section of a plant, retaining a part of the stem and root of the parent.   "Cuttings" (*sarmenta*) are clipped from terminal twigs; *cf. sarpo*, 'prune,' 'clip the ends.'   "Sprouts" (*plantae*) are the slender shoots that spring up about the base of a shrub or tree, or at times appear sporadically on the trunk itself.   "Mallets" (*malleoli*) differ from

" cuttings " in that they are cut in the particular shape indicated by their name.

PAGE 144, 1. nonne efficiunt ut delectent: merely a periphrasis for *nonne delectant? Cf.* p. 139, line 1, *invitus feci ut eicerem.*

2. quemvis: *i.e.* even the least appreciative observer.   cum admiratione delectent: *i.e.* fill with admiration and delight.

3. natura caduca est: *is naturally trailing.*   fertur: *sinks.*

4. eadem: to be taken with *vitis, — the vine again.*

5. serpentem multiplici lapsu et erratico: *winding in manifold and straggling course.*

6. ferro: *i.e.* the pruning-knife.

7. ars agricolarum: *the skilful husbandman,* the abstract for the concrete.

8. nimia: *too far.*

9. in eis: *i.e. in those shoots.*   quae relicta sunt: *viz.* after pruning, hence those shoots which have not been clipped in the pruning process.   tamquam ad articulos: *at the joints, so to speak; articulus* properly applies to the joint in an animal organism; hence the necessity of some apologetic particle here.

10. ea quae gemma dicitur: by attraction for *id quod gemma dicitur* (see note on p. 143, line 16); *gemma* meant originally ' outgrowth,' ' bud ' (*gemma* for **gen-ma,* root *gen-,* seen in *gen-us, genitus*) ; the meaning ' gem,' ' jewel,' was a secondary development.   Cicero apparently imagined the reverse to be true.

11. suco: *moisture.*

13. nec . . . et: correlative, as p. 143, line 7.

14. ardores: the plural as in *ortus, satus,* p. 143, line 23.

15. cum . . . tum: *either . . . or.*   fructu laetius, aspectu pulchrius: *pleasanter to enjoy, fairer to behold.*   Notice that *laetus* is here transferred in meaning from *glad* to *gladdening; fructu* and *aspectu* are nouns, not supines.

17. adminiculorum ordines: *rows of stakes,* to support the vines.

18. capitum jugatio: joining the tops of the stakes by crosspieces, a method still practised in Italian vineyards.   religatio et propagatio: *tying up and training; religatio* occurs only here ; *propagatio* refers to guiding the course of the new growth and giving the fresh shoots the proper direction.

20. aliorum immissio: *the allowing others to grow, viz.* those spoken of above as *quae relicta sunt; immissio* occurs only here in this sense, but *immitto* in the sense of ' let grow ' is well attested.

21. repastinationesque: *i.e.* digging up, or cultivating the earth with the *pastinum,* a two-pronged fork.

23. dixi: *i.e.* about those things.   **eo libro, quem de rebus rusticis scripsi**: the reference is to Cato's de Agri Cultura, a work on farming, which has come down to us. The discussion of manuring is in chapter 28 of that treatise.

24. de qua doctus Hesiodus: *about which Hesiod, with all his learning, said never a word, though he wrote on farming.* On Hesiod, see note on p. 130, line 11. Hesiod's treatment of farming is found in his Works and Days. Note the fine scorn of Cato at this serious defect in the work of his Greek predecessor.

25. at Homerus: Homer, in Cato's opinion, has done somewhat better.

26. multis ante saeculis fuit: *lived many generations earlier; fuit = vixit.*   **Laërtam lenientem desiderium**: *Laërtes endeavoring to assuage the longing;* conative use of the present participle. The allusion seems to be to the picture of Laërtes given in Odyssey, XXIV, 226, but in that passage there is no mention of manuring. Laërtes is simply represented as digging about the roots of the plants.

27. quod capiebat e filio: *which he felt for his son, viz.* the absent Ulysses, lit. *which he took from (in consequence of) his son.* **colentem et eum stercorantem**: these show the means, — *assuaging his longing by tilling the ground and manuring it.* When two verbs govern the same object, it is unusual to express the pronoun with the second as here.

28. facit: *represents.*   **segetibus**: standing crops of grain; this and the following ablatives denote cause.

29. res rusticae: *farm life.*   **laetae**: *pleasant,* as above, line 15.

30. hortis: *vegetable gardens.*

31. florum omnium: *flowers of all kinds.*

PAGE 145, 1. **consitiones, insitiones**: *planting* (of trees), *grafting.*

3. possum persequi: *I might enumerate.* The Latin commonly employs the indicative of *possum* in cases like this, where the English idiom would lead us to expect the subjunctive.

4. ea ipsa: *sc. oblectamenta, — these very attractions.*

5. longiora: *i.e.* have been dwelt upon at too great length. **ignoscetis autem**: *but pardon me;* as frequently, the future indicative has imperative force.

6. provectus sum: *I have been carried on.*   **loquacior**: *rather talkative.*

7. ne videar: see note on *ne indixisse videar*, p. 141, line 4. **ergo in hac vita**: the emphasis rests upon the phrase *in hac vita,* — *this, now, is the kind of life in which Manius Curius spent the close of his days.*

8. Curius: see note on p. 127, line 15.   **de Samnitibus:** *over the Samnites.*

10. cujus quidem, *etc.:* the mention of Curius's name irresistibly leads Cato to relate a famous incident illustrative of Curius's character.   That Cato himself feels this to be a digression, is clearly shown by the words below (line 17): *sed venio ad agricolas, ne a me ipso recedam.*

14. Samnites . . . repudiati sunt: this incident occurred after the subjugation of the Samnites.   Curius had become their *patronus* at Rome, and the gold had been brought as a gift, not as a bribe; nevertheless he refused it.   **non enim:** *non* belongs closely with *aurum habere,* — *he said it was not the possession of gold that seemed excellent to him, but commanding those who had it.*

16. poteratne: *-ne* regularly derives its force from the context; here it is equivalent to *num.*

17. non jucundam: *other than pleasant.   Cf.* p. 124, line 8, *non gravis.*

18. ne a me ipso recedam: *lest I wander from my subject.*   **in agris:** emphatic, — *the country in those days was the home of senators; tum* does not refer to the time of Curius, but simply in a general way to the early days.   Cincinnatus lived a century and a half before Curius.

19. id est senes: *i.e. senator* by its very derivation implies *senex.*   **si quidem aranti,** *etc.: aranti* is the emphatic word, — *if indeed L. Quinctius Cincinnatus was ploughing, when the news was brought, etc.*   **L. Quinctio Cincinnato:** Cincinnatus was twice dictator, 458 and 439 B.C.

20. esse factum: we should have expected *dictum esse, dictatorem dicere* being the technical phrase for ' to appoint a dictator.'

21. cujus dictatoris jussu: *by whose command when dictator;* another digression ; see note on p. 124, line 22.

22. Sp. Maelium: *viz.* in 439 B.C.   In a time of great scarcity Maelius had sold grain at a merely nominal price, and thus incurred the charge of aiming at regal power.   When summoned before Cincinnatus, he refused to appear.   Thereupon Ahala attacked and killed him ; but for this high-handed act, he was himself arraigned, and escaped punishment only by withdrawing into voluntary exile.   **occupatum interemit:** *forestalled and put to death; occupatum* means that Ahala prevented Maelius from executing his alleged design.

23. a villa, *etc.: 'twas from their country estates that Curius and the rest were summoned.*

24. ceteri senes: *i.e.* the others whom everybody recalls.   **ex quo :** *in consequence of which.*   **viatores:** lit. *travellers;* the

very name of the officials who gave the notification is held by
Cato to show that the men notified lived at a distance from the
city.

25. **horum qui**: not, *of those who* (which would be *eorum qui*),
but, *of these men* (*I have mentioned*), *inasmuch as they*, etc.

26. **agri cultione**: for the usual *agri cultura*.   **mea quidem
sententia**: *in my opinion*, *at least*, whatever others may think.

27. **haud scio an nulla**, *etc.*: *I am inclined to think that none*,
etc.   This is the regular force of *haud scio an* in Cicero.   B. 300, 5.

28. **officio**: *as regards the occupation*, lit. *function, duty*.

29. **salutaris**: *wholesome*.

31. **ad cultum deorum**: *i.e.* the farm supplies the first fruits
and the victims offered to the gods.

PAGE 146. 1. **ut in gratiam jam cum voluptate redeamus**: *so
that we are already getting on good terms again with pleasure;*
alluding to Cato's earnest invective against pleasure in chapter
xii.

3. **olearia**: *sc. cella*.   Butter was practically unknown to the
Romans; olive oil took its place, as it does still in Italy.   **pen-
aria** (*sc.* **cella**): *pantry, larder*.

4. **locuples**: *i.e.* richly supplied.   **porco, haedo, agno,
gallina**: *pork, kid's flesh, lamb, poultry;* all these words are
here used with collective force.

5. **jam**: *moreover;* here used as a particle of transition.

6. **succidiam alteram**: *the second meat supply*, lit. *the second
flitch; succidia* properly designates a ' side ' or ' flitch ' of bacon.
Cato means that the products of the garden are so many and so
valuable that they constitute a safe reliance, should flesh be lacking.   **conditiora**, *etc.*: *fowling and hunting give these things*
(*i.e.* the attractions already enumerated) *a greater zest by occupy-
ing one's leisure*.   Special emphasis rests upon *conditiora*, but it
is very difficult to bring this out in translation.

10. **brevi praecidam**: *I will cut off (all further remarks) with
(this) brief statement*.   As object of *praecidam* understand *sermo-
nem* or some similar word; *brevi* is explained by what follows.
agro bene culto, *etc.*: the emphasis rests on *agro*, — *as compared
with a well-tilled farm nothing can be*, etc.

12. **invitat atque allectat**: synonyms, as p. 135, line 9.

13. **illa aetas**: *i.e. men of that time of life*.

14. **calescere vel apricatione melius vel igni**: *bask more com-
fortably in the sun or by the fire*.

15. **aquis**: this probably refers to baths.   **refrigerari**: *cool
themselves;* reflexive.   **sibi habeant**: *let them keep to themselves;*
as subject of *habeant* understand *juvenes*.

16. clavam: the *clava* was a kind of foil used by soldiers in practice.

17. pilam: various games of ball were played by the Romans, but none in which the bat was used.

18. ex lusionibus multis: *out of many sports.* **talos et tesseras**: *tali,* lit. ' knuckle bones,' were dice with four flat sides and two round ones; *the tesserae* had six sides like our dice.

19. id ipsum ut lubebit: *even that (they may do or not) as they please; i.e.* they may either grant the dice or withhold them; *id ipsum* is the object of some verb to be supplied, — *faciant,* for example.

23. copiose: *eloquently,* lit. *abundantly, fully.*

24. qui est, qui inscribitur: we should naturally expect a connective with *qui inscribitur,* — 'and which is entitled'; its absence is usually explained as due to the parenthetical nature of the clause *qui est de tuenda re.* **de tuenda re familiari**: *on the care of property.* **Oeconomicus**: this work, as its name suggests, treats of the management of an estate.

25. ut intellegatis: see note on p. 143, line 24, *ut noscatis regale: princely, i.e.* worthy of a prince.

26. in eo libro: *viz.* in chapter iv, sections 20–25. **loquitur cum Critobulo**: *in conversation with Critobūlus says;* Critobulus was a disciple of Socrates.

27. Cyrum minorem, Persarum regem: Cyrus, the Younger, who fell at Cunaxa (401 B.C.) in the attempt to wrest the throne from his brother Artaxerxes. See Xenophon, Anabasis, I, 7–9. Cyrus was never king, but simply the son of King Darius, and satrap of the provinces of Lydia, Phrygia, and Cappadocia; hence *regem* in this passage means no more than ' prince,' ' ruler.'

28. Lysander Lacedaemonius: the distinguished Spartan leader; he commanded at Aegospotami, 405 B.C.

29. vir summae virtutis: *a man of the greatest ability; virtutis* here cannot refer to high moral worth; Lysander's character was not above reproach. **ad eum Sardis**: *to him at Sardis. Sardis* (= Σάρδεις) is accusative plural. B. 182, 2, *b*; A. 428, *j*; G. 337, 6. Sardis was the capital of Cyrus's satrapy.

PAGE 147, 1. a sociis: *i.e.* the Lacedaemonians and the other Peloponnesian states that were leagued against Athens in the Peloponnesian War. Cyrus assisted Lysander and the Spartans with large sums of money in this struggle. His object was to secure Spartan assistance in carrying out his designs upon the throne of Persia. **et (ceteris)**: *et* is correlative with *et* following *fuisse.*

2. humanum: *kindly.*

3. **consaeptum agrum**: *park;* this phrase is used to render the Greek παράδεισος; hence the absence of *et* before *consitum.* **consitum**: *planted* with trees, in rows or groups.

4. **proceritates**: the plural, because there were many trees (*arbores*), each of which was *procera.*

5. **in quincuncem**: *quincunx* was the name of the five-spot on dice ⁙ Hence *in quincuncem* is used to designate an arrangement of trees by which the lines run diagonally as in the following diagram.

6. **subactam**: *i.e.* carefully cultivated.   **puram**: *i.e.* free from weeds, stones, *etc.*

7. **afflarentur**: *were wafted.*   **eum dixisse**: dependent on *loquitur* above.

9. **dimensa atque discripta**: *laid out and arranged;* note the passive use of the deponent *dimensa; cf. adeptam,* p. 122, line 6.

10. **ego ista sum dimensus**: *ego* is emphatic; *I am the one who laid out these things that you see.*   **mei sunt ordines, etc.**: *mine are the rows, mine the arrangement.*

13. **purpuram**: *i.e.* his purple robe.   **nitorem corporis**: *the elegance of his person.*

14. **multo auro multisque gemmis**: Ablative of Quality. **rite, etc.**: *with reason do they call you happy.*

15. **ferunt**: the subject is general, — *people.*   **quoniam virtuti tuae fortuna conjuncta est**: as shown by the word order, the emphasis rests upon *virtuti,* — *with reason do people call you happy, since it is to inherent worth* (virtus) *that your prosperity is joined.* Cyrus's *virtus* is recognized by Lysander in his personal attention to the improvement of his estate ; *fortuna* refers to his advantages as a prince, — *purpura, nitor, gemmae, aurum.*

16. **hac igitur fortuna**: *this now is the happy lot; igitur,* as so frequently, simply resumes the substance of the foregoing discussion, — here of chapters xv and xvi on the delights of farm life.

17. **aetas**: *old age.*   **impedit**: the object (*nos*) is omitted, being readily supplied in thought from the following *quominus* clause.   **et (ceterarum rerum) et (agri colendi)**. the English idiom here is *either . . . or.*

18. usque ad ultimum: *up to the very last.*

19. M. Valerium Corvinum: in the Gallic War of 349 B.C.
M. Valerius Corvīnus defeated a gigantic Gaul in single combat.
During the struggle a raven (*corvus*) is said to have perched
upon Corvinus's helmet, and to have lent him assistance by
flying in the face of his antagonist; whence the surname
Corvinus.

20. perduxisse: *sc. studia agri colendi, — continued the pursuits of farming.*   **cum esset . . . coleret:** *still remaining on
the farm and cultivating it after his life was already spent; aetas*
here covers the period of an ordinary lifetime, corresponding to
our " three score years and ten." For the *cum*-clauses, see note
on p. 127, line 27; for *acta aetate* we should have expected *exacta
aetate.*

22. primum et sextum consulatum: Corvinus's first consulship was in 349 B.C., his sixth in 299. Cicero's reckoning, therefore, betrays an error.

23. majores: supply in sense *nostri.*

24. ad senectutis initium: *up to the beginning of old age, i.e.*
from birth. Old age (*senectus*) properly began at sixty, but Cicero
is here thinking rather of the *aetas seniorum*, the time when men
became exempt from military service; this was at forty-six.
esse voluerunt: *allowed,* lit. *wished to be.*   **cursus honorum:**
the technical expression denoting official career, including all
offices from the quaestorship to the consulship.

25. huius extrema aetas: *the latter part of his life.*   **hoc:**
explained by the clause *quod habebat.*

26. auctoritatis: *influence.*

27. apex: *the crowning glory; apex* primarily designated the
pointed piece of wood inserted in the top of the cap worn by the
flamens.

28. fuit: *sc. auctoritas.*   **L. Caecilio Metello:** see note on
p. 133, line 14.   **A. Atilio Calatino:** Calatīnus was twice consul
(258 and 254 B.C.) and once dictator (249 B.C.) in the First Punic
War.

29. illud: *the following.*   **elogium:** *epitaph.* The word is
derived from the Greek ἐλεγεῖον, ' epitaph,' ' sepulchral inscription.' English *eulogy* is not related.

30. hunc unum: *this man above all others.*   **gentes:** used in
the technical sense of the different Roman *gentes* (' clans ').

31. populi: with *virum.*

PAGE 148, 1. carmen: *i.e.* the entire epitaph, of which Cato
cites only two lines.   **incisum:** explanatory of *notum est;* the
epitaph is familiar because engraved upon his tomb.   **in se-**

pulcro: Calatinus was buried on the Appian Way, neaɪ the tombs of the Scipios.

2. **gravis, cujus esset**, *etc.*: *a man of weight, since all were unanimous in his praise; fama omnium* is literally the 'report of all,' *i.e.* the reputation which all men gave him. The clause *cujus esset* is one of Characteristic, with the accessory notion of cause; the clause, however, does not give the reason for Calatinus's influence, but simply a reason why we may infer that he was influential.

3. **quem virum nuper**, *eu.*: *what a man we saw recently in Publius Crassus!* lit. *what a man we saw Publius Crassus! video* here takes two accusatives, direct object and predicate accusative, like verbs of *calling, regarding, etc.* On Crassus, see note on p. 132, line 16.

4. **Lepidum**: pontifɔx maximus, 180 B.C. He twice led the Roman armies against the Ligurians, and was long *princeps senatus* ('leader of the house').

5. **Paulo**: see note on p. 133, line 4.

6. **Maximo**: see p. 124, line 17.   **quorum non in sententia solum**: *not merely in whose opinion; sententia* probably alludes to the formal expression of opinion when a vote was taken in the Senate. Each senator, as called upon, rose and explained his vote.

8. **honorata**: *i.e.* the old age of a man who had held offices (*honores*).

9. **pluris**: *of more account.*

11. **in omni oratione**: *in everything I say.*

13. **constituta sit**: *i.e. has been firmly established.*   **ex quo efficitur**: *and so it comes about.*   **id quod . . . dixi**: *a thing which I once remarked.*

14. **assensu omnium**: *i.e.* on the part of all.   **miseram esse,** *etc.*: logically this clause is the subject of *efficitur*, and would normally have been expressed by *ut misera sit senectus quae se defendat, — and so it comes about (as I once remarked) that that old age is wretched which has to defend itself by apologies.* But the proximity of *dixi* has evidently caused the writer to forget the structure of the sentence as begun with *efficitur*, and to make the clause which should have depended upon *efficitur* depend upon *dixi* instead. This has also involved the change of *defendat* to *defenderet*, according to the "sequence of tenses."

15. **non cani nec rugae**, *etc.*: *non* is emphatic, — *not gray hair nor wrinkles can suddenly lay hold on influence;* with *cani* understand *capilli;* this omission is elsewhere confined to poetry.

17. **fructus capit auctoritatis extremos**: *reaps influence as its final product; auctoritatis* is Appositional Genitive, — *the product, influence* (B. 202; A. 343, *d*; G. 361, 1; H. 440,

4); *extremos* is made emphatic by its position at the end of the sentence.

18. **haec**: explained by the following infinitives. **honorabilia**: *i.e.* tokens of honor; *honorabilis* occurs only here in good Latinity.

19. **salutari**: the reference is probably to the morning visit or *salutatio*, which the friends of a prominent man were wont to pay. **appeti**: *to be sought out.*

20. **decedi, assurgi**: these two infinitives, being intransitive, are used impersonally, — *to have people make way for one, rise in one's presence*, lit. (*for*) *it to be withdrawn, to be risen.* **deduci, reduci, consuli**: a return to the personal construction; *deduco* is the technical term for a formal escort of a man from his house to the Forum, *reduco* of the escort back to his house; *consuli* means merely to have one's opinion asked on any matter o. importance.

21. **ut quaeque optime morata est**: *according as each is most highly civilized*, lit. *best mannered.*

24. **honestissimum**: *most honorable.*

25. **nusquam enim**, *etc.*: *for nowhere is so much regard paid to age;* we should have expected this to be expressed as Lysander's thought, and accordingly to be in the infinitive dependent upon *dicere* above, but Cato gives it as his own justification of Lysander's statement.

26. **quin etiam**: *why actually.* **memoriae proditum est**: *the story goes*, lit. *it has been handed down to memory.*

27. **ludis**: Ablative of Time. The reference is probably to the festival of the great Dionysia, which occurred annually in March, and was celebrated with dramatic performances.

28. **magno consessu** Ablative Absolute with adversative force, — *although the throng was great*, implying that among so many some one might have been expected to offer the old man a seat.

PAGE 149, 1. **qui consederant**: an explanatory clause of the writer, and hence in the indicative. **certo in loco**: special seats in the orchestra were reserved for ambassadors and other distinguished guests.

2. **omnes illi**: *they all.*

3. **sessum**: *to a seat*, lit. *to sit down;* supine of *sedeo*, used to express purpose after the idea of motion involved in *recepisse.*

4. **dixisse**: dependent upon *proditum est* above.

5. **facere nolle**: not so much *were unwilling to do it*, as *lacked the disposition to do it.*

6. **vestro collegio**: *sc. augurum.*

8. sententiae principatum tenet: *enjoys precedence in giving his opinion; i.e.* in voting the augurs gave their opinions in the order of age.   **honore antecedentibus**: including all official positions, political or sacerdotal.

9. cum imperio: see note on p. 136, line 17.

12. quibus qui, *etc.: those who have made a fine use of these, viz.* of the *praemiis auctoritatis.*

13. fabulam aetatis: *the drama of life,* a common figure in all languages.   **peregisse**: *to have acted through to the end.*   **tamquam inexercitati histriones**: *like untrained players.*

14. corruisse: *to have broken down.*

15. at sunt: *at* as p. 129, line 11 and frequently.   **morosi**: *capricious;* by derivation *morosus* means *full of special habits* (*mores*), hence *crotchety, capricious.*

16. morum: *of the character.*

18. non illius quidem: *not, to be sure, a just one;* when an object has two attributes connected and contrasted by *quidem . . . sed,* the demonstrative pronoun (or personal pronoun) is usually present with the former attribute.

19. sed quae videatur: *but such as seems capable of being approved;* this is a Clause of Characteristic, and constitutes the second of the two attributes limiting *excusationis.*   **contemni, despici, illudi**: these words form a climax, — *ignored, despised, made sport of.*

21. omnis offensio: *every slight; offensio* is here used passively *i.e. a being offended.*

22. dulciora: *i.e.* less annoying.   **bonis**: modifying both *moribus* and *artibus.*

24. qui in Adelphis sunt: who appear in the *Adelphi,* an extant comedy of Terence (about 190–159 B.C.).

25. sic se res habet: *so it is* (*actually*) ; *sic* is best taken as referring back to the mellowing effects of good character and good breeding.

26. severitatem: *strictness* merely, a common meaning of the word.

28. avaritia vero: *but what sense avarice can have in an old man, I do not understand; avaritia* is emphatic by position, but it is difficult to bring this out in English translation, except by vocal stress.

30. quo viae minus, *etc.: i.e.* to seek more funds in proportion as the remainder of the journey diminishes; *quo* and *eo* are Ablatives of Degree of Difference.

PAGE 150, 2. sollicitam habere: *to keep in a state of unrest.*

4. esse longe: we should have expected *abesse* here instead of *esse.*

5. contemnendam: *i.e.* to be regarded with indifference.

7. etiam (optanda): *even.*   **aliquo**: the adverb.

8. sit futurus: *is destined to be.*   **tertium nihil**: *no third alternative.*

9. non miser: *non* is to be combined closely with *miser.*

10. beatus etiam: *happy even; etiam* receives additional emphasis by being placed after the word which it limits.   **quamquam**: corrective.

11. quamvis sit adulescens: *however young he be.*   **cui sit exploratum**: the expression is inexact. Cicero does not mean: *Who is so foolish as to have discovered?* but *Who is so foolish as to think he has discovered?*

12. quin etiam: as p. 148, line 26.

13. aetas illa: *i.e.* persons of that time of life.   **casus mortis**: *i.e.* the active life of young men makes them more liable to accidents.

15. tristius curantur: *they are treated by the application of severer remedies;* the frailer health of the aged calls for less heroic treatment.

16. ni: in classical prose *ni* is found almost exclusively in legal formulas and colloquial phrases.   **melius et prudentius viveretur**: *life would be better and wiser,* lit. *it would be lived, etc.*

17. mens, ratio, consilium: *ratio* ('reason') and *consilium* ('deliberation') are special functions of *mens* ('intellect').

18. qui si nulli fuissent: *and if there had never been any* (*sc. senes*).

19. ad mortem impendentem: *to death as* (*something*) *imminent.*

20. quod est istud, *etc.*: *how is that a charge against old age?* *i.e.* how does it constitute a valid charge?   **quod** as interrogative adjective means 'what kind of?' Hence here *quod crimen,* 'what kind of charge,' in the sense *how does it constitute a charge?* *istud* refers to the general idea of death impending, and is the subject of *est.*   **id**: *i.e.* the fact that death is imminent.   **ei**: *viz. senectuti.*

21. cum adulescentia: *cf. commune tecum,* p. 120, line 16. **sensi,** *etc.*: *sensi* is emphatic, — *we have had experience, I in the case of my most excellent son, you in the case of your brothers; sensi* is singular because agreeing with the nearer subject, *ego.* **in optimo filio**: Cato's son died in 152 B.C. while praetor-elect.

22. exspectatis . . . fratribus: a peculiar expression for: *brothers who were expected to arrive at the highest honors.* Cato refers to the two sons of Lucius Aemilius Paulus, one of whom, aged 12, died five days before his father's triumph, the other, aged 14, three days after the triumph.

24. quod idem: *etc.: which the old cannot likewise hope,* lit. *which same thing, etc.*

25. insipienter sperat: *i.e.* he is foolish to cherish such a hope; *insipienter* is emphatic.

26. incerta pro certis habere: *to regard as certain what is uncertain.*

27. at senex, *etc.: but, it is alleged, the old man has not even anything to hope for;* the clause *quod speret* is one of purpose.

PAGE **151**, 1. **at est**: *at* here introduces Cato's own reply to the argument of his imaginary opponent.

2. ille, hic: *ille* refers to the youth, *hic* to the old man, as the one really nearer in thought, though not last mentioned in the preceding context.

5. Tartessiorum: the Tartessians dwelt in southern Spain.

6. Gadibus: the modern Cadiz.

7. centum viginti: there are other indications in Latin literature that one hundred and twenty years was regarded by the Romans as the ultimate limit to which the life of man might extend.

8. sed mihi, *etc.:* there is a slight anacoluthon here; we should have expected this clause to be introduced by *tamen,* since *da* and *exspectemus* have the force of ' though you grant,' ' though we look forward to.' **ne diuturnum quidem**: *not even of any considerable duration,* — to say nothing of its being "long."

9. in quo est: we might have expected the Subjunctive of Characteristic here; but the indicative is regularly used in any characterizing clause that has the force of a condition; thus here *in quo est, etc.* = *if there is something final in it.*

10. quod praeteriit, effluxit: *what has passed has vanished.* **tantum remanet**: *there remains only so much.*

11. consecutus sis: the indefinite 2d singular; hence the subjunctive.

12. horae et dies et menses et anni: note the rhetorical force of the polysyndeton. B. 341, 4, *b.* The asyndetic form of expression is, however, much more usual.

13. quid sequatur: *i.e. what the future will be;* the clause is the logical subject of *sciri potest.*

16. neque enim: *for neither; neque* is correlative with *neque* in line 17. **histrioni . . . peragenda fabula est**: *i.e.* the actor, in order to please his audience, does not need to act through the piece, — does not need to appear in every act.

17. modo probetur: *provided only he meet approval.* **in quocumque fuerit**: the subjunctive is purely the result of attraction. **neque sapienti usque ad Plaudite veniendum est**

nor does a wise man need to come to the very ' Plaudite ' (of life).
Plaudite was the regular appeal made by one of the troupe at the
close of the play; hence, in a transferred sense, it means ' the
end,' ' conclusion.'

20. **processerit**: as subject supply in sense *quis*, ' one.'

21. **verni temporis suavitate** = *the pleasant spring-time.*

22. **tamquam**: *tamquam* qualifies the entire phrase *adulescentiam significat,* — *typifies youth, as it were.*

23. **ostenditque fructus futuros**: *i.e.* gives promise of the
fruits that are to come.

24. **tempora**: *seasons.* **demetendis et percipiendis**: *reaping
and gathering;* another illustration of Cicero's fondness for group-
ing synonyms in pairs.

26. **ante partorum bonorum**: *of blessings previously acquired.*

28. **sunt habenda**: *are to be reckoned.*

29. **quod idem**: *which likewise.*

PAGE **152**, 1. **adversante et repugnante natura**: the Ablative
Absolute here has adversative force, — *though nature resists and
rebels.*

3. **ut cum**: *as when.*

4. **flammae vis**: *a vigorous flame.*

5. **nulla adhibita vi**: *without the application of any force.*
consumptus ignis exstinguitur: *a fire is extinguished as a result
of burning out; consumptus* takes the chief stress in this sentence,
and is used in a middle sense, — *having burnt itself out.*

6. **quasi**: here equivalent to *sicut;* this use is archaic.

7. **si matura**: we should have expected *sin* instead of *si* to
introduce this second protasis. B. 306, 3; G. 592.

8. **sic . . . vis aufert**: the emphasis rests upon *vis,* — *so
'tis force that takes life from the young; adulescentibus* is dative.
B. 188, 2, *d*; A. 381; H. 427.

9. **quae quidem**, *etc.*: grammatically *quae* can refer only to
maturitas, but such is not Cicero's meaning; the logical antecedent is the substance of the whole preceding sentence; hence
this thought is so pleasant to me.

10. **quo propius accedam**: Subjunctive by Attraction; we
should have expected this clause to be followed by one containing
a comparative with *eo,* corresponding to *quo propius.*

14. **recte vivitur**: *i.e.* one is justified in remaining alive.
quoad possis: *as long as one can;* the indefinite 2d singular leads
to the use of the subjunctive. **munus offici exsequi et tueri** ·
to discharge and attend to the performance of one's duty.

17. **hoc illud est**, *etc.*: *this is the significance of the famous reply
of Solon.* **Pisistrato**: tyrant of Athens in the sixth century B.C.

Plutarch, in his life of Solon, chapter 31, says this reply was made to inquiring friends; yet he elsewhere confirms the account here given.

18. illi: *i.e.* Pisistratus.   **qua tandem:** *tandem* emphasizes the interrogative, — *what pray!*

19. audaciter: archaic for *audacter*.   **obsisteret:** Solon's opposition was directed against Pisistratus's usurpation in 560 B.C.

20. ' senectute ': *sc. fretus;* Solon was seventy-five years old at this time.   **integra mente certisque sensibus:** *with the mind sound and the faculties unimpaired.*

22. coagmentavit: *put together.*   **dissolvit:** *takes apart.*

25. iam: *now,* continuing the argument; so below, p. 153, line 8.   **omnis conglutinatio recens:** lit. *every construction when fresh, i.e.* everything newly made.   **inveterata:** *if of long standing.*

26. illud breve vitae reliquum: *reliquum* is here a substantive, — an infrequent use of the word.

27. nec sine causa deserendum sit: *i.e.* suicide must not be resorted to except in a special exigency.

28. vetatque: *-que* is here 'epexegetic,' *i.e.* explanatory of what has just preceded, — *and so, and accordingly.*

29. praesidio et statione: *post and station.*

PAGE 153. 1. elogium: here in the sense of ' couplet.'   **se negat velle:** *says he does not wish.*

2. suam mortem: *suam* is emphatic; these lines of Solon were directed against Mimnermus, a contemporary elegiac poet, who had given expression to a contrary sentiment.

3. vult, credo, se esse carum: the construction of infinitive with subject accusative after *volo, nolo, malo,* is less usual, if the subjects of the main and dependent verbs are the same; but it is permissible in case of *esse* and passive infinitives. B. 331, iv, *a.* **haud scio an melius Ennius:** *I am inclined to think Ennius utters a better sentiment;* with *melius* understand some such verb as *dicat.* On *haud scio an, cf.* note on p. 145, line 27, *haud scio an nulla beatior possit.*

5. nemo me dacrumis decoret, etc.: *dacruma* is an archaic form of *lacruma.* Notice the alliteration in *dacrumis decoret,* and in *funera fletu faxit; fletu* is Ablative of Attendant Circumstance. B. 221. *faxit* is an archaic form of *fecerit* (perfect subjunctive); as subject supply in sense *quisquam* from *nemo.* The second line is given in full by Cicero, Tusculan Disputations, I, 34:

> Faxit. Cur? Volito vivos per ora virum.
> *' Why? I still live and flit about in the mouths of men.'*

9. isque: *-que* is here adversative.   **ad exiguum tempus:** *i.e.* only for a short time.

10. aut nullus est: *nullus* here has the force of an emphatic *non;* *est* is almost equivalent to *adest;* hence *is not present.*

11. hoc meditatum ab adulescentia debet esse: *this (lesson) ought to be rehearsed by us from youth up; meditor* is to go over a thing again and again by way of preparation, as a lesson or a speech; *hoc* is explained by the following *ut mortem neglegamus, i.e.* the lesson is : ' disregard of death.' Notice the passive use of the participle of *meditor,* like *adeptam,* p. 122, line 6; *dimensa,* p. 147, line 9. The tense of *meditatum esse* is also peculiar; we should have expected the present, but with *debeo* and *oportet* the perfect infinitive occasionally appears used for the present. B. 270, 2, *a;* A. 486, *e.*

12. sine qua meditatione: *a practice without which.*

13. moriendum enim certe est: *moriendum* takes the emphasis, — *for die we surely must.* **et incertum an:** *and possibly,* lit. *and it (is) uncertain (whether at some other time) or.*

14. mortem . . . impendentem: as the position shows, this phrase takes the chief emphasis of the sentence, — *with death imminent at all hours, how can one who fears it be of a tranquil heart?* *qui* is the interrogative adverb; as subject of *poterit* an indefinite *quis* must be supplied in thought; *consistere* literally means ' to stand firm,' and so, ' to be tranquil.'

16. non ita longa: *i.e.* no very long.

17. cum recordor: *when I recall;* the clause, however, is strongly causal; hence the subjunctive.   **L. Brutum:** this and the following accusatives *Decios, Atilium,* are to be taken as the subjects of some verb to be supplied from *profectas (esse)* in line 27. **in liberanda patria:** the Tarquins, after their expulsion, endeavored to regain the throne; Brutus, while resisting their attempts, was killed in single combat with Arruns Tarquinius.

18. duos Decios: see note on p. 139, line 21.

19. M. Atilium: Marcus Atilius Regulus, the famous general of the First Punic War. The story of his return to Carthage to keep his plighted faith is probably apocryphal.

21. duos Scipiones: see p. 133, line 3.

22. Poenis: dative of reference, — lit. *to obstruct the way to the Carthaginians.*   **vel:** intensive.

23. avum tuum: this is addressed to Scipio. His grandfather by blood, L. Aemilius Paulus (father of Macedonicus, conqueror of Perseus), had commanded at the disaster of Cannae, 216 B.C. **collegae:** C. Terentius Varro.

24. M. Marcellum: M. Claudius Marcellus, an eminent

general of the Second Punic War. He was lured into ambush and slain by the troops of Hannibal in 208 B.C.

25. interitum: *i.e.* his dead body. **crudelissimus hostis**: Hannibal's conduct never justified this epithet. He was characterized rather by generosity and even chivalry.

27. in Originibus: see note on p. 136, line 26.

PAGE 154, 2. indocti: referring particularly to lack of training in philosophy. **rustici**: *i.e.* not merely devoid of the higher culture, but lacking all training whatsoever. The Roman army was recruited chiefly from the country districts.

3. omnino: *all in all.*

5. studia certa: *definite interests, pursuits.*

7. constans jam aetas: like *jam constantis aetatis*, p. 134, line 31; in the present passage note that *jam*, at variance with the usual practice, follows the word it modifies.

8. ne ea quidem: *i.e.* old age does not pine even for the occupations of middle life, much less, then, for those of youth and boyhood.

12. maturum: best taken as a predicate modifier of *tempus*, lit. *brings the time of death ripe*, *i.e.* makes the time ripe for death.

13. cur non audeam: *why I should not venture;* the indirect question here represents a Deliberative Subjunctive of direct discourse.

14. quod: relative, referring to *quid ipse sentiam.* **eo melius quo ab ea propius absum**: *the better, the nearer I am to it;* nearness *from* a thing is a favorite mental attitude with Latin writers.

15. cernere: *discern;* used of clear vision.

16. tuumque, Laeli: Laelius's father also bore the name C. Laelius; he was an intimate friend of the elder Africanus.

20. munere quodam necessitatis: *i.e.* a function imposed by necessity.

21. est animus caelestis, etc.: *the soul is from heaven; animus* is further modified by the participle *depressus,* 'lowered.'

22. quasi demersus: *quasi* apologizes for the figure; *demergo* ordinarily applies to what is sunk in water.

25. qui terras tuerentur: *to care for, protect, the earth,* lit. *lands.* **caelestium**=*caelestium rerum; of celestial things.*

27. ratio, disputatio: *reflection, discussion.*

28. nobilitas: *reputation.*

29. Pythagoram: see note on p. 130, line 13.

PAGE 155, 1. incolas paene nostros: the seat of the Pythagorean school was Crotona in southern Italy. **qui essent nominati**: this clause seems to be introduced merely as an explanation of the speaker, and as such would naturally have stood in the indicative. The subjunctive indicates that it is here felt to be a part of the indirect discourse.

3. ex universa mente divina: *i.e.* from the world-soul. **delibatos:** *i.e.* souls which are emanations of the world-soul; *delibo* literally means *to take a taste* or *a sip* of something; then figuratively *to draw, pluck, gather.*

4. haberemus: in English we should use the present; but in Latin even subordinate clauses expressing general truths conform to the sequence of tenses. **quae . . . disseruisset:** implied indirect discourse, — *the views which Socrates was said to have set forth.* B. 323; A. 341.

5. immortalitate animorum: note the plural in *animorum.*

6. esset judicatus: Subjunctive by Attraction; the clause is an integral part of the clause on which it depends. B. 324, 1; A. 592, 2; G. 508, 4; H. 649, I.

7. quid multa: *sc. dicam.* **sic persuasi mihi, sic sentio:** *sic* is explained by what follows. The arguments for the soul's immortality are four in number:

(1) Its capacity (*cum tanta celeritas, etc.*).
(2) Its original activity (*cumque agitetur, etc.*).
(3) Its indivisibility (*cum simplex animi esset natura, etc.*).
(4) Its preëxistence (*scire pleraque ante quam, etc.*).

8. celeritas: *i.e.* the rapidity of thought.

9. memoria praeteritorum futurorumque prudentia: note the chiastic arrangement. Observe that *prudentia* here has its primitive meaning of ' foresight.'

10. tot artes: such as *rhetoric, music, geometry, astronomy, etc.;* each of these was an *ars,* — *ars rhetorica, ars musica, etc.* **tantae scientiae:** *so vast branches of knowledge;* the plural of *scientia* is extremely rare, but its occurrence is justified by the neighboring plurals, *tot artes, tot inventa.*

12. semper agitetur: *is always active; agitetur* has here a reflexive or middle sense, — lit. *moves itself; cf. erecta,* p. 143, line 19.

13. quia se ipse moveat: this is said in justification of the previous statement *nec principium motus habeat,* and does not refer at all to *agitetur.* **ne finem quidem,** *etc.: no end of motion either.*

14. numquam sit relicturus: almost equivalent to ' can never leave.'

15. cum simplex animi esset: the previous dependent clauses (beginning with line 8), *cum sit, quae contineat, cumque agitetur, quia moveat, quia sit relicturus,* have all depended upon *persuasi* taken as a principal tense, but with line 15 *persuasi* comes to be felt as historical; hence the secondary sequence in *esset, haberet, posset,* followed, however, by a return to primary sequence in *nati sint, discant, etc.* In English we should render the imperfects of this passage by presents. **simplex:** *i.e.* as opposed to composite.

17. **quod si non posset:** *and if it* (the soul) *cannot, i.e.* cannot be divided; with *posset* supply *dividi* from the preceding *dividi posse.* **non posse interire:** *sc. animum.*

18. **magnoque esse argumento:** *and (I am convinced, — persuasi mihi) that it is (for) a great argument, viz.* in favor of the immortality of the soul; the subject of *esse* is *homines scire, etc.; i.e.* knowledge anterior to birth is a great argument.

19. **quod jam pueri discant:** this gives the reason, not for men's foreknowledge, but for our feeling assured of such foreknowledge. The force of the clause may best be seen in the following free paraphrase of the whole passage, beginning with *magnoque argumento:* ' and I am convinced that a strong argument in favor of immortality is furnished by the fact that men know many things before they are born, — and that they do is clear, because children, when they are learning difficult subjects, lay hold of innumerable things so rapidly that they seem not to be learning them then for the first time, but to be remembering and recalling them.'

22. **haec Platonis fere:** *these are substantially (the arguments) of Plato;* they are taken chiefly from Plato's Phaedo and Phaedrus.

23. **autem:** *again;* used to introduce other arguments in support of the soul's immortality.

24. **Cyrus major:** Cyrus the Elder; see note on p. 133, line 11. **haec dicit:** the passage is in the Cyropaedia, VIII, 7, 17. Though attributed to Cyrus, these views are really Xenophon's, and were gathered by him from the teachings of Socrates, like those of Plato above enumerated.

26. **nullum:** *non-existent; cf. nullus,* p. 153, line 10.

28. **eundem esse:** *that it still exists.*

29. **creditote:** for the use of the future tense here, *cj. attribuito,* p. 121, line 18. **nullum:** here equivalent to *non.* **nec clarorum virorum post mortem honores permanerent:** *i.e.* the souls of great men after death consciously endeavor to keep alive their fame among posterity; only so, it is urged, can we account for the perpetuation of their glory.

PAGE 156, 2. **quo teneremus:** we should have expected *ut teneremus, ut* being the regular particle to introduce a substantive clause after *efficio;* *quo,* however, occurs occasionally for *ut* when the substantive clause contains a comparative, as here.

3. mihi quidem numquam persuaderi potuit: *I at least could never be convinced,* lit. *it could never be convinced to me.*

4. dum essent, cum excessissent, cum evasisset, cum coepisset: in Latin all these clauses, following the principle for the ' sequence of tenses,' stand in the imperfect and pluperfect, since *vivere,* taking its time from *potuit,* is historical; in English we should use the present and perfect, *viz. while they are, when they have departed, when it has gone out, when it has begun.* Similarly we should render *vivere, emori, etc.,* by the present, — *live, die, etc.* Note the adversative asyndeton in *vivere, emori,* — *live while they are in the body, but die when they have departed.*

5. insipientem: *without consciousness.*

8. tum esse sapientem: *is then really conscious; esse* depends upon *mihi persuasum est* to be supplied in thought from *mihi numquam persuaderi potuit.*

9. ceterarum rerum: dependent upon *quaeque; ceterarum* means ' the rest ' as opposed to *animus;* for this proleptic use of *ceteri, cf. ceteris,* p. 121, line 9.

13. atqui: *now.*

19. hanc omnem pulchritudinem: *i.e.* all this beautiful universe.

21. servabitis: the future indicative, as often, has here the force of an imperative.

22. nostra: *i.e.* views of our own countrymen as opposed to those of a foreigner like Cyrus.

26. multos: here as elsewhere for *multos alios.*

27. tanta esse conatos: *would have attempted so great enterprises;* we should have expected *conaturos fuisse,* since the infinitive represents the apodosis of a condition contrary-to-fact in indirect discourse. B. 321, 2, *a* ; A. 589, *b*, 2 ; G. 597, R. 4 ; H. 647. **quae . . . pertinerent:** the clause expresses purpose, — *to have to do with the memory of posterity, i.e.* deeds which they intended should have to do with posterity.

28. nisi cernerent: *had they not discerned;* in conditions contrary-to-fact, the imperfect subjunctive is used in preference to the pluperfect, to denote a *continued* action belonging to past time. B. 304, 2 ; A. 517, *a* : G. 597. R. 1 ; H. 579, 1. The sam thought occurs also in Cicero's oration for Archias, § 28 f.

PAGE 157, 1. **an censes:** *you don't think, do you?* **ut aliquic glorier:** *to boast a bit; cf. idem gloriari,* p. 134, line 4.

3. si essem terminaturus: Cato really means *si credidissem me terminaturum esse.*

5. **otiosam**: see note on *otiosa*, p. 142, line 9.

6. **nescio quo modo**: *somehow.*

7. **ita**: correlative with the following *quasi.*

8. **cum excessisset**: the subjunctive is purely the result of attraction.

9. **victurus esset**: *i.e.* truly live. *Cf.* p. 154, line 17.   **quod ni ita se haberet**: *unless it were so; quod* is further explained by the appositional clause *ut . . . essent;* on *ni* see note on p. 150, line 16.

10. **ut animi immortales essent**: *that souls are immortal;* for the imperfect, see note on *ut intellegeretis*, p. 138, line 23.   **haud niteretur** and **haud retraxerit** (line 20, below): in his orations, Cicero confines the use of *haud* to adjectives, adverbs, and the verb *scio;* in the philosophical writings it occurs with other verbs, as here.   **optimi cujusque animus**: *the souls of all the best men,* lit. *the soul of each best man.*

11. **maxime niteretur**: *i.e.* strive in proportion to their strength of character, hence the best men the most earnestly.   **immortalitatem et gloriam**: Hendiadys.

12. **quid, quod**: *what of the fact that?*

13. **iniquissimo**: *sc. animo; with the greatest reluctance.*

14. **qui plus cernat et longius**: *which sees deeper and farther;* for the force of *plus, cf.* note on p. 125, line 6.

15. **ille autem**: *i.e. ille animus.*

16. **non videre**: *to fail to see.*   **efferor**: *I am carried away.*

18. **aveo**: used of intense and eager longing; *cf. avidus.* **cognovi**: *I have known.*

20. **quo quidem, etc.**: *and when I set out for them; quo* here =*ad quos,* just as *unde* often =*a quibus, a quo.*

21. **retraxerit, recoxerit**: Potential Subjunctive, but differing only slightly in force from a future indicative.   **tamquam Peliam recoxerit**: *boil me back to life again like Pelias.* Cicero seems to have confounded Pelias with Aeson; it was the latter whom Medea restored to life by boiling.

22. **ex hac aetate**: *at* (lit. *from*) *my present time of life.*   **repuerascam**: only here apparently in this sense; the clause *ut repuerascam* is the object of *largiatur.*

23. **quasi decurso spatio ad carceres a calce revocari**: *quasi* modifies the entire expression, — *after finishing the course, to be recalled from the goal to the starting-point, so to speak.* The comparison is borrowed from the race-course; *carceres* were the stalls at the end of the course, from which the chariots started; the *calx* (lit. *lime*) was a chalk-line marking the limit of the race.

25. **quid laboris**: *sc. habet.*

PAGE **158**, 1. **sed habeat sane**: *but grant that it really has* (*advantages*); *habeat* is a Jussive Subjunctive with concessive force. B. 278; A. 440; G. 264; H. 559, 3.

3. **et ei docti**: *and those, too, philosophers.*

6. **commorandi, non habitandi**: *for tarrying at, not for dwelling in;* a peculiar use of the genitive of the gerund to denote purpose.

11. **ad Catonem meum**: *i.e.* his son, mentioned p. 127, line 15.

12. **nemo vir**: a stronger *nemo;* sometimes we find *nemo homo.*

14. **quod contra**, *etc.: whereas on the contrary mine ought to have been burned by him; quod* is governed by *contra*, lit. *opposite to which;* on the anastrophe of the preposition see B. 144, 3; A. 435; H. 676, 1.   **meum**: *i.e. meum corpus cremari.* **animus**: *i.e.* the soul of his son.

16. **quo** =*ad quae*, as above, p. 157, line 20.   **mihi ipsi esse veniendum**: *that I myself must come.*

18. **non quo aequo animo ferrem**: *not that I bore it with resignation.* B. 286, 1, *b;* A. 540, N. 3; G. 541, N. 2; H. 588, 2.

19. **digressum et discessum**: *parting and separation;* synonyms; *cf. officia et munera*, p. 135, line 9.

21. **his rebus**: emphatic by position, — *these are the things whereby old age is easy to me.* **id**: *emphatic,* — *for 'twas that you said you wondered at; id* anticipates *levis est senectus.*

23. **in hoc**: explained by the following *qui*-clause, — *in this, viz. that I believe the souls of men to be immortal.*

24. **mihi**: Dative of Separation.

26. **mortuus**: *when dead.* **ut censent**: modifying *nihil sentiam.* **quidam minuti philosophi**: *certain petty philosophers;* the reference is to the Epicureans, who denied the immortality of the soul. **nihil sentiam**: *i.e. have no consciousness.*

27. **philosophi mortui irrideant**: they will be unable to scoff if death brings annihilation, for they too will be annihilated.

31. **peractio tamquam fabulae**: *the last act of a play, so to speak; peractio* is found only here.

PAGE **159**, 3. **haec habui quae dicerem**: *this was what I had to say on old age; haec* is emphatic; *quae dicerem* is a clause of purpose.

4. **re experti**: *by actual experience,* lit. *experiencing it in fact; re* is opposed to *quae audivistis.*

VOCABULARY AND INDEX OF PROPER NAMES

VOCABULARY.

[References are to Roman Numerals and Sections *in the text.*]

ā, ab, prep. [abl.] *by,* of the agent, 5, 13, etc.; *from,* 2, 4, etc.

absēns, -utis, adj. *absent,* 7, 24.

abstergō, -ere, -ersī, -ersum, *to wipe away,* to obliterate, 1, 2.

absum, -esse, -fuī, *to be absent,* 16, 55; **propius abesse,** *to be nearer,* 21, 77.

absurdus, -a, -um, adj. *absurd, unreasonable,* 18, 65.

abundē, adv. *abundantly,* 14, 48.

abundō, -āre, -āvī, -ātum, *to abound, to be well supplied,* 16, 56.

āc, 15, 51, see **atque.**

accēdō, -ere, -ēssī, -ēssum, 3 v. n. *to go towards, to approach,* 18, 63; 19, 71; *to come near to,* 15, 51; **accēdere ad,** *to be added to,* 6, 15; 11, 35.

accidō, -ere, -idī, *to happen, to fall out,* 3, 7; 10, 31.

accipiō, -ere, -ēpī, -eptum, *to receive,* 13, 55; 15, 51; *to listen to, to learn, to be informed,* 5, 13; 12, 39, 41; 21, 78.

accommodō, -āre, -āvī, -ātum, *to make to suit, to fit,* 19, 70.

accubitiō, -ōnis, f. *a lying at table, reclining,* 13, 45.

accūsō, -āre, -āvī, -ātum, *to accuse, to find fault with,* 3, 7; 5, 13.

acerbitās, -ātis, f. *bitterness,* 18, 65.

aciēs, -ēī, f. *eye-sight,* 23, 83.

acinus (or **-um,** n.), -ī, m. *a berry, a grape,* 15, 52.

āctus, -ūs, m. *an act* of a play, 2, 5; 18, 64; 19, 70.

acūtus, -a, -um, adj. *acute, keen,* 14, 50.

ad, prep. [acc.] *to,* 13, 43; **accēdere ad,** 15, 51; **pertinet ad,** 16, 56; **usque ad,** *up to,* 14, 50; 17, 60; *in addition to,* 11, 35; *with a view to,* 10, 31; 17, 59; 19, 86.

addīscō, -ere, -didicī, *to learn in addition, to increase one's knowledge by,* 8, 26; 14, 50.

addūcō, -ere, -ūxī, -ūctum, *to induce,* 10, 34.

adeptus, -a, -um, past part. pass. of depon. v. **adipīscor,** *obtained,* 2, 4.

ᴧdfor, -ārī, -ātus, to address, 1, 1.

adferō, -rre, adtulī, adlātum, to bring to, 16, 55; to bring in, 11, 38.

adhibeō, -ēre, -uī, -itum [ad-habeō], to apply, to make use of, 11, 36; 14, 46; 19, 71.

adjungō, -ere, -nxī, -nctum, to join on, to add, 23, 86.

adjuvō, -āre, ūvī, -ūtum, to assist, 1, 1.

adminiculum, -ī, n. [ad-manus] a support, a prop, 15, 53.

admīrābilis, -e, n. admirable, worthy of admiration, 4, 12.

admīrātiō, -ōnis, f. wonder, admiration, 15, 52.

admīror, -ārī, -ātus sum, to wonder at, to express admiration, 1, 3; 23, 85.

admisceō, -ēre, -cuī, -īxtum, to mix with, 21, 78.

admīxtiō, -ōnis, f. admixture, 22, 80.

admodum, adv. considerably, very, 4, 10; 9, 30; 14, 46; [ad modum 'up to a measure'].

adolēscō, -ere, -ēvī, adultum, to grow, to come to maturity, 15, 51.

adoptō, -āre, -āvī, -ātum, to adopt as a son, 11, 35.

adsentior, -īrī, -sēnsus, to assent to, to agree with, 10, 32.

adsequor, -ī, -secūtus, to come up with, to attain, 3, 8.

adsurgō, -ere, -surrēxī, -sur-

rēctum, to rise up before, in pass. to have the honor paid one of having men rise at one's approach, 18, 63.

adspiciō, -ere, -ēxī, -ectum, to look at, to behold, 9, 27.

adsum, -esse, -fuī, to be present, 10, 33; to appear in court for, 11, 38.

adulēscēns, -ntis, m. a young man, between the ages of 17 and 30 [originally partic. of adolēscō], 12, 39, etc.

adulēscentia, -ae, f. manhood, youth [opposed to senectus], 2, 4, etc.

adulēscentulus, -ī, m. a very young man, 4, 10; 9, 29; with contemptuous meaning, 6, 20.

adulterium, -ī, n. adultery, 12, 40.

adveniō, -īre, -vēnī, -ventum, to come, to arrive, 8, 25.

adventō, -āre, -āvī, -ātum, to be coming, to approach, 1, 2.

adversor, -ārī, -ātus, to oppose, to resist, 19, 71.

aedificium, -ī, n. a building, 20, 72.

aegrē, adv. with difficulty, painfully, 20, 72.

aegrōtō, -āre, -āvī, -ātum, to be ill, 19, 67.

aequālis, -e, adj. of the same age, 3, 7; 14, 46; contemporaneous, lasting the same time, 7, 23.

aequitās, -tātis, f. fairness, calmness, 1, 1.

aequus, -a, -um, adj. placid

VOCABULARY.

undisturbed, 23, 85; **aequis-
simus**, 23, 83.

aestās, -tātis, f. *summer*, 19,
70.

aetās, -tātis, f. *age, time of
life*, 2, 4; 19, 66, etc.; **aetātem agere**, *to spend one's life*,
17, 60; *a generation*, 10, 31.

aeternitās, -tātis, f. *eternity,
perpetuity*, 21, 77.

aeternus, -a, -um, adj. *ever-
lasting, immortal*, 19, 66.

adficiō, -ere, -ēcī, -ectum, *to
affect, to affect unfavorably,
to weaken*, 14, 47.

adflīgō, -ere, -īxī, -īctum, *to
depress, to bring down*, 10,
32.

adflō, -āre, -āvī, -ātum, *to
breathe out, to waft towards*,
17, 59.

ager, -rī, m. *a field, a farm*, 7,
24; 15, 54; **agrī**, 16, 56; *a
district*, 4, 11; *land*, 16, 56.

agitātiō, -ōnis, f. *a spending*
of time, 7, 23.

agitō, -āre, -āvī, -ātum, freq.
to move, to keep in motion,
21, 78; **agitāre mente**, *to
reflect upon, to ponder*, 12,
41.

āgnus, -ī, m. *a lamb*, 16, 56.

agō, -ere, ēgī, āctum, *to act, to
do*, 6, 15; 8, 26; 9, 27; *to
spend* time, 2, 4; 10, 32; **aetātem**, 17, 60; **vītam**, 11, 38;
age, *come! well then!* 7, 23.

agrestis, -e, adj. *rustic, savage*,
14, 47.

agricola, -ae, m. *a husbandman, cultivator of land*, 7,
24; 15, 51.

āiō, **ais**, **ait**, **āiunt**, *to say*,
7, 21.

alacer, -cris, -cre, adj. [al-, cf.
alō] *brisk, cheerful*, 20, 75.

aliās, adv. *at other times*,
15, 51.

aliquandō, adv. *eventually*,
11, 35; *at length*, 19, 71.

aliquī, -qua, -quod, indef. pro-
nom. adj. *some*, 3, 6; 14, 49,
etc.

aliquis [-qua (rare)], -quid,
indef. pron. *some one, something*, 8, 26; 14, 49, etc.

aliquō, adv. *somewhither*, 19, 66.

alius, -a, -ud [gen. alīus], adj.
other, something else, 2, 5.

adlectō, -āre, -āvī, -ātum, *to
entice, to allure* [freq. of
adliciō], 16, 57.

alter, -era, -erum [gen. alterius,
dat. alterī], adj. *another*, 8,
25; *a second*, 5, 15; 9, 27, 30.

ambitiō, -ōnis, f. lit. *a going
round canvassing for office*,
etc., hence, *ambition*, 14, 49.

amīcus, -ī, m. *a friend*, 10, 32.

amīcus, -a, -um, adj. **amīcis-
simus**, *friendly*, 21, 77.

āmittō, -ere, -īsī, -issum, *to lose*,
4, 11; 6, 20; 9, 27.

amplus, -a, -um, adj. *ample,
grand, honorable;* **amplis-
simus**, 6, 20; 19, 68.

amputātiō, -ōnis, f. *a cutting
off, a pruning*, 15, 53.

amputō, -āre, -āvī, -ātum, *to
cut off, to prune*, 15, 52.

an, interrog. particle, *is it?*
6, 15: in indirect questions,
whether, 20, 74 ; with the
latter of two alternatives, the
first introduced by **utrum**,
or, 10, 33.

angō, -ere, anxī, anctum or
anxum, *to give pain to, to
make anxious*, 19, 66.

animus, -ī, m. *the soul*, 19, 66,
etc.; *mind, feeling*, 23, 83,
etc.

animōsus, -a, -um, adj. *cour-
ageous, spirited*, 20, 72.

annus, -ī, m. *a year*, 5, 13, etc. ;
annī, *age*, 9, 28.

ante, (1) prep. [acc.] *before* of
time or place; *in preference
to*, 4, 10. (2) adv. *beforehand, earlier*, 14, 49; 15, 54;
ante . . . **quam**, 6, 18; 10, 33;
14, 50.

antecēdō, -ere, -cēssī, -cēssum,
to precede, to be superior,
18, 64.

antehāc, adv. *heretofore*, 6, 16.

antepōnō, -ere, -posuī, -positum,
to place before, to prefer.

antīquitās, -tātis, f. *antiquity,
ancient times*, 4, 12; 11, 38.

antīquus, -a, -um, adj. *ancient ;*
antīquī, *the ancients, the men
of past time*.

anxius, -a, -um, adj. *anxious*,
18, 65.

apex, -icis, m. *the highest
point, the chief glory*, 17, 60.

apis, -is, f. *a bee*, 15, 54.

appāreō, -ēre, -uī, *to appear*,
22, 80.

appellō, -āre, -āvī, -ātum, *to
call, to name*, 6, 19; 11, 36.

adpetō, -ere, -īvī or -iī, -tītum,
to seek for, to make for, 16,
56; 18, 63; 20, 72.

adportō, -āre, -āvī, -ātum, *to
bring*, 8, 25.

adpropīnquātiō, -ōnis, f. *a
nearing, an approaching, the
near approach*, 19, 66.

aprīcātiō, -ōnis, f. *a warming
in the sun*, 16, 57.

aptus, -a, -um, adj. [apo] **ap-
tissimus**, *fitting, suitable*,
3, 9.

apud, prep. [accus.] *with,
among*, 6, 20; 18, 63; *at or
near*, 10, 32; *at the house of*,
1, 3; *at the headquarters of*,
13, 43; *in the writings of*,
9, 30; 10, 31; 21, 78.

aqua, -ae, f. *water*, 19, 71.

arbitror, -ārī, -ātus, *to think*,
10, 33; 20, 75; 21, 77.

arbor, -oris, f. *a tree*, 2, 5, etc.

arbustum, -ī, n. [arbosētum]
orchard used as a vineyard,
15, 54.

arcessō, -ere, -īvī, -ītum, *to
summon*, 16, 56.

arcus, -ūs, m. *a bow*, 11, 37.

ārdor, -ōris, m. *heat*, 15, 53.

argūmentum, -ī, n. *an argument*, 21, 78.

arista, -ae, f. *the beard of an
ear of corn*, 15, 51.

arma, -ōrum, n. *arms*, 3, 9.

arō, -āre, -āvī, -ātum, *to plough*,
16, 56.

arripiō, -ere, -uī, -eptum, *to*

VOCABULARY.

snatch, *to catch eagerly at*,
8, 26; 21, 78; 18, 62.

ars, -rtis, f. *art, skill*, 5, 52;
artēs, *accomplishments*, 3,
9; 9, 29; 18, 65.

articulus, -ī, m. *joint knot in
a plant*, 15, 53.

arx, -rcis, f. *a citadel*, 4, 11.

ascendō, -ere, -ndī, -nsum, *to
ascend, to mount*, 10, 34.

aspectus, -ūs, m. *sight, appearance*, 15, 53.

aspernor, -ārī, -nātus, *to reject,
to despise*, 12, 42.

assēnsus, -ūs, m. *assent, approbation*, 18, 62.

assiduus, -a, -um, adj. *careful,
diligent*, 16, 56.

at, conj. *but, yet*, 15, 54; introducing a supposed objection = at enim, *but it is* or
may be said, 7, 21; 9, 33;
11, 35; 13, 44; 14, 47; 18, 65;
19, 68; the answer is also
introduced sometimes by *at*,
as in 11, 35; as an exclamation, *ah but! ah well!* 9, 27,
cf. 14, 49.

Athēniēnsis, -e, adj. *Athenian*,
12, 41.

āthlēta, -ae, m. *an athlete*,
9, 27.

atque, conj. *and, and as well*,
14, 49; *and therefore*, 14, 46;
and besides, or, *now!* 14,
50.

atqui, conj. *and yet, however,
why!* 2, 6; 14, 50; 17, 59;
19, 66; introducing the minor
of a syllogism, *now*, 22, 81.

attribuō, -ere, -uī, -ūtum, *to
attribute, to set down to*, 1, 3.

auctōritās, -tātis, f. *influence,
authority*, 6, 15; 11, 37; 21,
77 ; senātūs auctōritās, *a
resolution of the senate*, 4,
11.

aucupium, -ī, n. *fowling, the
sport of taking birds* [avis-
capio], 16, 56.

audāciter, adv. *audaciously,
boldly*, 20, 72.

audeō, -ēre, ausus sum, a. *to
dare, to venture*, 21, 77.

audientia, -ae, f. *a hearing;*
facere, a. *to secure a hearing*, 9, 28.

audiō, -īre, -īvī or -iī, -ītum,
to hear, 4, 11; *to be told*, 21,
78; 23, 83.

auferō [ab- ferō], -erre, abstulī,
ablātum, *to take away*, 12, 39;
19, 71.

augeō, -ēre, auxī, auctum, *to
make to increase*, 6, 17.

augēscō, -ere [augeō], incept.
to begin to grow, to increase,
14, 46; 15, 53.

augur, -uris, m. [avis] *an
augur*, one of the college of
augurs, 4, 11; 7, 22.

augurium, -ī, n. *augury, the
art of making predictions
from birds*, 4, 12; 11, 38.

aurum, -ī, n. *gold*, 16, 55.

auspicium, -ī, n. [avis- spiciō]
*a divine premonition, an
omen derived from observing
birds*, 4, 11.

aut, disjunct. *either, or*.

autem, conj. *but, moreover, however,* 3, 8, etc.

autumnus, -ī, m. *autumn,* 19, 70.

avāritia, -ae, f. *avarice,* 18, 65.

avārus, -a, -um, adj. *greedy, avaricious,* 18, 65.

āvellō, -ere, -vellī or -vulsī, -vulsum, *to pull or tear off,* 19, 71.

aveō, -ēre, *to wish eagerly, to desire,* 23, 83.

avidē, adv. *eagerly, greedily,* 20, 72.

aviditās, -tātis, f. *a longing for, an eager desire,* 14, 46.

avis, -is, f. *a bird,* 15, 51.

avītus, -a, -um, adj. *belonging to a grandfather, ancestral,* 10, 34.

āvocō, -āre, -āvī, -ātum, *to call away, to call off from,* 5, 15.

avus, -ī, m. *a grandfather,* 6, 19.

bāca, -ae, f. *a berry,* 2, 5.

beātē, adv. *happily,* 2, 4.

beātus, -a, -um, adj. *happy, prosperous,* 9, 29; **beātior**, 16, 56.

bellō, -āre, -āvī, -ātum, *to wage war.* 2, 5.

bellum, -ī, n. *war,* 14, 46, etc.

bene, adv. *well,* 3, 9; 13, 45; 14, 47, etc.

blanditiae, -ārum, f. *charms, soothing influence,* 13, 44.

bona, *property,* 7, 22; 19, 71.

bonum, -ī, n. *a good thing, a blessing,* 10, 33; 19, 71, etc.

bonus, -a, -um, adj. *good, virtuous:* **melior, optimus.**

bōs, bovis, m. *an ox,* 10, 33.

brevis, -e, adj. *short;* **brevī**, adv. *shortly, soon,* 10, 31; *in few words,* 16, 57.

cadūcus, -a, -um, adj. *perishable,* 2, 5; *liable to fall,* 15, 52.

caecus, -a, -um, adj. *blind,* 6, 6; 11, 37.

caelestis, -e, adj. *of heaven, heavenly,* 21, 77; **caelestia**, *the heavenly bodies,* ib.

caelum, -ī, n. *heaven, the sky,* 14, 49.

calēscō, -ere, incept. *to grow warm,* 16, 57.

calor, -ōris, m. *warmth, heat,* 15, 53.

calx, -cis, f. *chalk* or *lime:* used for the *alba linea* across a race-course, from which the chariots started and to which they returned, 23, 83.

canōrus, -a, -um, adj. *tuneful,* 9, 28.

cānus, -a, -um, adj. *white;* **cānī**, *white hair,* 18, 62.

capiō, -ere, cēpī, captum, *to take, to receive,* 15, 54; 18, 62; *to catch, to take in,* 13, 44.

capitālis, -e, adj. *fatal, mortal,* 12, 39; **rēs capitālis**, *a capital offence,* 12, 42.

caput, -itis, n. *a head,* 10, 34; *top of vines,* 15, 53.

carcer, -eris, m. *a barrier* or *stall,* behind which the racing chariots were stationed before advancing to the *calx*, 23, 83.

căreō, -ēre, -uī, *to be without, to lack*, 3, 7, etc.

carmen, -inis, n. *a poem*, 6, 16; 7, 22; *an inscription*, 17, 61.

cārus, -a, -um, adj. *dear*, 11, 37; 20, 73; **cārissimus**, 22, 79.

cāseus, -i, m. *cheese*, 16, 56.

cāsus, -ūs, m. *a chance, an accident*, 19, 67; *a misfortune*, 23, 85.

Caudīnus, -a, -um, adj. *of Caudium, Caudine*, 12, 41.

causa, -ae, f. *a cause, a reason*, 5, 15; *a law-suit*, 11, 38.

cavea, -ae, f. *the auditorium of a theatre*, 14, 48.

cēdō, -ere, -ssī, -ssum, *to give place, to depart*, 19, 69.

cedō, cette, old imperative form [probably from particle ce- and do], *here! pray tell me!* 6, 20.

celeritās, -tātis, f. *swiftness*, 21, 78.

cella, -ae, f. *a chamber, closet;* c. **vīnāria**, *cellar*, 16, 56.

cēna, -ae, f. *dinner, supper*, the principal meal of the Romans which took place about three P.M., 13, 44.

cēnseō, -ēre, -uī, **cēnsum**, *to think, hold as an opinion*, 20, 74; 23, 82.

cēnsor, -ōris, m. *a Censor*, a Roman magistrate, 6, 16; 12, 42.

centēsimus, -a, -um, ordin. num. adj. *hundredth*, 17, 60.

centum, indecl. num. adj. *a hundred*, 5, 13.

centuriō, -ōnis, m. *a centurion*, an officer in a legion next in rank to the tribunus, 10, 33.

cēreus, -a, -um, adj., *of wax, waxen, wax*, 13, 44.

cernō, -ere, crēvī, crētum, a. *to perceive, to see*, 21, 77; 23, 82.

certē, adv. *at least*, 1, 2; 8, 26; *certainly*, 4, 11; 14, 50; 20, 74.

certō, adv. *certainly, for certain*, 1, 2.

certus, -a, -um, adj. *fixed, certain*, 18, 63; 19, 68; *to be relied upon*, 20, 72.

cēssō, -āre, -āvī, -ātum, *to be idle, to do nothing*, 5, 13; 6, 18.

cēterus, -a, -um, adj. *the other, the rest* [rare in sing.], 1, 3, etc.

cibus, -ī, m. *food*, 11, 36.

citō, citius, adv. *quickly*, 2, 4; 6, 20.

cīvīlis, -e, adj. *of a city or citizen, civil*, 11, 38.

cīvis, -is, m. *a citizen*, 4, 12; 18, 63.

cīvitās, -tātis, f. *a state*, 18, 63.

clandestīnus, -a, -um, *secret, clandestine*, 12, 39.

clāreō, -ēre, -uī, *to be bright, to be famous*, 4, 10.

clārus, -a, -um, adj. *illustrious* 3, 8; 4, 12; 7, 22.

classis, -is, f. *a fleet*, 13, 44.

clāva, -ae, f. *a club, a foil*, 16, 51.

clāvicula, -ae, f. *tendril*, 15, 52.

clāvus, -ī, m. *a tiller, a helm*, 6, 17.

cliēns, -ntis, m. *a client*, 10, 32.

clientēla, -ae, f. *a band* or *number of clients*, 11, 37.

coacēscō, -ere, incept. *to begin to turn sour*, 18, 65.

coāgmentō, -āre, -āvī, -ātum, 1 v. a. *to weld* or *cement together*, 20, 72.

coepī, -isse, defect. *to begin*, 14, 49.

coerceō, -ēre, -cuī, -citum, 2 v. a. *to compel*, 15, 52.

coetus, -ūs, m. *a company, an assembly*, 13, 45; 23, 84.

cōgitātiō, -ōnis, f. *thinking, thought*, 12, 41.

cōgitō, -āre, -āvī, -ātum, *to think of*, 6, 18; *to reflect upon, to ruminate*, 11, 38.

cōgnōmen, -inis, n. *a surname, a title of honor*, 1, 1; 2, 5.

cōgnōscō, -ere, -nōvī, -nitum, 3 v. a. *to know, to be acquainted with*, 3, 7; 4, 12; *to learn, to be assured*, 6, 18.

cōgō, -ere, coēgī, coactum, *to force, to compel*, 2, 4; 7, 23.

cohibeō, -ēre, -uī, -itum, *to keep*, 15, 51.

conlēga, -ae, m. *a colleague* in an office, 18, 64.

conlēgium, -i, n. *a number of colleagues*, as the college of augurs, etc., 18, 64.

conligō, -ere, -ēgī, -ectum, *to collect*, 11, 38.

conloquium, -ī, n. *parley, conference*, 12, 40.

conluviō, -ōnis, f. *foul medley, offscouring*, 23, 84.

colō, -ere, -uī, -cultum, *to cultivate*, 17, 59; *to pay respect* or *court to*, 3, 7; 8, 26; 23, 83; *to worship*, 22, 81.

Colōnēus, -a, -um, adj. *of Colonus*, a deme in Attica, 7, 22.

cōmicus, -a, -um, adj. *belonging to* or *represented in a comedy, comic*, 11, 36.

comminus, adv. *at close quarters* [com- manus], 6, 19.

cōmitās, -tātis, f. *courtesy, politeness*, 4, 10; 18, 65.

cōmitātus, -ūs, m. *society*, 9, 29.

commemorō, -āre, -āvī, -ātum, *repeat to myself*, 11, 38; *to commemorate, to mention*, 14, 15; 15, 52.

commercium, -ī, n. *intercourse* [properly ' mutual trading '], *connection*, 12, 42.

commodum, -ī, n. *convenience, advantage*, 23, 84.

commoror, -ārī, -ātus, *to stay temporarily, to be on a visit*, 23, 84.

commoveō, -ēre,- ōvī, -ōtum, *to move thoroughly, to affect*, 1, 1.

commūnis, -e, adj. *common, shared with*, followed by *cum* 1, 2; 19, 67; *ordinary*, 18, 63; *condescending, polite*, 17,

59; *universal, shared in by
all*, 11, 35; 19, 68.
commūniter, adv. *in common,
mutually*, 1, 2.
compāges, -is, f. *a fastening,
a structure*, 21, 77.
comparō, -āre, -āvī, -ātum, *to
compare*, 5, 14; 14, 50; 18,
64.
compēnsō, -āre, -āvī, -ātum, *to
compensate, to make good*,
11, 35.
complector, -ī, -xus, *to embrace*, 15, 52.
compleō, -ēre, -ēvī, -ētum, *to
fill*, 5, 13; 14, 46.
compositus, -a, -um, adj. *se-
date*, 9, 28.
compōtātiō, -ōnis, f. *a drinking together*, 13, 45.
compressus, -ūs, m. *close pres-
sure*, 15, 51.
concēdō, -ere, -cēssī, -cēssum,
*to allow, to grant as a privi-
lege*, 9, 30.
concēnātiō, -ōnis, f. *a dining
or supping together*, 13, 55.
concilium, -ī, n. *council, assembly*, 23, 85.
condiō, -īre, -īvī or -iī, -ītum,
to flavor, to season, 4, 10.
conditiō, -ōnis, f. *terms, position*, 19, 68.
conditus, -a, -um, **condītior**,
part. adj. [condiō] *seasoned,
well-flavored*, 16, 56.
condō, -ere, -didī, -ditum, *to
store up*, 7, 24.
cōnfectiō, -ōnis, f. *a making,
a composition*, 1, 2.

cōnferō, -erre, -tulī, -lātum, *to
bestow upon*, 5, 14.
cōnficiō, -ere, -fēcī, -fectum, *to
complete, to prepare thor-
oughly*, 18, 38.
conglūtinātiō, -ōnis, f. *a glue-
ing together, a compacting*,
20, 72.
conglūtinō, -āre, -āvī, -ātum,
*to glue together, to unite se-
curely*, 20, 72.
congregor, -ārī, -ātus, *to asso-
ciate together*, 3, 7.
coniūnctiō, -ōnis, f. *union*, 13,
45.
coniungō, -ere, -nxī, -nctum,
to join together, 12, 42; 17,
59.
cōnor, -ārī, -ātus, *to try, to attempt*, 23, 82.
cōnsaepiō, -īre, -īvī or -iī,
-aeptum, *to enclose with a
fence*, 17, 59.
cōnscientia, -ae, f. *consciousness, inward feeling*, 3, 9.
cōnscrībō, -ere, -psī, -ptum, *to
compose, to write*, 1, 1; 23,
83.
cōnsenēscō, -ere, -senuī, incept. *to grow old, to begin
to decay*, 1, 29.
cōnsentiō, -īre, -nsī, -nsum, *to
agree*, 17, 61.
cōnsequor, -ī, -secūtus sum,
to follow, 6, 19; v. a. *to obtain*, 12, 41; 19, 68.
cōnserō, -ere, -sēvī, -situm, *to
sow* or *plant with*, 17, 59.
cōnservō, -āre, -āvī, -ātum, *to
preserve*, 10, 34; 20, 75.

cōnsessus, -ūs, m. *assemblage, a company* or *audience seated together,* 18, 63.

cōnsīdō, -ere, -sēdī, -sessum, *to be seated, to take one's seat,* 18, 63.

cōnsilium, -ī, n. *a counsel, plan, prudence,* 4, 11; 6, 15; *deliberation,* 42.

cōnsistō, -ere, -stitī, 3 v. n. *to stand firm, to be unshaken,* 12, 41; 20, 74.

cōnsitiō, -ōnis, f. *a planting* in groups, 15, 54.

cōnsōlātiō, -ōnis, f. *consolation,* 1, 1; 2, 4.

cōnsōlor, -ārī, -ātus, a. *to console,* 23, 85.

cōnstāns, -ntis, adj. *constant, settled,* 10, 33; 20, 76.

cōnstat, impers. v. *it is certain, it is well known,* 1, 3.

cōnstituō, -ere, -uī, -ūtum, *to set up, to settle,* 13, 45; **vadimonia cōnstitūta,** *engagements at court,* 7, 21.

cōnstruō, -ere, -strūxī, -strūctum, *to construct, to build,* 20, 72.

cōnsuēscō, -ere, -suēvī, -suētum, *to be accustomed,* 1, 3.

cōnsul, -ulis, m. *a consul,* a Roman magistrate, 4, 10.

cōnsulāris. -is, m. *one who has been consul, an ex-consul, a consular,* 3, 7; 4, 12.

cōnsulātus, -ūs, m. *a consulship,* 6, 16.

cōnsulō, -ere, -uī, -ultum, *to consult,* 18, 63.

cōnsūmō, -ere, -ūmpsī, -ūmptum, *to use up, to spend,* 16, 55; 19, 71.

cōnsurgō, -ere, -surrēxī, -surrēctum, *to rise together,* 18, 63.

contemnō, -ere, -mpsī, -mptum, *to despise, to make light of,* 4, 12; 13, 43; 18, 65.

contemplor, -ārī, -ātus, *to contemplate, to look at,* 5, 15; 16, 55; 21, 77.

contemptus, -a, -um, partic. contemptior, *more despicable,* 9, 27.

contentiō, -ōnis, f. *rivalry,* 14, 49; *earnest striving,* 23, 82.

contentus, -a, -um, adj. *content,* 19, 69.

continentia, -ae, f. *self-control, moderation,* 15, 55.

contineō, -ēre, -uī, -ntum, *to contain, to include,* 21, 78.

contingō, -ere, -igī, -tāctum, *to happen, to befall,* 3, 8; 19, 70.

contrā, prep. [acc.] *opposite to, against,* 4, 11; adv. *on the other hand,* 23, 84.

contrārius, -a,-um, adj. *uncongenial,* 21, 77.

conveniō, -īre, -vēnī, -ventum, *to meet* some one, 10, 32; 23, 83.

convīvium, -ī, n. *a banquet, a party,* 12, 42; 13, 44; 13, 45; 14, 46.

cōpia, -ae, f. *abundance,* 16, 56; 19, 71: **cōpiae,** *large means,* 3, 8.

cōpiōsē, adv. *largely, copiously*, 17, 59.

coquō, -ere, coxī, coctum, *to burn, to torture*, 1, 1; coctus, *ripe*, 19, 71.

corpus, -oris, n. *a body*, 5, 15, etc.

corruō, -ere, -uī, *to fall altogether, to fail*, 18, 64.

cotīdiē [quot- dies], adv. *every day, daily*, 8, 26.

crēdō, -ere, -didī, -ditum, *to believe*, 21, 77.

crēdulus, -a, -um, adj. *easily persuaded, credulous*, 11, 36.

cremō, -āre, -āvī, -ātum, *to burn*, 23, 15.

creō, -āre, -āvī, -ātum, *to create, to appoint to an office*, 6, 19.

crēscō, -ere, crēvī, crētum, incept. *to grow*, 14, 50.

crīmen, -inis, n. *accusation, charge against*, 19, 67.

Crotōniātēs, -ae, m. *an inhabitant of Crotona*, 9, 27.

crūdēlis, -e, adj. *cruel;* crūdēlissimus, 20, 75.

crūditās, -tātis, f. *indigestion*, 13, 44.

crūdus, -a, -um, adj. *raw, unripe*, 19, 71.

culmus, -ī, m. *a stalk*, 15, 51.

culpa, -ae, f. *fault*, 3, 7.

cultiō, -ōnis, f. *the practice of cultivation*, 16, 56.

cultūra, -ae, f. *cultivation*, 15, 53; 16, 56.

cum, (1) prep. [abl.] *with, together with*, 3, 7, etc.; placed after its case with

pers. and rel. pron. as *tecum.* 1, 2, etc.

(2) (quom), as (locative) relative conjunction, originally locative, afterward temporal, *when, whereas, although*, 1, 2, etc.; cum ... tum, *both* ... *and*, 2, 4, etc.; nunc cum māximē, *at this very time*, 11, 38; with indic. *when, at the time when*, purely temporal, 10, 32; 22, 79.

cūnae, -ārum, f. *a cradle*, 23, 83.

cunctor, -ārī, -ātus sum, *to delay*, 4, 10.

cūnctus, -a, -um, adj. *all together* [co(m)vinctus], 18, 64.

cupidē, adv. *greedily, eagerly*, 4, 12.

cupiditās, -tātis, f. *greed, greedy desire*, 14, 49.

cupidus, -a, -um, adj. *eager, desirous of*, 14, 47.

cupiō, -īre, -īvī or -iī, -ītum, *to desire*, 8, 26.

cūr, adv. *why?* 5, 14, etc.

cūra, -ae, f. *care, anxiety, carefulness*, 1, 1, etc.

cūria, -ae, f. *the Senate-house*, 10, 32.

cūrō, -āre, -āvī, -ātum, *to treat, to cure*, 19, 67; *to care for*, 7, 21.

curriculum, -ī, n. *a race-course, an exercise ground*, 9, 27; 11, 38.

cursō, -āre, -āvī, ātum, freq. *to run backwards and forwards, to keep moving quickly*, 6, 17.

o

cursus, -ūs, m. *a course, a fixed period,* 10, 33; 17, 60; *a running, a gallop,* 20, 75.

damnō, -āre, -āvī, -ātum, *to condemn;* **capitis damnātus**, *condemned to death,* 12, 42.

dē, prep. [abl.] *concerning,* 10, 31; 13, 43, etc.

dēbeō, -ēre, -uī, -itum, *I owe, I ought,* 7, 21; 10, 33.

dēcēdō, -ere, -cēssī, -cēssum, *to depart from, to quit,* 20, 72; *to make way for,* and in pass. *to have way made for one,* 18, 63.

decem, indecl. num. adj. *ten,* 10, 31.

decet, -ēre, -cuit, impers. *to be becoming to; it is right,* 9, 27.

dēclārō, -āre, -āvī, -ātum, *to declare, to make manifest,* 22, 81.

decorō, -āre, -āvī, -ātum, 1 v. a. *to adorn,* 20, 73.

decōrus, -a, -um, adj. *becoming,* 9, 27.

dēcurrō, -ere, -cucurrī, -cursum, *to run through, to complete,* 23, 83.

dēdecus, -oris, n. *disgrace,* 12, 42.

dēdūcō, -ere, -dūxī, -ductum, *to conduct, to bring,* 19, 26; *to escort,* as a **mark of re**spect, 18, 63.

dēfatīgātiō, -ōnis, f. *a tiring out, weariness;* 23, 86.

dēfectiō, -ōnis, f. *a failing,* 9, 29; **dēfectiō sōlis**, *a solar eclipse,* 14, 49.

dēfendō, -ere, -ndī, -nsum, *to defend,* 11, 38; 6, 15; *to act as advocate, counsel,* 11, 38; *to ward off,* 15, 53.

dēficiō, -ere, -fēcī, -fectum, *to fail, to fall away,* 9, 29.

dēgō, -ere, *to pass, to spend,* 1, 2.

deinde, adv. *then, in the next place,* 2, 4.

dēlectātiō, -ōnis, f. *delight, pleasurableness,* 14, 46; 15, 41; 16, 56.

dēlectō, -āre, -āvī, -ātum, *to please, to delight,* 5, 14; 8, 26.

dēlībō, -āre, -āvī, -ātum, *to take a little from, to skim, to sip,* 21, 78.

dēlīrātiō, -ōnis, f. *dotage, imbecility,* 11, 36.

dēmēns, -ntis, adj. *distraught, out of one's mind,* 6, 16.

dēmergō, -ere, -rsī, -rsum, *to cause to sink, to drown,* 21, 77.

dēmetō, -ere, -messuī, -messum, 3 v. a. *to reap,* 19, 70.

dēmōnstrō, -āre, -āvī, -ātum, 1. v. a. *to point out,* 21, 78.

dēnique, adv. *in fine, in fact,* 10, 33; with *tum,* 23, 82.

dēnūntiō, -āre, -āvī, -ātum, *to denounce, to declare,* 6, 18.

dēplōrō, -āre, -āvī, -ātum, *to deplore,* 3, 7; 13, 84.

dēportō, -āre, -āvī, -ātum, *to bring home, to import,* 1, 1.

dēprimō, -ere, -essī, -essum, *to depress, to bring down,* 21, 77.

dēpūgnō, -āre, -āvī, -ātum, *to be actively engaged in a battle,* 10, 32.

dēputō, -āre, -āvī, -ātum, *to make up one's mind, to be of opinion,* 8, 25.

dēscendō, -ere, -ndī, -nsum, *to descend, to dismount,* 10, 34.

dēscrībō, -ere, -īpsī, -īptum, *to draw, to describe,* as a mathematical figure, 14, 49; *to write out, to compose,* 2, 5.

dēserō, -ere, -ruī, -ertum, *to desert,* 3, 9; 20, 72; 23, 85.

dēsiderātiō, -ōnis, f. *a feeling regret, a feeling the loss of,* 14, 47.

dēsiderium, -ī, n. *regret, a missing,* 10, 33; 15, 54.

dēsiderō, -āre, -āvī, -ātum, *to miss, to regret,* 9, 27; 14, 47.

dēsinō, -ere, -siī, *to cease,* 6, 18.

dēsipiēns, -ntis, adj. *out of one's mind, foolish,* 7, 22.

dēspiciō, -ere, -exī, -ectum, *to despise,* 3, 7.

dēstruō, -ere, -ūxī, -ūctum, *to destroy,* 20, 72.

dēsūdō, -āre, -āvī, -ātum, *to keep at work, to work hard,* 11, 38.

dētēstābilis, -e, adj. *execrable, abominable,* 12, 41.

dēvincō, -ere, -vīcī, -victum, *to conquer entirely,* 13, 44.

dēvorsōrium, -ī, n. *a place for halting, an inn,* 23, 84.

dēvoveō, -ēre, -vōvī, -vōtum, *to devote, to vow to death,* 13, 43.

dīcō, -ere, -xī, -ctum, *to speak, to say,* 14, 50, etc.

dictātor, -ōris, m. *a Dictator,* an extraordinary magistrate at Rome, 16, 56.

diēs, -ēī, m. and f. *a day,* 19, 69; in diēs, *every day, day by day,* 13, 45; 14, 50.

differō, -erre, distulī, dīlātum, *to postpone, to put off,* 1, 1.

difficilis, -e, adj. *difficult,* 2, 4; 21, 78; *ill-tempered,* 3, 7; 18, 65.

diffundō, -ere, -fūdi, -fūsum, *to expand,* 15, 51.

dignē, adv. *in a worthy manner, worthily,* 1, 2.

dignitās, -tātis, f. *rank, estimation,* 2, 8.

dignus, -a, -um, adj. *worthy,* 1, 2; 5, 14.

digressus, -ūs, m. *separation, parting,* 23, 85.

dīligentia, -ae, f. *diligence, earnestness,* 11, 35; 17, 59, etc.

dīligō, -ere, -ēxī, -ēctum, *to love, to esteem,* 4, 10; 8, 26; 23, 83.

dīmētior, -īrī, -mēnsus [part. pass. dīmēnsus, 17, 59], *to calculate the measurement of, to lay out,* 14, 49; 17, 59.

dīrigō, -ere, -ēxī, -ēctum, *to arrange in a straight line,* 17, 59.

dīritās, *harshness,* 18, 65.

discēdō, -ere, -ēssī, -essum, *to go away from, to depart*, 22, 79.

discēssus, -ūs, m. *departure, separation*, 23, 84.

disciplīna, -ae f. *discipline, rule of conduct*, 11, 37; 16, 55.

discō, -ere, didicī, *to learn*, 4, 12, etc.

discrībō, -ere, -psī, -ptum, *to lay out, to arrange on a plan*, 17, 59.

discrīptiō, -ōnis, f. *a laying out, an arrangement on a plan*, 17, 59.

disertus, -a, -um, adj. [dissero] *eloquent*, 9, 28.

dispār, -aris, adj. *dissimilar, unequal*, 21, 78.

disputātiō, -ōnis, f. *discussion*, 20, 74; 21, 77.

disputō, -āre, -āvī, -ātum, *to discuss, to conduct an argument*, 1, 3.

disserō, -ere, -uī, -ertum, *to argue, to state in discussion*, 24, 78.

dissimilis, -e, adj. *unlike*, 21, 78.

dissolūtus, -a, -um, adj. *lax, careless*, 11, 36.

dissolvō, -ere, -vī, -solūtum, *to dissolve, to break up*, 20, 72; 22, 82.

diū, adv. *for a long time*, **diū multumque**, 3, 9; **diūtius**, 22, 80.

diurnus, -a, -um, adj., *by day, in the daytime*, 23, 82.

diūturnitās, -tātis, f. *long duration, length of time*, 11, 38.

diūturnus, -a, -um, adj. *lasting long, long continued*, 8, 26; 19, 69.

dīvellō, -ere, -vellī, -vulsum, *to tear asunder, to pull to pieces* 20, 72.

dīvidō, -ere, -īsī, -īsum, *to divide*, 4, 11; 21, 78.

dīvīnē, adv. *divinely, extraordinarily*, 13, 44.

dīvīnitās, -tātis, f. *divinity, divine origin*, 22, 81.

dīvīnō, -āre, -āvī, -ātum, *to divine, to forebode*, 4, 12.

dīvīnus, -a, -um, adj. *godlike, divine*, 7, 24; *from God*, 12, 40.

dō, dare, dedī, datum, *to give, to grant*, 13, 43, 44; 19, 69.

doceō, -ēre, -uī, -ctum, *to teach*, 9, 29; **docēre fābulam**, *to exhibit a tragedy*, 14, 50.

doctrīna, -ae, f. *learning*, 11, 35; 14, 49.

doctus, -a, -um, adj. **doctior**, *learned*, 15, 54, etc.

doleō, -ēre, -uī, -itum, *to grieve*, 19, 70.

dolor, -ōris, m. *grief, pain*.

domesticus, -a, -um, adj. *belonging to home, internal*, 4, 12.

domī, locative case of **domus**, *at home*, 4, 12; 23, 82.

domicilium, -ī, n. *dwelling, abode*, 13, 63; 21, 77.

dominor, -ārī, -ātus, *to be master, to exercise authority*, 11, 38; 12, 41.

VOCABULARY.

dominus, -ī, m. *a master of a family* or *of slaves*, 16, 56.

domus, -ūs, loc. ī, f. *a house, an establishment*, 11, 37.

dōnum, -ī, n. *a gift*, 4, 10; 17, 59.

dormiō, -īre, -īvī, -ītum, *to sleep*, 22, 81.

dubitō, -āre, -āvī, -ātum, *to doubt*, 7, 24; d. quīn, 10, 31.

dubius, -a, -um, adj. *doubtful*, 12, 41.

dūcō, -ere, dūxī, ductum, *to lead, to guide*, 8, 26.

dulcēscō, -ere, incept., *to grow sweet*, 15, 53.

dulcis, -e, adj. *sweet, pleasant;* dulcior, 18, 65.

dum, conj. *whilst, as long as*, 23, 85.

duo, duae, duo, num. adj. *two*, 5, 14.

dux, ducis, m. and f. *a leader, a guide*, 2, 5; 10, 31.

ē, see ex.

ecquis, -quid, interrog. pron. *who? what? is there any who?* 1, 1.

edepol, indecl. expletive, *by Pollux! in faith!* 8, 25.

efferō, -rre, extulī, ēlātum, *to raise, to elate;* efferor, *I am enraptured*, 23, 83.

effētus, -a, -um, adj. *worn out, effete*, 9, 29.

efficiō, -ere, -fēcī, -fectum, *to make, to render*, 1, 2; 9, 29; 16, 56; *to cause,* efficit ut, 12, 42; 15, 52.

effluō, -ere, -uxī, *to flow away, to elapse*, 2, 4; 19, 69.

effrēnātē, adv. *in an unbridled manner, intemperately*, 12, 39.

effugiō, -ere, -fūgī, *to escape, to avoid*, 11, 35.

egeō, -ēre, -uī, *to be in need of*, 10, 31.

ego, meī, pers. pron. *I*, 4, 10, etc.

ēiciō, -ere, -iēcī, -ectum, *to eject*, 12, 42.

ēlābor, -ī, -psus, *to glide out, to escape*, 12, 42.

ēlabōrō, -āre, -āvī, -ātum, *to work earnestly*, 7, 24; 8, 26; 11, 38.

ēleganter, adv. *tastefully, elegantly*, 5, 13.

elephantus, -ī, m. *an elephant*, 9, 27.

ēliciō, -ere, -icuī, -licitum, *to draw forth*, 15, 51.

ēlogium, -ī, n. *an inscription*, 17, 61; *an epigram*, 20, 73.

ēmancipō, -āre, -āvī, -ātum, *to transfer from one authority to another*, 11, 38.

ēmereō, -ēre, -uī, -itum, *to earn fully;* ēmerēre stīpendia, *to serve one's full time*, and so, *to be discharged*, 14, 49.

ēminus, adv. *at a distance* [opp. to comminus], 6, 19.

ēmorior, -ī, -mortuus, *to die off, to die*, 19, 71; 22, 80.

412

ēnervō, -āre, -āvī, -ātum, to
deprive of bodily strength, to
enervate, 10, 32.

enim, conj. for, 4, 10: introducing examples of a general
statement, 19, 70.

ēnumerō, -āre, -āvī, -ātum, to
enumerate, to give a list of,
23, 32.

eō, īre, īvī or iī, itum, irreg.
v. to go.

eō [is], on that account, 19, 68;
eō . . . quō, 21, 77.

epulae, -ārum, f. a banquet,
13, 44; 14, 50.

epulāris, -e, adj. belonging to
a banquet, 13, 55.

epulor, -ārī, -ātus, to feast,
13, 55.

equidem, adv. certainly, at all
events, 7, 21; 8, 26; 9, 27.
[e interj. and quidem. Cf.
enim.]

equus, -ī, m. a horse, 5, 14;
10, 34.

ergā, prep. [acc.] towards,
17, 59.

ergō, conj. therefore, 6, 15.

ērigō, -ere, -ēxī, -ēctum, to
raise, to erect, 15, 51, 52; 20,
75; 23, 82.

errāticus, -a, -um, adj. straggling, straying, 15, 52.

errō, -āre, -āvī, -ātum, to wander, to be mistaken, to err,
23, 86.

error, -ōris, m. an error, a
mistake, 23, 85.

ērudītē, -ius, learnedly, 1, 3.

ēsca, -ae, f. bait, 13, 44.

et, conj. and, even; et . . . et
que . . . et, both . . . and.

etenim, conj. for indeed, 10, 31.

etiam, adv. even, also; nōn
sōlum . . . sed etiam, 1, 2,
etc.

etsī, conj. and yet, 1, 2.

ēvādō, -ere, -āsī, -āsum, to go
out of, to escape from, 22, 80.

ēveniō, -īre, -vēnī, -ventum, to
happen, 20, 76.

ēversiō, -ōnis, f. an overthrow,
ruin, 12, 40.

ex, prep. [abl.] out of, from,
20, 72; after, 19, 71.

exāmen, -inis, n. a swarm,
15, 54.

excēdō, -ere, -ssī, -ssum, to
depart, 23, 82.

excellēns, -ntis, adj. excellent,
superior, 2, 4.

excīdō, -ere, -cīdī, -cīsum, to
cut down, to destroy utterly,
6, 18.

excipiō, -ere, -ēpī, -eptum, to receive, 15, 51; to keep up, 6, 19.

excitō, -āre, -āvī, -ātum, to
excite, to call into being,
12, 49.

excursiō, -ōnis, f. expedition,
active service, 6, 19.

excūsātiō, -ōnis, f. excuse,
defence, plea, 18, 65.

exemplum, -ī, n. an example,
precedent, 8, 26; 13, 44.

exerceō, -ēre, -uī, -itum, to keep
at work, to exercise, 7, 21;
11, 38; 14, 50.

exercitātiō, -ōnis, f. practice,
exercise, 3, 9; 10, 34; 11, 36.

VOCABULARY.

exhauriō, -īre, -ausī, -austum, *to draw out*, 6, 17.

exiguus, -a, -um, adj. *small, short*, 20, 74.

existimō, -āre, -āvī, -ātum, *to think*, 23, 84.

exōrō, -āre, -āvī, -ātum, *persuade by entreaty*, 12, 42.

experior, -īrī, -ertus, *to have experience of*, 23, 85.

expleō, -ēre, -ēvī, -ētum, *to fill up, to satisfy*, 8, 26; 14, 47.

explicō, -āre, -uī (-āvī), -itum (ātum), *to unfold, to explain*, 1, 3.

explōrō, -āre, -āvī, -ātum, *to investigate;* **explōrātus**, *certain, assured*, 19, 67.

expūgnātiō, -ōnis, f. *a taking by storm*, 5, 13.

exsequor, -ī, -secūtus, *to follow up, to obtain*, 9, 28; *to keep up*, 20, 72.

exsistō, -ere, -stitī, -stitum, *to come into existence, to grow*, 15, 53.

exspectō, -āre, -āvī, -ātum, *to expect, to wait for*, 19, 68.

exstinguō, -ere, -nxī, -nctum, *to extinguish, to put out*, 4, 12; 11, 36, 38; 12, 41.

exstō, -āre, -stitī, *to be extant, to survive*, 6, 16.

exstruō, -ere, -ūxī, -ūctum, *to build up, to furnish elaborately*, 13, 44.

exsultāns, -ntis, part. of **exsultō**, *exulting*, 4, 10.

externus, -a, -um, adj. *external, foreign*, 4, 12; 6, 20.

extimēscō, -ere, -timuī, incept. *to begin to dread, to shrink from*, 20, 75.

extorqueō, -ēre, -orsī, -ortum, *to wrench away*, 23, 85.

extrēmus, -a, -um [superl. adj. from **extrā**], *furthest, last*, 2, 5; 9, 27; 19, 69.

fābula, -ae, f. *a fable, a myth*, 1, 3; *a play*, 7, 22; 14, 50; 18, 64; 19, 70; 23, 85.

facile, adv. *easily*, 1, 3; 13, 44; **facilius**, *more easily*, 13, 43; 19, 67; **facillimē**, *with the greatest ease*, 3, 7; 20, 72.

facinus, -oris, n. *a crime*, 12, 39.

faciō, -ere, fēcī, factum, *to do, to make, to cause*, 9, 27; *to represent*, 1, 3; **facere . . . ut**, 11, 38; 12, 42; **faxim**, -īs, -it [old aor. opt. formed by adding -sim to root **fac-**], 20, 73.

factum, -ī, n. *a deed*, 13, 43.

falsus, -a, -um, adj. *untrue, false*, 2, 4; 18, 68.

fāma, -ae, f. *common report, fame*, 17, 61.

familiāris, -e, adj. *intimate*, 7, 24; 14, 49.

faxit, see **faciō**.

fēcundus, -a, -um, adj. *fertile;* **fēcundior**, 15, 53.

fēnus, -oris, n. *interest, profit*, 15, 51.

ferē, adv. *just about, usually, nearly*, 21, 78.

feriō, -īre [no perfect or supine], *to strike*, 12, 42.

ferō, ferre, tuli, lātum, *to carry, to bear, to report*, 17, 59.

ferōcitās, -tātis, f. *high spirit, exuberant courage*, 10, 33.

ferrum, -ī, n. [no plur.] *iron*, 15, 52.

fervor, -ōris, m. *heat, exuberance*, 13, 45.

fibra, -ae, f. *a fibre, a filament*, 15, 51.

ficus, -ī [and -ūs], f. *a fig*, 15, 52.

fidēs, -eī, f. *good faith*, 20, 75; *honor, trustworthiness*, 1, 1.

fidēs, -ium, f. *a lyre*, 8, 26.

figō, -ere, -xī, -xum, *to fix, to fasten*, 1, 1.

fīlia, -ae, f. *a daughter*, 11, 37.

fīlius, -ī, m. *a son*, 4, 11; 22, 79.

fingō, -ere, -nxī, fictum, *to make up, to construct;* **fingere animō**, *to imagine*, 12, 41.

fīnis, -is, m. and f. *an end*, 20, 72.

fīō, fierī, factus, *to be made, to become*, 9, 30; 18, 65, etc.; **fit ut**, *it comes about that*, 20, 72.

flāgitiōsus, -a, -um, adj. *infamous*, 12, 42.

flāgitium, -ī, n. *sin*, 12, 40.

flagrō, -āre, -āvī, -ātum, *to be burning, to be inflamed with*, 14, 50.

flamma, -ae, f. *a flame*, 19, 71.

flectō, -ere, -xī, -xum, *to bend*, 6, 6.

flētus, -ūs, m. *weeping*, 20, 73.

flōreō, -ēre, -uī, *to flourish*, 6, 20.

flōs, flōris, m. *a flower*, 15, 54.

fluō, -ere, -xī, -ctum, *to flow*, 10, 31.

focus, -ī, m. *a hearth*, 16, 55.

foedus, -eris, n. *a treaty*, 6, 16.

fore [fut. infin. of **sum**], 23, 84, etc.

fortāsse, adv. *perhaps*, 3, 8; 8, 25.

forte, adv. [abl. of **fors**] *by chance;* **nisi forte**, *unless by chance*, introducing some absurd or unlikely proposition, 6, 18; 10, 33.

fortis, -e, adj. *brave*, 5, 14; **fortior**, 20, 72.

fortiter, adv. *bravely*, 23, 85.

fortūna, -ae, f. *fortune*, 17, 59.

fortūnātus, -a, -um, adj. [fortuno] *fortunate, lucky*, 9, 29.

forus, -ī, m. *a gangway*, 6, 17.

fossiō, -ōnis, f. *a digging*, 15, 53.

fragilis, -e, adj. *easily broken, fragile*, 18, 65.

frangō, -ere, frēgī, fractum, *to break*, 11, 38.

frāter, -tris, m. *a brother*, 18, 65; 19, 68.

frequēns, -ntis, adj. and adv *frequent*, 13, 44; *frequently* 11, 38.

frētus, -a, -um, adj. *relying on, supported by*, 20, 72.

frīgus, -oris, n. *cold*, 10, 34.

frūctus, -ūs, m. *fruit, profit*, 3, 9; 15, 51, 53.

fruor, -ī, frūctus, *to take pleasure in, to enjoy*, 16, 57.

frūstrā, adv. *in vain*, 23, 84.

[frūx], frūgis, f. *corn*, 15, 51.

fugiō, -ere, fūgī, fugitum, *to fly*, 4, 11.

fulciō, -īre, fulsī, fultum, *to prop*, 15, 52.

fūnāle, -is, n. *torch*, 13, 44.

fundō, -ere, fūdī, fūsum, *to pour out*, 15, 51; *to spread*, 15, 52.

fundāmentum, -ī, n. *foundation*, 18, 62.

fūnus, -eris, n. *a funeral*, 20, 73.

furiōsus, -a, -um, adj. *mad, furious*, 14, 47.

futūrus, -a, -um, partic. adj. *future, about to be*, 21, 78; 22, 81.

gallīna, -ae, f. *a hen, fowl*, 16, 56.

gaudeō, -ēre, gāvīsus sum, *to rejoice*, 8, 26.

gemma, -ae, f. *a bud*, 15, 53; *a gem, a jewel*, 17, 59.

generō, -āre, -āvī, -ātum, *to beget*, 15, 52.

geniculātus, -a, -um, adj. [genu] *knotted, jointed*, 15, 51.

gēns, -ntis, f. *a clan, a family, nation*, 17, 61.

genus, -eris, n. *sort, kind, class*, 6, 8; 13, 45; *a race*, 16, 56.

gerō, -ere, -ssī, -stum, *to carry on, to conduct*, 4, 10; 6, 18, etc.; **rem gerere**, *to be engaged in* or *to transact business*, 5, 15; 6, 17; 7, 22.

gladius, -ī, m. *a sword*, 6, 19.

glōria, -ae, f. *glory*, 3, 8; 4, 10; 13, 44; 17, 59.

glōrior, -ārī, -ātus, n. *to boast*, 4, 11; 8, 26; 10, 32; 23, 82.

grandis, -e, adj. *heavy, heavy with years, old*, 6, 16; or joined with **natū**, 4, 10; 18, 63.

grānum, -ī, n. *a grain, a seed*, 15, 52.

grātia, -ae, f. *gratitude; thanks*, 12, 42; 14, 46; *favor*; **in grātiam redīre**, *to become reconciled*, 16, 56.

grātus, -a, -um, adj. *pleasant, grateful*; **grātissimus**, 2, 6.

gravis, -e, adj. *heavy, oppressive*, 2, 4; 3, 8; 21, 78; *respectable, dignified*, 17, 61; **gravior**, -ius, 2, 4.

gravitās, -tātis, f. *gravity, seriousness*, 4, 10; 10, 33.

graviter, gravius, gravissimē, adv. *heavily, severely*, 1, 1; 19, 67; *with weight, weightily*, 6, 16.

gremium, -ī, n. *bosom, lap*, 15, 51.

gubernātor, -ōris, m. *a steersman, a pilot*, 6, 17.

gustātus, -ūs, m. *taste, flavor*, 15, 53.

habeō, -ēre, -uī, -itum, *to have*, 11, 37; 16, 58, etc.; *to reckon to consider*, 19, 71; **habēre grātiam**, *to be grateful*, 12, 42; 14, 46; **habēre ratiōnem**, *to have regard for, to pay attention to*, 11, 35; 15, 51;

habēre sermōnem, *to deliver a discourse,* 9, 30; **sē habet** = ἔχει, *is,* 18, 65; 23, 82.

habitō, -āre, -āvī, -ātum, *to reside, to live, to inhabit,* 23, 83.

haedus, -ī, m. *a kid,* 16, 56.

hāmus, -ī, m. *a hook,* 13, 44.

hasta, -ae, f. *a spear,* 6, 19; 16, 58.

haud, neg. particle, *not;* **haud sciō an,** *I rather think,* 16, 56; 20, 73.

herbēscō, -ere, incept. *to sprout into blade, to grow up,* 15, 51.

herculē, *by Hercules! truly!* [probably a vocative of *Hercules* on the analogy of the Greek oath 'Ηράκλεις], 3, 8.

hībernus, -a, -um, adj. *of the winter, wintry,* 14, 46.

hīc, haec, hōc, hūius, demonstr. pron. *this, this much, such as this,* 16, 55; 17, 60; **his diēbus,** *within these last days,* 14, 50.

histriō, -ōnis, m. *an actor,* 18, 64; 19, 70.

hodiē, adv. [hoc die], *to-day,* 10, 34.

homō, -inis, m. and f. *a human being, a man,* 10, 31, etc.

honestē, adv. *with honor, respectably,* 19, 70.

honestus, -a, -um, adj. *honorable, respectable,* 11, 38; 14, 50; **honestissimus,** 18, 63.

honor, -ōris, m. *honor,* 20, 75; *office,* 17, 60.

honōrābilis, -e, adj. *honorable,* 18, 63.

honōrō, -āre, -āvī, -ātum, *to endue with honor, to bestow office upon,* 7, 22; 17, 61; **honōrātus honōrātior,** *honored,* 18, 63.

hōra, -ae, f. *an hour,* 19, 69.

hortus, -ī, m. *a garden,* 15, 54.

hospes, -itis, *a guest-friend,* 10, 32.

hospitium, -ī, n. *a place of entertainment, an inn,* 23, 84.

hostis, -is, m. *a public enemy,* 20, 75.

hūmānitās, -tātis, f. *culture, gentle breeding,* 1, 1.

hūmānus, -a, -um, adj. *human, of men,* 21, 77; *polite,* 17, 59.

humus, -ī, f. *the ground, soil,* 17, 59.

idcircō, adv. *therefore, on that account,* 10, 33.

idem, eadem, idem, ēiusdem, adj. *the same;* **idem quod,** 10, 32.

igitur, conj. *therefore,* 5, 13; 13, 43.

ignāvus, -a, -um, adj. *idle, spiritless,* 11, 36.

ignis, -is, m. [abl. īgnī, 16, 57], *fire,* 19, 71.

ignōminia, -ae, f. *disgrace,* 20, 75.

ignōscō, -ere, -nōvī, -nōtum *to pardon,* 16, 55.

ille, -a, -ud, illīus, demonstr. pron. *he, that one, the famous*

VOCABULARY.

one; **nōn illīus quidem,** 18, 65.

illūc, adv. *thither,* 22, 70.

imbēcillus, -a, -um, adj. *weak,* 11, 35; **imbēcillior,** 9, 30.

imber,-bris [abl.-brī], m. *rain,* 10, 34.

imitor, -ārī, -ātus, *to imitate,* 21, 77.

immissiō, -ōnis, f. *setting,* 15, 53.

immoderātus, -a, -um, adj. *immoderate, excessive,* 13, 44.

impediō, -īre, -īvī, -itum, *to hinder,* 12, 42.

impellō, -ere, -pulī, -pulsum, *to impel, to urge on,* 12, 40; 21, 77.

impendeō, -ēre, *to threaten, to hang over, to be near,* 19, 69; 20, 74.

imperātor, -ōris, m. *a military commander,* 20, 72.

imperium, -ī, n. *absolute power,* 11, 37 ; *authority,* 15, 51 ; 17, 59; **cum imperiō esse,** *to be in possession of imperium,* i.e. to be one of the curule magistrates who had *imperium* bestowed on them by a vote of the *comitia curiata,* 18, 64.

imperō, -āre, -āvī, -ātum, *to command,* 16, 55.

importūnitās, -tātis, f. *unreasonableness, insolence,* 3, 7.

in, prep. I. with acc. *into,* 7, 22, etc.; **in suōs,** *in regard to, over his family,* 11, 37 ;

in diēs, *day by day,* 13, 45; 14, 50 ; **in omnēs partēs,** *in every direction,* 15, 52. II. with abl. *in,* 2, 4, etc.; *in the case of,* 2, 5; 7, 22.

incertus, -a, -um, adj. *uncertain,* 19, 68; 20, 74.

incidō, -ere, -īdī, -īsum, *to cut, to engrave,* 17, 61.

incidō, -ere, -cidī, *to fall into,* 19, 67.

incitō, -āre, -āvī, -ātum, *to incite, to urge,* 12, 41; 20, 75.

inclīnō, -āre, -āvī, -ātum, *to incline,* 6, 16.

inclūdō, -ere, -ūsī, -ūsum, *to enclose, to shut in,* 15, 51; 21, 77.

incola, -ae, m. *an inhabitant, a fellow countryman,* 21, 78.

incōnstantia, -ae, f. *inconsistency,* 2, 4.

incrēdibiliter, adv. *in an incredible manner,* 15, 51.

incrēmentum, -ī, n. *increase, growth,* 15, 52.

incurrō,-ere,-cucurrī,-cursum, 3 v. n. *to run upon,* 8, 25.

indīcō, -ere, -īxī, -ictum, *to proclaim;* **bellum indīcere,** 14, 46.

indoctus, -a, -um, adj. *unlearned,* 20, 75.

indolēs, -is, f. *disposition, character, natural ability,* 8, 26. Found only once in plural. Gell. xix. 12, 5.

industria, -ae, f. *industry,* 7, 22.

meō, -īre, -īvī or -iī, -ītum, *to begin*, 15, 53; 20, 76.

iners, -rtis, adj. *idle, inactive*, 2, 5; 8, 26.

'nexercitātus, -a, -um, adj. *unpractised*, 18, 64.

īnfīrmitās, -tātis, f. *weakness*, 10, 33.

īnfīrmus, -a, -um, adj. -ior, -ius, 5, 15, *weak, in bad health*, 11, 35.

ingenium, -ī, n. *intellect, character*, 7, 22; 9, 28, etc.

ingravēscō, -ere, incept. *to grow heavy, to become burdensome*, 2, 6; 11, 36.

ingredior, -ī, -gressus, *to enter upon*, 2, 6; *to set about, to begin*, 14, 49; v. n. *to enter, to come forward*, 10, 33.

inhūmānitās, -tātis, f. *roughness, ill-temper, want of refinement*, 3, 7.

inhūmānus, -a, -um, adj. *unkind, unsocial, unrefined*, 3, 7.

inimīcitia, -ae, f. *enmity*, 14, 49.

inimīcus, -a, -um, adj. *unfriendly, hostile*, 12, 40, 42.

inīquus, -a, -um, adj. *disturbed, uneasy;* inīquissimus, 23, 83.

initium, -ī, n. *a beginning*, 17, 60.

iniūssū (only as the ablative case), *without the command of*, 20, 72.

inlacrimō, -āre, -āvī, -ātum, *to shed tears*, 9. 27.

inlecebra, -ae, f. *charm, enticement*, 12, 40.

inlūdō, -ere, -ūsī, -ūsum, *to deceive, to mock*, 18, 65.

inlustris, -e, adj. *illustrious*, 11, 38.

inmortālis, -e, adj. *immortal*, 7, 25; 23, 85.

innumerābiliter, adv. *innumerably*, 21, 78.

inopia, -ae, f. *poverty, want*, 3, 8.

inquam, -is, -it, defect. *I say*, 5, 13.

īnscrībō, -ere, -psī, -ptum, *to inscribe, to give a title to*, 5, 13; 17, 59.

īnsipiēns, -ntis, adj. *unwise*, 3, 8; 22, 80.

īnsipienter, adv. *unwisely*, 19, 68.

īnsitiō, -ōnis, f. *grafting*, 15, 54.

insolēns, -ntis, adj. *presumptuous*, 10, 31.

īnsomnium, -ī, n. *sleeplessness*, 13, 44.

īnstīllō, -āre, -āvī, -ātum, *to drop into*, 11, 36.

īnstituō, -ere, -uī, -ūtum, *to educate, to instruct*, 9, 29; 14, 50.

īnstitūtum, -ī, n. *a doctrine, an established custom*, 11, 34.

īnstruō, -ere, -ūxī, -ūctum, *to furnish, to make accomplished*, 9, 29.

integer, -gra, -grum, adj. *untouched, whole, sound*, 20, 72; 22, 80.

VOCABULARY.

intellego, -ere, -exi, -ectum, *to understand,* 8, 26; 11, 38; 12, 42.

intemperāns, -ntis, partic. adj. *intemperate,* 9, 29.

intentus, -a, -um [intendo], partic. adj. *at full stretch,* 11, 37.

interdīco, -ere, -īxī, -ctum, *to interpose, to prohibit from,* 7, 22.

interdum, adv. *sometimes.*

intereō, -īre, -īvī or -iī, -itum, *to perish,* 22, 81; 21, 78.

interficiō, -ere, -fēcī, -fectum, *to kill,* 20, 74.

interimō, -ere, -ēmī, -ēmptum, *to kill, to destroy,* 16, 56.

interitus, -ūs, m. *death,* 20, 75.

intersum, -esse, -fuī, *to be present, be a witness of,* 3, 7; 12, 41; *to intervene, to be between,* 6, 16; 17, 60.

intueor, -ērī, -tūtus, *to look at, to behold,* 14, 48; 17, 59.

intus, adv. *within, in private,* 4, 12.

inveniō, -īre, -vēnī, -ventum, *to discover, to invent,* 15, 54.

inventum, -ī, n. *a discovery, an invention,* 21, 78.

inveterāscō, -ere, -veterātus, incept. *to grow old, to become inveterate,* 20, 72.

inviolātē, adv. *inviolably,* 22, 81.

invītō, -āre, -āvī, -ātum, *to invite,* 16, 57.

invītus, -a, -um, adj., *unwilling, involuntary,* 12, 42.

ipse, -a, -um, ipsīus, pron. *self, himself, herself, itself,* 8, 26, etc.; **tū ipse**, 9, 27.

īrācundus, -a, -um, adj. *given to anger, ill-tempered,* 18, 65.

irrīdeō, -ēre, -rīsī, -rīsum, *to laugh at, to mock,* 23, 85.

irrigātio, -ōnis, f. *irrigation,* 15, 53.

is, ea, id, ēius, demonstr. pron. *that one, that, such,* 9, 27, etc.; **eō,** *on that account, so much,* 21, 74; **et eī,** *and they too,* 23, 84; 20, 74; **eaque,** *and that too,* 10, 33.

iste, -a, -ud, istīus, demonstr. pron. *that one by you, he whom you see, yours,* 7, 24, etc.

istīc, istaec, istūc [and -ōc], demonstr. pron. *that, what you mention,* 3, 8.

istinc, adv. *thence, from that, from what you mention,* 14, 47.

istūc, adv. *in your direction, to your point,* 2, 6.

ita, adv. *so,* 11, 35; *in such manner,* followed by *quasi,* 4, 12; 23, 83; followed by *ut,* 4, 10; 23, 84; *on such condition,* followed by *si,* 11, 38.

itaque, conj. *and so, therefore,* 19, 66, etc.

iter, itineris, n. *a journey, a march,* 20, 74.

iterum, adv. *a second time, again,* 4, 11, etc.

iam, adv. *now, even, already,* 4, 12, etc.; *nay more,* 16, 56;

iam diū, *this long time past,* 6, 18; introducing a new point or step in an argument, *now,* 20, 72; or **iam vērō,** 22, 80.

iūcundus, -a, -um, adj. *pleasant,* 8, 56; **iūcundior,** -ius, 14, 47; **iūcundissimus,** 3, 9.

iūdex, -icis, m. *a judge,* 7, 22.

iūdicium, -ī, n. *a legal decision, a legal inquiry.*

iūdicō, -āre, -āvī, -ātum, *to judge, to come to a conclusion,* 13, 43; v. a. *to adjudge, to decide upon,* 21, 78.

iugātiō, -ōnis, f. *a joining, a yoking together,* 15, 53.

iūre, adv. [abl. of **iūs**] *rightly,* 17, 61.

iūrgium, -ī, n. *a quarrel, a wrangle,* 3, 8.

iūs, iūris, n. *right, prerogative,* 11, 38; *law,* 9, 27; *a body of law,* **iūs augurium pontificium cīvīle,** *the augural, pontifical, civil code,* 11, 38; 14, 50, cf. 4, 12; **iūris cōnsultī,** *jurists,* 7, 22.

iūssus, -ūs, m. *a command,* 16, 56.

iūstus, -a, -um, adj. *just, right, complete,* 18, 65.

iuvenīliter, adv. *like a young man, insolently,* 4, 10.

iuventūs, -tūtis, f. *youth,* 6, 15; *a band of youths,* 9, 28.

labefactō, -āre, -āvī, -ātum, *to shake, to make to totter,* 6, 20.

labor, -ōris, m. *labor, trouble, sorrow,* 23, 84.

lāc, lactis, n. *milk,* 16, 56.

lacertus, -ī, m. *an arm,* 9, 27.

lacrima [or **lacruma,** 20, 73], -ae, f. *a tear.*

laetor, -ārī, -ātus, *to be rejoiced,* 14, 48.

laetus, -a, -um, adj. *glad, joyful;* **laetior,** -ius, 15, 53.

lāmentum, -ī, n. *a lamentation, a mourning,* 20, 73.

languēscō, -ere, incept. *to languish, to become feeble,* 9, 28; 11, 37.

languidus, -a, -um, adj. *languid, feeble,* 8, 26.

lāpsus, -ūs, m. *a gliding, a spreading,* 15, 52.

largior, -īrī, -ītus, *to bestow as a favor,* 23, 83.

latus, -eris, n. *a side;* in plur. *lungs,* 5, 14; 9, 28; *body,* 9, 27.

laudātiō, -ōnis, f. *a panegyric, a funeral oration,* 4, 12.

laudō, -āre, -āvī, -ātum, *to praise, to quote frequently,* 10, 32.

laus, laudis, f. *praise,* 13, 44; 17, 62.

laxō, -āre, -āvī, -ātum, *to loosen, to release,* 3, 7.

lectulus, -ī, m. *a couch,* 11, 38.

lēgātus, -ī, m. *a lieutenant, a legatus,* an officer in a province next in rank to the consul or proconsul, 6, 18; *an ambassador,* 13, 43; 18, 63.

VOCABULARY.

legiō, -ōnis, f. *a legion*, 24, 75.

legō, -ere, lēgī, lēctum, *to read*, 4, 12; 6, 20.

lēniō, -īre, -īvī or -iī, -ītum, *to soothe, to assuage*, 15, 54.

lēnis, -e, adj. *gentle, unruffled*, 15, 54.

levis, -e, adj. *light, easy to bear*, 3, 8; levior, 8, 26, *frivolous*, 11, 36; 18, 63; levior, *simpler*, 14, 50.

levō, -āre, -āvī, -ātum, *to lighten, to relieve of*, 1, 1; 11, 36.

lēx, lēgis, f. *a law*, 4, 10, etc.

libenter, libentius, adv. *with pleasure, readily*, 14, 47, 48; 23, 85.

līber, -era, -erum, adj. *free*, 22, 81.

liber, -brī, m. *a book*, 11, 38; 17, 59.

līberō, -āre, -āvī, -ātum, *to acquit*, 7, 22; *to set free*, 20, 75; 22, 80.

libet, libuit or libitum est, impers. *it pleases*, 12, 42.

libīdinōsus, -a, -um, adj. *licentious*, 9, 29.

libīdō, -inis, f. *lust, licentious desires*, 3, 7; 11, 36.

licet, licuit or licitum est, impers. *it is allowed, it is lawful*, 17, 60; licet mihi, *I may*, 1, 1.

litterae, -ārum, f. *literature, language*, 1, 3; 4, 12; 11, 38.

locuplēs, -ētis, adj. *rich, well supplied*, 16, 56.

locus, -ī, m. [in plur. -ī or -a,

23, 85] *a place*, 21, 77; *a subject, a topic*, 9, 27.

longē, adv. *afar, far off*, 19, 66; 16, 55.

longinquus, -a, -um, adj. *long continued*, 12, 41; 23, 84.

longus, -a, -um, adj. *long*, 2, 6; longior, *too long*, 16, 55.

loquāx, -ācis, adj. *garrulous*, 10, 31; loquācior, 16, 55.

loquor, -ī, locūtus, *to speak, to say*, 12, 41.

lubet, impers. *it pleases*, 16, 58; 23, 84.

lūdus, -ī, m. *a game*, 14, 50; *theatrical exhibition*, 18, 63, cf. 6, 20.

lūgeō, -ēre, -xī, -ctum, *to mourn for, to bewail*, 20, 74.

lūmen, -inis, n. *light*, 12, 41; *a lamp*, 11, 36; *ornament*, 11, 35.

lūna, -ae, f. *the moon*, 14, 49.

luō, -ere, -luī, *to atone for, to expiate*, 20, 75.

lūsiō, -ōnis, f. *playing, a game*, 16, 58.

lūx, lūcis, f. *daylight*, 14, 49; in lūce, *in public*, 4, 12.

magis, adv. *more, rather*, 11, 36, etc.

magister, -trī, m. *master, teacher*, 5, 13; 9, 29; magister equitum, *master of the horse*, a magistrate nominated by and next in rank to the dictator, 16, 56.

magisterium, -ī, n. *office of master of a feast*, 14, 46.

magistrātus, -ūs, m. *office*, 4, 10.

māgnitūdō, -inis, f. *greatness*, 11, 35.

māgnus, -a, -um, adj. *great*, 1, 1; *loud*, 5, 14; **māgnō opere**, *greatly*, 13, 44.

māior, -ōris, compar. adj. *greater, too great*, 1, 1; *elder*, 22, 79; **māiōrēs nātū**, *elders*, 3, 7; 12, 1; 13, 43; **māiōrēs**, -um, m. *ancestors*, 7, 25; 13, 45.

male, adv. *ill, badly*, 7, 22.

malleolus, -ī. m. *mallet-shoot, a hammer-shaped slip*, 15, 52.

mālō, māvis, māvult, mālle, -uī, *to prefer, to wish in preference*, 10, 32.

malum, -ī, *an evil*, 13, 44.

malus, -a, -um, adj. *evil, bad.*

mālus, -ī, m. *a mast*, 6, 17.

maneō, -ēre, -nsī, -nsum, *to remain*, 7, 22.

manus, -ūs, f. *a hand;* **in manibus esse, habēre**, 4, 12; 7, 22; 11, 38.

māter, -tris, f. *a mother*, 13, 45.

mātūrē, adv. *early, quickly*, 10, 32.

mātūritās, -tātis, f. *maturity, ripeness*, 2, 5; 10, 33; 19, 71.

mātūrō, -āre, -āvī, -ātum, *to make ripe, to bring to maturity*, 15, 53.

mātūrus, -a, -um, adj. *ripe, mature*, 19, 71; 20, 76.

māximē, superl. adv. *chiefly, especially*, 2, 4; 13, 45; **quam māximē**, *as much as possible*, 14, 46; **nunc cum māximē**, *at this very time*, 11, 38.

meditātiō, -ōnis, f. *preparation*, 20, 74.

meditor, -ārī, -ātus, *to prepare, to meditate on;* pass. part. **meditātus**, 20, 74.

medius, -a, -um, adj. *middle*, 20, 76.

medulla, -ae, f. *marrow*, 14, 50.

mel, mellis, n. *honey*, 10, 36; 16, 56.

melior, -ius, -ōris, compar. adj. *better*, 23, 84; **dī meliōra**, *heaven forbid!* 14, 47.

melius, compar. adv. *better, in a better way*, 13, 45; 19, 67; 20, 73.

meminī, -isse [no pres. or imperf.], defect. v. a. *to remember*, 9, 30, etc.; **mementōte**, 18, 62.

memoria, -ae, f. *memory*, 4, 12; 7, 21; 19, 71.

mēns, -ntis, f. *mind, intellect*, 6, 16; 11, 36, 38; 12, 40, 42.

mēnsa, -ae, f. *a table*, 13, 44.

mēnsis, -is, m. *a month*, 19, 69.

mentiō, -ōnis, f. *mention*, 5, 14; 18, 63.

mētior, -īrī, mēnsus, *to measure*, 13, 45.

metuō, -ere, -uī, *to fear*, 11, 37.

mīles, -itis, m. *a common soldier*, 4, 10; 6, 8; 10, 32.

mīlitia, -ae, f. *military service;* **mīlitiae**, *on service, abroad*, opposed to *domi*, 23, 82.

minimus, -a, -um, superl. adj. *least*, 13, 45.

minor, -us, -ōris, compar. adj *less*, 15, 51; *younger*, 17, 59.

minuō, -ere, -uī, -ūtus, to
diminish, 7, 21.
minus, compar. adv. less, 2, 4;
8, 26; 10, 32; n. subst. 10, 33.
minūtus, -a, -um, adj. small,
14, 46; insignificant, 23, 85;
minūtissimus, 15, 52.
mīrificus, -a, -um, adj. aston-
ishing, wonderful, 3, 9.
miror, -ārī, -ātus, to wonder
at, to express admiration of,
13, 43.
miser, -era, -erum, adj. miserable, 5, 13; miserrimus,
8, 25.
miserābilis, -e, adj. to be pitied,
miserable, 16, 56.
mītis, -e, mītior, adj. gentle,
quiet, 9, 28; 13, 45.
moderātiō, -ōnis, f. reasonable-
ness, moderation, 1, 1; a
moderate use, an economy,
10, 33.
moderātus, -a -um, adj. moderate, reasonable, 3, 7.
modicē, adv. temperately, with
moderation, 1, 2; 13, 45.
modicus, -a, -um, adj. moderate, within reasonable limits,
11, 36; 13, 44.
modo, adv. lately, 9, 27; only,
nōn modo . . . sed etiam,
7, 21, 22; 11, 37; 15, 51; 19, 70;
nōn modo . . . verum etiam,
8, 26; 16, 57.
modus, -ī, m. manner, method,
3, 8; 21, 77; a limit, 14, 46;
23, 84.
molestē, adv. with offence,
with dislike, 3, 7.

molestia, -ae, f. trouble, annoyance, 1. 2.
molestus, -a, -um, adj. trouble-
some, offensive, 2, 6; 14, 47;
23, 85.
mōlior, -īrī, -ītus, to attempt,
8, 26.
molliō, -īre, -īvī or -iī, -ītum,
to soften, 15, 51; to subdue
by degrees, to wear out, 4,
10.
mollis, -e, adj. soft, easy, 1, 2.
molliter, adv. gently, easily,
2, 5.
moneō, -ēre, -uī, -itum, to
warn, to advise, 10, 32.
monumentum, -ī, n. a record,
a memorial, 11, 38.
mōrātus, -a, -um, adj. endowed
with morals, 18, 63.
morbus, -ī, m. a disease, 11, 35;
19, 67.
morior, -ī, mortuus, to die,
5, 13, etc.
mōrōsitās, -tātis, f. ill-temper,
18, 65.
mōrōsus, -a, -um, adj. ill-tem-
.pered, 18, 65.
mors, -rtis, f. death, 5, 15, etc.
morsus, -ūs, m. bite, pecking,
15, 51.
mortālis, -e, adj. mortal, subject to death, 22, 80; 21, 78.
mortuus, -a, -um, adj. dead,
7, 21; 9, 27.
mōs, mōris, m. manner, custom, 7, 22; 14, 46; 23, 82;
mōrēs, character, habits,
3, 7: 18, 65.
mōtus, -ūs, m. motion, 21, 78.

P

moveō, -ēre, mōvī, mōtum, *to move*, 21, 78.

multiplex, -plicis, adj. *manifold*, 15, 52; *often repeated*, 18, 64.

multitūdō, -inis, f. *a great quantity*, 19, 71.

multō, adv. *by much*, 11, 36; 15, 53.

multum, adv. *much*, 11, 38, etc.

multus, -a, -um, adj. *much*, 14, 44, etc.; **ad multam noctem**, *till late at night*, 14, 46.

mūniō, -īre, -īvī or -iī, -ītum, 4 v. a. *to fortify, to entrench*, 15, 51.

munus, -eris, n. *a gift*, 1, 2; 12, 39; **lēx dē mūneribus**, 4, 10; *a duty*, 9, 27, 29; 10, 34; 21, 77.

mūtō, -āre, -āvī, -ātum, *to change*, 4, 10.

nam or **namque**, conj. *for*.

nancīscor, -ī, nactus, *to obtain, to catch hold of*, 15, 52.

nāscor, -ī, nātus, *to be born*, 23, 84.

natātiō, -ōnis, f. *swimming*, 16, 58.

nātūra, -ae, f. *nature*, 15, 52, etc.

nātūrālis, -e, adj. *of nature, arising from nature, natural*, 10, 33; 14, 46.

nātus, -ūs, m. *birth*, 3, 7, etc.

nāvālis, -e, adj. *of ships, naval*, 5, 13.

nāvigātiō, -ōnis, f. *a voyage, a sailing*, 19, 71.

nāvigō, -āre, -āvī, -ātum, *to sail, to manage a ship*, 6, 17.

nē, adv. *not*, in final clauses; **ne . . . quidem**, *not even*, 3, 8, 9, etc.; *neither*, 10, 33; 11, 34; 14, 47; *with imperative or subjunctive, do not*, prohibitive; conj. *lest, that not*, 9, 27, etc.

ne, interrog. enclitic, 10, 31, etc.

nē, *truly, verily*, 10, 33.

necesse, neut. adj. *necessary*, 2, 5.

necessitās, -tātis, f. *necessity, natural law*, 2, 4; 21, 77.

nefās, n. indeclin. *wrong, impiety*, 5, 13.

neglegō, -ere, -ēxī, -ēctum, *to neglect, to disregard*, 20, 74; *to do carelessly*, 2, 5.

negō, -āre, -āvī, -ātum, *to deny*, 6, 17; 9, 30.

nēmō, -inis, m. *no one*, 11, 38; 23, 85.

nēquāquam, adv. *by no means*, 3, 8.

neque, **nec**, conj. *nor, and not*, 12, 41, etc.

nequeō, -is, -it, -īre, -īvī, *to be unable*, 9, 28.

nesciō, -īre, -īvī or -iī, -ītum, *to be ignorant of, not to know*; **nesciō quō modō** or **pāctō**, *somehow or another*, 9, 28.

neutiquam, adv. *in no case, by no means*, 12, 42.

nī, conditional neg. = *nisi, unless*, 23, 82.

nihil [or **nīl**, 8, 25], n. indeclin. *nothing*, 22, 80, etc.

nimis, adv. *too, too much*, 10, 31.

nimius, -a, -um, adj. *excessive, too much*, 15, 52, 53, etc.

nisi, conditional neg. *unless*, 23, 82, etc.; **nisi forte**, 6, 18, see **forte**.

nitor, -ōris, m. *brilliance*, 17, 59.

nītor, -i, nīsus or nīxus, *to attempt, strive for*, 10, 33; 23, 82; *to rest on*, 15, 51.

nōbilis, -e, adj. *noble, famous*, 3. 8: 9, 29.

nōbilitās, -tātis, f. *fame, great reputation*, 21, 77.

nōbilitō, -āre, -āvī, -ātum, *to make famous*, 9, 27.

noctū, adv. *by night*, 14, 49.

nocturnus, -a, -um, adj. *nocturnal, of the night*, 23, 80.

nōlō, nōnvis, nōnvult, nōlle, nōluī, *not to wish, to be unwilling*, 8, 35.

nōmen, -inis, n. *name*, 7, 21.

nōminō, -āre, -āvī, -ātum, *to name, to call*, 6, 20; 13, 55; 15, 51; 16, 56.

nōn, neg. adv. *not*.

nōnāgintā, indeclin. num. adj. *ninety*, 10, 34.

nōnne, interrog. particle expecting affirmative answer, *is it not?*

nōscō, -ere, nōvī, nōtum, *to know*, 8, 26; 17, 61. [**nōrat** = noverat, 13, 43.]

noster, -tra, -trum, poss. pron. *our*, 7, 22; 23, 82.

nostrūm, gen. plur. of **ego**, 1, 2.

nōtitia, -ae, f. *knowledge*, 4, 2.

notō, -āre, -āvī, -ātum, *to mark, to brand* (of the censor's stigma), 12, 42.

novem, indeclin. num. adj. *nine*, 6, 19.

novus, -a, -um, adj. *new*, 6, 20.

nox, -ctis, f. *night*, 14, 48; **multa nox**, *late*, 14, 46.

nūgātor, -ōris, m. *a trifler*, 9, 27.

nūllus, -a, -um [gen. -īus], adj. *none, no*, 2, 4, etc.; *non-existent*, almost = *non*, 19, 67; 22, 79; *not to be counted, worthless*, 3, 7; subst. *no one*.

num, interrog. particle expecting negative answer, *is it? it is'nt, is it?* 6, 19, etc.

numquam, adv. *never*, 1, 2, etc.

nunc, adv. *now, at the present time*, 1, 1, etc.

nūntiō, -āre, -āvī, -ātum, *to announce*, 16, 56.

nūper, adv. *lately*, 17, 61.

nusquam, adv. *nowhere*, 10, 31; 18, 63.

nūtus, -ūs, m. *a nod*, 17, 61.

ō, interject. *oh!* with voc. 1, 1; with nom. 19, 69; with accus. 19, 66: 23, 84.

oblectāmentum, -ī, n. *source of pleasure, delight*, 15, 52; 16, 55.

oblectō, -āre, -āvī, -ātum, *to please, to delight*, 11, 38; 16, 56.

426

CATŌ MĀIOR.

oblīviōsus, -a, -um, adj. *for-getful*, 11, 36.
oblīviscor, -ī, oblītus, *to forget*, 7, 21.
obmūtēscō, -ere, -tuī, incept. *to become dumb*, 7, 23.
brēpō, -ere, -psī, -ptum, *to creep up*, 2, 4; 11, 38.
obruō, -ere, -uī, -utum, *to hide, to cover up*, 7, 21.
observō, -āre, -āvī, -ātum, *to observe, to keep up*, 18, 63.
obstruō, -ere, -ūxī, -ūctum, *to block up*, 20, 75.
obtūsus, -a, -um [obtundo], obtūsior, adj. *blunted, dim*, 23, 83.
occaecō, -āre, -āvī, -ātum, *to hide up, to conceal* [ob-caeco]. 51, 51.
occātiō, -ōnis, f. [occo. root ac-, as in acuō], *harrowing*, 15, 51.
occidō, -ere, -idī, -cāsum, *to fall, to perish*, 20, 76.
occupō, -āre, -āvī, -ātum, *to seize* (with the idea of 'surprise'), 16, 56; *to forestall, to engage*, 10, 32.
occurrō, -ere, -currī, -cursum, *to occur, to come into the mind*, 1, 2.
octingentēsimus, -a, -um, ordinal num. adj. *eight hundredth*, 2, 4.
octōgēsimus, -a, -um, ordinal num. adj. *eightieth*, 2, 4; 5, 13; 10, 32.
octōgintā, indeclin. num. adj. *eighty*, 19, 69.

oculus, -ī, m. *an eye*, 4, 12.
odiōsus, -a, -um, adj. *hateful*, 2, 4; 8, 25; 18, 65.
odor, -ōris, m. *scent, smell*, 17, 59.
offēnsiō, -ōnis, f. *offence* received, *vexation*, 18, 65.
officium, -ī, n. *a duty*, 9, 29; 10, 34; *employment*, 16, 56.
oleārius, -a, -um, adj. *of olives*, or, *of olive oil*, 16, 56.
oleum, -ī, n. *oil*, 11, 36.
olīvētum, -ī, n. *an olive grove*, 16, 57.
Olympius, -a, -um, adj. *of Olympia;* Olympia, 'the Olympic games,' 5, 14.
omittō, -ere, -īsī, -issum, *to omit, to pass over*, 7, 24.
omnīnō, adv. *altogether*, 14, 46; 14, 48; 19, 66; *at all*, 7, 24; 10, 34; *however*, 9, 28; 3, 9; *certainly, on the whole*, 13, 45.
omnis, -e, adj. *all, every*, 1, 2, etc.
onus, -eris, n. *a burden*, 2, 4; 5, 14.
opera, -ae, f. *pains, labor*, 4, 11.
operiō, -īre, -ruī, -rtum, *to cover;* opertus, *covered*, i.e. *wearing a hat*, 10, 44.
operōsus, -a, -um, adj. *active, busy*, 8, 26.
opīnio, -ōnis, f. *opinion*, 2, 5.
oportet, -ēre, -uit, impers. *it behoves, it is right*, 12, 42.
oppidum, -ī, n. *a town*, 4, 11.
opprimō, -ere, -essī, -essum, *to*

crush, to overpower, 11, 36; to smother, 19, 71; to surprise, 14, 49.

[ops], opis, f. help, 2, 4; opēs, -um, resources, 3, 8.

optābilis, -e, adj. to be wished, desirable, 13, 85.

optimē, adv. best, in the best way, 20, 72.

optimus, -a, -um, superl. adj. best, 4, 11.

optō, -āre, -āvī, -ātum, to wish, 13, 43; 18, 66; 20, 74.

opus, -eris, n. a work, a deed, employment, 5, 13; 9, 29; need, 1, 3; 20, 74.

ōrāculum, -ī, n. an oracle, the answer of an oracle, 21, 78.

ōrātiō, -ōnis, f. a speech, an oration, 6, 16; a discourse in proof of something, a pleading, 1, 3; 18, 62.

ōrātor, -ōris, m. a speaker, an orator, 6, 20.

orbō, -āre, -āvī, -ātum. to deprive, to bereave, 6, 17.

ōrdō, -inis, m. a row, 15, 53; 16, 57; 17, 59.

orīgō, -inis, f. origin; Orīginēs, the title of a book of Cato's, 11, 38.

orior, -īrī, ortus, to rise, 15, 53.

ōrnātior, -iōris, -ius, comp. adj. [from partic. of ōrnō], more adorned, 16, 67.

ōrnātus, -ūs, m. adornment, 17, 59.

ortus, -ūs, m. a growing, sprouting, 15, 52.

ostendō, -ere, -ndī, -nsum, to

show, to point out, 15, 53; 19, 70.

ōtiōsus, -a, -um, adj. at leisure, 14, 49; 23, 82.

pābulum, -ī, n. food, provender, 14, 49.

pāctum, -ī, n. [pacīscor] a way, a method, 9, 28.

paene, adv. almost, 5, 14; 21, 77.

paenitet, -ēre, -uit, impers. it repents one, 6, 19; 23, 84.

palma, -ae, f. a palm, a crown of victory, 6, 19.

pampinus, -ī, m. and f. a tendril, 15, 53.

pār, paris, adj. like, equal, 3, 7.

pāreō, -ēre, -uī, -itum, to obey, 1, 2; 2, 5.

pariō, -ere, peperī, partum, to beget, to produce, to obtain, 19, 21.

pariter, adv. equally, contemporaneously, 14, 50.

pars, partis, f. part, portion, side, 15, 52; partēs, a part in a play, 2, 5.

parum, adv. not sufficiently; subst. indeclin. n. not enough, 1, 3.

parvulus, -a, -um, adj. [dimin. of parvus] small, mean, insignificant, 14, 48.

parvus, -a, -um, adj. small.

pāstus, -ūs, m. pasturing feeding, 15, 54.

pater, -tris, m. a father, 12, 41, etc.

paternus, -a, -um, adj. of a father, paternal, 11, 35.

patientia, -ae, f. *endurance, persistence*, 4, 10.

patria, -ae, f. *a fatherland, country*, 12, 40.

patrius, -a, -um, adj. *ancestral*, 11, 37.

patruus, -ī, m. *a father's brother, an uncle*, 11, 37; 23, 83.

paucus, -a, -um, adj. *few*, 19, 59.

paululum, adv. *a little*, 10, 33.

paupertās, -tātis, f. *poverty*, 5, 15.

pāx, pācis, f. *peace*, 6, 16.

pectus, -toris, n. *a breast*, 1, 1.

pecus, -udis, f. *a sheep*, 15, 54.

pedester, -tris, -tre, adj. *on foot, on land*, 5, 13, where it is equal to *terrestris*.

penārius, -a, -um, adj. *belonging to provisions;* **cella p.** *store cupboard*, 16, 56.

per, prep. [acc.] *through, by means of.*

peracerbus, -a, -um, adj. *very bitter*, 15, 53.

perāctiō, -ōnis, f. *a complete performance*, 23, 85.

peragō, -ere, -ēgī, -āctum, *to perform, to act throughout*, 18, 64; 19, 70.

percipiō, -ere, -cēpī, -ceptum, *to conceive in the mind*, 12, 41; *to learn*, 7, 21; *to gather, to harvest*, 7, 24; 19, 70.

percontor, -ārī, -ātus, *to ask, to put questions*, 6, 20.

perditus, -a, -um, adj. *abandoned, wicked*, 12, 42.

perdō, -ere, -didī, -ditum, *to lose*, 7, 21.

perdūcō, -ere, -ūxī, -uctum, *to keep up, to continue*, 17, 60.

pereō, -īre, -īvī or -iī, -itum, *to perish*, 10, 31.

perfectus, -a, -um, adj. *perfect, consummate*, 2, 4.

permaneō, -ēre, -nsi, -nsum, *to be permanent, to remain*, 7, 22; 12, 41; 22, 80.

permulceō, -ēre, -mulsī, -mulsum, *to soothe, to console,* 2, 4.

persaepe, adv. *very often*, 9, 28

persequor, -ī, -secūtus, *to go through, to retail*, 6, 16; *to follow up, to put a finishing stroke to*, 6, 19; *to give a list of, to go through*, 16, 55.

perspicuus, -a, -um, adj. *clear*, 22, 80.

perstudiōsus, -a, -um, adj. *very eager for, very fond of*, 1, 3.

persuādeō, -ēre, -suāsī, -suāsum, *to persuade, to convince*, 13, 43; 21, 78; 22, 80.

pertineō, -ēre, -uī, *to belong, to pertain*, 7, 24; 16, 56; 23, 82.

perūtilis, -e, adj. *very useful*, 17, 52.

perveniō, -īre, -vēnī, ventum, *to arrive*, 2, 6; 23, 86.

perversitās, -tātis, f. *perversity, wrong-headedness*, 2, 4.

pēs, pedis, m. *a foot*, 10, 34.

pestifer, -era, -erum, adj. *pestilent, destructive*, 12, 41.

pestis,-is, f. *a pest, destruction,* 12, 39.

petō, -ere, -īvī or iī, -ītum, *to seek,* 13, 43.

petulantia, -ae, f. *wantonness,* 11, 36.

philosophia, -ae, f. *philosophy,* 1, 2.

philosophus, -ī, m. *a philosopher,* 4, 12; 7, 22; 23, 85.

piē, adv. *piously,* 22, 81.

pietās, -tātis, f. *piety,* 23, 84.

pila, -ae, f. *a ball,* 16, 58.

piscis, -is, m. *a fish,* 13, 44.

placeō, -ēre, -cuī, -citum, *to please,* 19, 70; impers. **placet,** *it pleases;* **sī placet,** *if you please,* 23, 82.

placidus, -a, -um, adj. *pleasing, peaceful,* 5, 13.

plānē, adv. *plainly, quite,* 4, 10; 22, 81.

planta, -ae, f. *a cutting, a slip,* 15, 52.

plaudō, -ere, -ausī, -ausum, *to clap the hands, to applaud,* 19, 70.

plausus, -ūs, m. *a clapping of the hands, applause,* 18, 64.

plēbs, plēbis, f. *people, the Plebs,* 4, 11.

plēnus, -a, -um, adj. *full,* 1, 1.

plērīque, -aeque, -aque, adj. *very many, most,* 2, 4; 21, 78.

plērumque, adv. *more often than not, generally,* 15, 51.

plūrimus, -a, -um, superl. adj. *the greatest number, most,* 17, 61.

plūs, -ūris [comp. of **multus**],

adj. **plūris,** *of more value,* 17, 61; 19, 66; subst. n. *more, a greater amount,* 17, 60; in plur. **plūrēs, plūra,** subst. and adj. *more,* 1, 3; adv. *any more,* 9, 27.

pōculum, -ī, n. *a cup,* 13, 44.

poēta, -ae, m. *a poet,* 2, 5.

polliceor, -ērī, -icitus, *to make a promise,* 2, 6.

pōmārium, -ī, n. *an apple orchard,* 15, 54.

pōmum, -ī, *an apple,* 19, 71.

pondus, -eris, n. *weight,* 16, 55.

pōnō, -ere, -osuī, -ositum, *to place, to reckon,* 4, 10.

pontifex, -ficis, m. *a priest, one of the college of pontifices,* 7, 22; **Pontifex Māximus,** *the head of the college,* 17, 61.

pontificius, -a, -um, adj. *belonging to or concerning the Pontifices,* 11, 38.

populus, -ī, m. *a people,* 12, 41; 17, 61.

porrō, adv. *in succession, in their turn,* 13, 43.

portus, -ūs, m. *a port, a harbor,* 19, 71.

post, prep. [acc.] *after,* 16, 16; adv. *after, later;* followed by *quam,* 4, 10.

posteā, adv. *afterwards,* 5, 13; 17, 61.

posteritās, -tātis, f. *posterity,* 23, 82.

posterus, -a, -um, adj. *posterior, coming after;* **posterī,** *posterity,* 7, 25.

pōstulō, -āre, -āvī, -ātum, *to demand, to expect*, 11, 34.

pōtiō, -ōnis, f. *a drinking*, 11, 36; 14, 46.

potior, -īrī, -ītus, *to become possessed of, to get possession*, 12, 39; 14, 48.

potius [pote], adv. *rather*, 11, 35; 23, 84.

praeceptum, -ī, n. *a precept, a rule*, 4, 12; 8, 26.

praecīdō, -ere, -cīdī, -cīsum, *to cut short*, 16, 57.

praecipiō, -ere, -cēpī, -ceptum, *to enjoin, to instruct*, 9, 28.

praeclārē, adv. *admirably, splendidly*, 4, 10.

praeclārus, -a, -um, adj. *admirable, splendid*, 4, 12; 5, 14; 16, 55; **praeclārior**, -ius, 9, 29.

praedicō, -āre, -āvī, -ātum, *to speak openly, to harangue*, 10, 31.

praedīcō, -ere, -īxī, -ictum, *to predict, to foretell*, 14, 49.

praeditus [do], -a, -um, adj. *endowed with, possessed of*, 8, 26; 17, 61.

praemium, -ī, n. *reward*, 1, 1; 18, 64.

praescrībō, -ere, -psī, -ptum, *to lay down a rule, to prescribe*, 6, 13; *to write out for public use*, 9, 27.

praesertim, adv. *especially*, 2, 6; 17, 61; 23, 85.

praesidium, -ī, n. *intrenchment, post*, 20, 72.

praestābilis, -e, adj. *choice-worthy, excellent;* **praestābilior**, -ius, 12, 40.

praestāns, -ntis, adj. *excellent, eminent*, 17, 59; **praestantior**, -ius, 4, 11; 10, 23; 23, 84.

praestringō, -ere, -nxi, -ictum, *to blind*, 12, 42.

praesum, -esse, -fuī, *to be at the head of*, 9, 30.

praetereā, adv. *besides*, 18, 65; 21, 78.

praetereō, -īre, -īvī or iī, -itum, irreg. v. *to pass*, 19, 69.

praeteritus, -a, -um [praetereō], adj. *past*, 2, 4; 19, 69, 70.

prātum, -ī, n. *a meadow*, 15, 54; 16, 56.

prīmārius, -a, -um, adj. *of the first rank*, 17, 61.

prīmō, adv. *at first*, 15, 53.

prīmum, adv. *in the first place*, 2, 4; 13, 45; *for the first time*, 4, 10.

prīmus, -a, -um, ordinal num. adj. *first;* **in prīmīs**, *among the first, especially*, 2, 4; 6, 20; 12, 39; 17, 60; 18, 64.

prīncipātus, -ūs, m. *the lead, the right of being first*, 18, 64.

prīncipium, -ī, n. *the beginning*, 21, 78.

prīstinus, -a, -um, adj. *early, pristine*, 10, 34.

prīvātus, -a, -um, adj. *private*, 7, 22; 12, 42; 13, 44.

prīvō, -āre, -āvī, -ātum, *to deprive*, 5, 15.

VOCABULARY.

prō, prep. [abl.] *for, in behalf of,* 2, 6; 4, 11; *in proportion to,* 9, 27.

probē, adv. *well,* 5, 14.

probō, -āre, -āvī, -ātum, *to approve,* 11, 38; 18, 65; 19, 70; *to prove,* 23, 85.

probrum, -ī, n. *disgrace,* 12, 42.

probus, -a, -um, adj. *good, moral,* 11, 36.

prōcēdō, -ere, -cēssī, -cēssum, *to proceed, to advance,* 7, 21; 14, 50; 19, 70.

prōcēritās, -tātis, f. *tallness, height,* 17, 59.

prōcreō, -āre, -āvī, -ātum, *to produce,* 15, 52.

procul, adv. *far, far off,* 5, 15.

prōditiō, -ōnis, f. *a handing over, treason,* 12, 40.

prōdō, -ere, -didī, -ditum, *to hand down,* 7, 25; 18, 63.

prōdūcō, -ere, -ūxī, -uctum, *to prolong,* 14, 46.

proelium, -ī, n. *a battle,* 12, 41.

profectō, adv. *certainly, assuredly,* 13, 43; 23, 83; *at once, thereupon,* 5, 13.

prōferō, -ferre, -tulī, -lātum, *to bring forth, to make known.*

proficīscor, -ī, -fectus, *to set out,* 20, 75; 23, 83.

profiteor, -ērī, -fessus, *to profess,* 13, 43.

profugiō, -ere, -fūgī, -fugitum, *to run away, to escape,* 14, 47.

prōgredior, -ī, -gressus, *to advance,* 13, 45.

propāgātiō, -ōnis, f. *propagation,* 15, 53.

propāgō, -inis, f. *a layer,* 15, 52.

prope, adv. *near, nearly;* **propius,** 19, 71; 21, 77; **proximē,** 15, 51.

proprius, -a -um, adj. *proper, peculiar,* 11, 35.

propter, prep. [acc.] *on account of,* 14, 46; adv. *near at hand, close,* 14, 48.

prōspiciō, -ere, -exī, -ectum, *to look forward to,* 23, 82; v. n. *to take thought for, to be anxious beforehand,* 8, 25.

prōsum, prōdesse, prōfuī, *to be of advantage,* 7, 24.

prōvehō, -ere, -exī, -ectus, *to carry forward, to prolong, to advance,* 4, 10; 9, 27; 16, 55.

prōveniō, -īre, -vēnī, -ventum, *to come forward,* 6, 20.

prōverbium, -ī, n. *a proverb,* 3, 7; 10, 32.

proximē, superl. adv. *next, nearest,* 15, 51; *last, most recently,* 7, 22.

proximus, -a, -um, superl. adj. [see **prope**] *nearest,* 12, 42.

prūdēns, -ntis, **prūdentior,** -ius, adj. *prudent,* 14, 50: 19, 67.

prūdentia, -ae, f. *good sense,* 1, 1; 6, 20; *practical* or *legal knowledge,* 9, 27; *foreknowledge,* 21, 78.

pūbēscō, -ere, pūbuī, incept. *to be coming to full growth,* 15, 5.

puer, -erī, m. *a boy, a child,* 10, 33.

pueritia, -ae, f. *boyhood, childhood,* 2, 4, etc.

pūgna, -ae, f. *a battle,* 5, 13.

pūgnō. -āre, -āvī, -ātum, *to fight,* 11, 35.

pulcher, -chra, -chrum; **pulchrior**, -ius, adj. *beautiful,* 15, 53.

pulchritūdō, -inis, f. *beauty,* 22, 81.

puppis, -is, f. *the stern of a vessel,* 6, 17.

pūrē, adv. *with purity,* 5, 13.

purpura, -ae, f. *a purple garment,* 17, 59.

pūrus, -a, -um, adj. *clean, pure,* 17, 59; 22, 80.

putō, -āre, -āvī, -ātum, *to think, to believe,* 7, 24.

quādrāgintā, indeclin. num. adj. *forty,* 17, 60.

quādrennium, -ī, n. *a space of four years,* 4, 10; 9, 30.

quaerō, -ere, quaesīvī, quaesītum, *to seek, to inquire,* 7, 22, 25; 20, 76.

quaesō, *to pray, to beg,* 17, 59.

quaestor, -ōris, m. *a quaestor, a financial officer either at Rome or serving under the commander of an army or of a province,* 10, 32; 13, 55.

quālis, -e, adj. correlative of **tālis**, *such as,* 8, 26; without *talis,* 5, 13; as a relative, *of what kind,* 2, 6.

quam, adv. *how,* 5, 15; after comparatives, *than,* 9, 27, etc.; with superlatives, *as much as possible,* 14, 46, etc.

quamquam, conj. *and yet,* 1, 1; *although, though as a fact,* 9, 30; 13, 44; 14, 47.

quamvīs, conj. and adv. *although, however much,* 2, 4; 7, 25.

quandō, adv. and conj. *when, at what time,* 11, 38.

quantus, -a, -um, adj. *how great,* 5, 15; correlative of **tantus**, *as great as,* 12, 41; 17, 60; *how great!* 4, 12; **quantī**, *of what value!* 14, 49.

quārtum, adv. *for the fourth time,* 4, 10.

quārtus, -a, -um, ordinal num. adj. *fourth,* 5, 13.

quasi, conj. *as if, as it were.*

que, enclit. conj. *and,* see **et**: *and so, accordingly,* cf. 9. 28; 14, 46; **isque**, *and that too,* 10, 33.

querēlla, -ae, f. *a complaint,* 3, 7.

quī, **quae**, **quod**, gen. cūius, I. relat. pron. *who, which.* II. interrog. adj. *which? what?* or in indirect questions, *who, which, what.* **quod āiunt**, *as the saying is,* 7, 21.

quī, adv. [old abl. of **quī**] *how? in what way?* 2, 4; 20, 74.

quia, conj. *because,* 21, 78, etc

quīcumque, **quaecumque**, **quodcumque**, indef. pron *whosoever, whatsoever.*

quidam, quaedam, quoddam, pron. *a certain one.*

quidem, adv. *indeed,* 2, 3; 15, 51, etc.: **ne ... quidem,** see **ne.**

quiēscō, -ere, -ēvī, -ētum, incept. *to grow quiet, to rest,* 4, 11; 5, 14.

quiētē, adv. *quietly,* 5, 13.

quiētus, -a, -um, adj. *quiet,* 6, 7; 7, 22; 9, 28; 23, 82.

quin, conj. [quī non] *but that, lest, by which the less,* after words of doubt as *dubito* and *dubium,* 10, 31; 12, 41; 21, 78; **quin etiam,** *nay more,* 18, 63; 19, 67.

quincunx, -ncis, m. (lit. *five twelfths of an as*) *trees planted in groups of five,* 17, 59.

quīnque, indeclin. num. adj. *five,* 5, 13; 11, 37.

quinquennium, -ī, n. *a space of five years,* 5, 13.

quintus, -a, -um, ordinal num. adj. *fifth,* 4, 10.

quis, quae and **qua, quid,** interrog. pron. *who? what? what sort of?* 4, 11; in conditional sentences, *any one,* as **sī quis,** 1, 1; 23, 83; **sīve quis,** 12, 40; **quod sī quem,** 14, 46; **haud quis,** 23, 83; with suffix *quam,* **quisquam,** in neg. and interrog. sentences, *any one,* 8, 25.

quispiam, quaepiam, quodpiam (quidpiam, subst.), *some one,* 3, 8.

quisque, quaeque, quodque and **quidque,** indef. pron. *each,* especially with superlative adjectives, 13, 43; 23, 82.

quisquis, quodquod (quidquid, subst.), *whosoever, whatsoever,* 15, 52.

quīvīs, quaevīs, quidvīs, indef. pron. *any one you please, any one,* 15, 52.

quō, adv. *whither? to which place,* 6, 16; 23, 85; *whereby,* 1, 3; **quō magis,** *whereby the more,* 12, 41; **quō diūtius,** *whereby the longer,* 22, 80; *in proportion as,* 19, 71; **eō ... quō,** 21, 77.

quoad, adv. *as far as, as long as,* 4, 11; 20, 72.

quōcircā, adv. *wherefore, on which account,* 2, 5; 12, 41.

quod, conj. *because, in that,* 3, 7; **quod sī,** *but if,* 14, 46.

quōminus, conj. *that not,* 17, 60.

quō modō, adv. *in which way, how,* 4, 11; 6, 18.

quondam, adv. *formerly,* 18, 62.

quoniam, adv. *since,* 2, 5; 13, 44; 17, 59.

quoque, adv. *also,* 14, 46.

quōrsus [quo-versus], *to what end?* 5, 13; 12, 42; 13, 44.

quotiēns, adv. *how often,* 14, 49.

rāmus, -ī, m. *a bough,* 15, 32.

ratiō, -ōnis, f. *reason, the faculty of reason,* 12, 41, 42; *a*

method, **2**, 6: **habēre ratiōnem**, *to have an account,*
11, 36, cf. 15, 51.

recēdō, -ere, -cēssī, -cēssum, *to
retire, to leave,* 16, 56.

recēns, -ntis, adj. *new, fresh,*
20, 72.

recipiō, -ere, -cēpī, -ceptum, *to
take again, to recover,* 4, 10;
to receive, 18, 63.

recitō, -āre, -āvī, -ātum, *to read
or recite aloud,* 7, 22.

recoquō, -ere, -xī, -ctum, *to
boil up again,* 23, 83.

recordātiō, -ōnis, f. *recollec-
tion, a recalling to mind,* 3, 9.

recordor, -ārī, -ātus, *to recall
to mind,* 5, 13; 20, 74; 21, 78.

rēctē, adv. *rightly,* 17, 59; 20,
72.

rēctus, -a, -um, adj. *upright,
right,* 6, 10; 18, 64.

recūsō, -āre, -āvī, -ātum, *to re-
fuse,* 23, 83.

reddō, -ere, -didī, -ditum, *to
give back,* 15, 51.

redeō, -īre, -īvī or -iī, -itum, *to
go back, to return,* 19, 67; **in
grātiam redīre**, *to be reconciled,* 16, 56.

redūcō, -ere, -ūxī, -ctum, *to
lead back, to bring back,* 18,
63.

referciō, -īre, -ersī, -ertum, *to
stuff, to fill full,* 16, 56.

referō, -ferre, rettulī, relātum,
3 v. a. *to carry back, to refer,*
13, 43.

reficiō, -ere, -fēcī, -fectum, *to
restore,* 11, 36.

refrīgerātiō, -ōnis, f. *a making
cool,* said of the room, 14, 46.

rēgālis, -e, adj. *royal,* 17, 59.

rēgnō, -āre, -āvī, -ātum, *to
reign,* 19, 69.

rēgnum, -ī, n. *royal power,* 16,
57; *a realm,* 12, 41.

regō, -ere, -xī, -ctum, *to rule,*
11, 37; 22, 81.

relaxō, -āre, -āvī, -ātum, *to
loosen, to release,* 22, 81.

religātiō, -ōnis, f. *a tying up,*
15, 53.

relinquō, -ere, -līquī, -lictum,
to leave, to abandon, 21, 78.

reliquus, -a, -um, adj. *left, remaining:* **reliquum**, -ī, n.
the remainder, 20, 72.

remaneō, -ēre, -nsi, -nsum, *to
remain,* 19, 69.

reminīscor, -ī, *to recall, to
remember,* 21, 78.

remissus, -a, -um, adj. *released
from control,* 22, 81; *gentle,*
9, 28.

removeō, -ēre, -mōvī, -mōtum,
to remove, 7, 22.

repastinātiō, -ōnis, f. *a digging up again,* 15, 53.

repente, adv. *suddenly, without preparation,* 18, 62.

reperiō, -īre, repperī, reper-
tum, *to find,* 12, 41.

repudiō, -āre, -āvī, -ātum, *to
reject,* 16, 55.

repuerāscō, -ēre, incept. *to
become a child again,* 23, 83.

repūgnō, -āre, -āvī, -ātum, *to
fight against, to resist,* 2, 5;
19, 71.

requies, -ētis, acc. requiem or -ētem, f. *repose, rest*, 15, 52.

requīrō, -ere, -quīsīvī, -quīsītum, *to seek for*, 20, 75; 10, 33; *to miss*, 9, 30.

rēs, reī, f. *a thing;* **rēs gerendae**, *business*, 5, 15; 6, 17; cf. 22, 79; **rēs capitālis**, *a capital charge*, 12, 42; **rēs rūsticae**, *farming*, 15, 54; **rēs veneriae**, *lasciviousness*, 14, 47; *property*, 1, 1; **rēs familiāris**, *private property*, 7, 22; 17, 59; *the public prosperity*, 4, 10; **rē**, *adverbial, practically*, 23, 85.

reservō, -āre, -āvī, -ātum, *to keep in store, to reserve*, 6, 19.

resideō, -ēre, sēdī, sessum, [re-sedeo], *to rest, remain*, 17, 61.

resistō, -ēre, -stitī, *to resist, to stand against*, 11, 35.

respectō, -āre, -āvī, -ātum, *to look back upon*, 23, 84.

respondeō, -ēre, -ndī, -nsum, *to answer*, 1, 3; 7, 25; 20, 72.

respōnsum, -ī, n. *an answer*, 5, 14.

rēs pūblica, -ae, f. *the Republic, the state, public business*, 6, 15, 20, etc.

restituō, -ere, -uī, -ūtum, *to restore*, 4, 10; 6, 20.

restō, -āre, -stitī, *to remain, to be over*, 18, 65.

retardō, -āre, -āvī, -ātum, *to make slow, to retard*, 16, 57.

retineō, -ēre, -uī, -entum, *to maintain, to keep*, 11, 38.

retrahō, -ere, -xī, -ctum, *to drag back*, 23, 83.

revertor, -ī, -rsus, *to return*, 13, 55; 19, 69.

revocō, -āre, -āvī, -ātum, *to recall*.

rēx, rēgis, m. *a prince*, 17, 59.

rīdeō, -ēre, rīsī, rīsum, *to laugh*, 4, 11.

rīte, adv. *rightly*.

rōbur, -oris, n. *strength*, 10, 34.

rōbustus, -a, -um, adj. *strong, robust*, 11, 37.

rōrō, -āre, -āvī, -ātum, [ros], *to drop, to trickle*, 14, 46.

rōstra, -ōrum, n. *the Rostra,* the platform or pulpit between the Comitium and Forum, supported by the *columna rostrata*, on which the Roman orators stood to address the people, 10, 32.

rūga, -ae, f. *a wrinkle*, 18, 62.

rūmor, -ōris, m. *rumor*, 4, 10.

rūsticus, -a -um, adj. *of the country, rustic*, 7, 24; 20, 75; 15, 54.

sacer, sacra, sacrum, adj. *sacred;* **sacra**, -ōrum, n. *sacred rites, festival*, 13, 45.

sacerdōtium, -ī, n. *the office of priest, priesthood, membership of the college of sacerdotes*, 7, 30; 17, 61.

saeculum (saeclum, 7, 24), -ī, n. *an age, a generation*, 15, 54.

saepe, adv. *often*, 3, 7, etc.; **saepius, saepissimē**, 10, 31.

saepe numerō, adv. *frequently,* 1, 3.

saltus, -ūs, m. *leaping,* 6, 19.

salūbris, -e, adj. **salūbrior,** -ius, *healthy,* 16, 57.

salūs, -ūtis, f. *safety,* 4, 10.

salūtāris, -e, adj. *healthy, beneficial to health,* 16, 56.

salūtō, -āre, -āvī, -ātum, *to salute,* 7, 21.

Samnītis, -is, adj. *of Samnium, a Samnite,* 12, 4; **Samnītēs,** -ium, m. *the Samnites,* 13, 43: 16, 55.

sānē, adv. *certainly,* 6, 16: **haud sānē,** *not at all,* 2, 4; 23, 83.

sapiēns, -ntis, adj. *wise,* 22, 79, etc.; **sapientissimus,** 21, 78; subst. *a wise man, a philosopher,* 15, 51.

sapienter, adv. *wisely,* 1, 2.

sapientia, -ae, f. *wisdom, philosophy,* 2, 4; 12, 42, etc.

sarmentum, -ī, n. *a twig, a cutting,* 15, 52.

sat [8, 25; 14, 48] and **satis** [19, 70], adv. *enough, sufficiently;* or as n. subst. followed by gen. *enough.*

satietās, -tātis, f. *satiety, weariness,* 20, 76; 23, 83.

satiō, -āre, -āvī, -ātum, *to satiate,* 14, 47; 15; 41.

saturitās, -tātis, f. *fulness, abundance,* 16, 56.

satus, -ūs, m. *planting,* 15, 52.

scandō, -ere, -dī, -sum, *to climb,* 6, 17.

scelus, -eris, n. *wickedness, a crime,* 12, 39.

scaena, -ae, f. *a stage,* 18, 65.

scientia, -ae, f. *knowledge,* 4, 12.

scīlicet, adv. *that is to say, of course,* 8, 26.

sciō, -īre, -īvī, -ītum, *to know,* 1, 2.

scortum, -ī, n. *a harlot,* 12, 42; 14, 50.

sē, see **suī.**

sēcum [sē-cum], *to himself, apart from others,* 14, 49.

secundum, adv. *according to,* 19, 71.

secūris, -is, f. *an axe,* 12, 42.

sed, conj. *but,* 1, 2, etc.

sedeō, -ēre, sēdī, sessum, *to sit,* 18, 63.

seges, -etis, f. *a cornfield,* 15, 54.

sēmen, -inis, n. *seed,* 15, 51.

semper, adv. *always,* 8, 26, etc.

senātus, -ūs, m. *the Senate,* 6, 16; 12, 42.

senecta, -ae, f. *old age,* 8, 25.

senectūs, -tūtis, f. *old age,* 1, 1, etc.

senēscō, -ere, -nuī, incept. *to grow old,* 6, 20; 11, 38.

senex, senis, m. *an old man.*

senīlis, -e, adj. *belonging to an old man, senile,* 9, 30; 18, 65.

senium, -ī, n. *the weakness of old age, old age,* 5, 14.

sēnsim, adv. *gradually,* 11, 38; 15, 51.

sēnsus, -ūs, m. *sensation, sense.*

VOCABULARY.

feeling, 11, 30; 14, 46; 20, 72, 74.

sententia, -ae, f. *opinion*, 6, 16; *a formal expression of opinion* in the Senate or elsewhere, 6, 17, 19; 17, 61; *a vote, a giving a vote*, 7, 22; 18, 64.

sentīna, -ae, f. *bilge-water*, 6, 17.

sentiō, -īre, -nsī, -nsum, *to feel, to perceive*. 2, 4; 8, 25; 21, 77.

septem, indeclin. num. adj. *seven*, 5, 13: **septemdecim**, *seventeen*, 6, 16.

septimus, -a, -um, ordinal num. adj. *seventh*, 11, 38.

septuāgintā, indeclin. num. adj. *seventy*, 5, 14.

sepulcrum, -ī, n. *a tomb, a grave*, 7, 21; 17, 61.

sepultūra, -ae, f. *burial*, 20, 75.

sequor, -ī, secūtus, *to follow, to keep in view*, 11, 38.

sermō, -ōnis, m. *a discourse, speech*, 1, 3, etc.; *style*, 9, 28.

serō, -ere, sēvī, satum, *to sow, to plant*, 7, 24; 17, 59.

serpō, -ere, -psī, -ptum, *to creep, to spread*, 15, 52.

servō, -āre, -āvī, -ātum, *to keep, to preserve*, 22, 81.

seu, see **sīve**.

sevēritās, -tātis, f. *gravity*, 18, 65.

sex, indeclin. num. adj. *six*, 14, 50; 17, 60.

sexāgintā, indeclin. num. adj. *sixty*, 5, 14.

sextus, -a, -um, ordinal num. adj. *sixth*, 17, 60.

sī, conj. *if;* **sī quem**, 14, 46:

siquidem, *since*, 16, 56; 12, 41: **sīn**, *but if*, 23, 85; 19, 70.

sīc, adv. *thus, so*, 2, 4, etc.: **sīcut**, *as, like*, 1, 2; 14, 47: **sīc . . . quasi**, 8, 26.

siccitās, -tātis, f. *dryness*, absence of unhealthy humors, 10, 34.

sīgnificō, -āre, -āvī, -ātum, *to indicate, to mean*, 19, 70.

silvēscō, -ere, incept. *to grow into a wood, to become bushy*, 15, 52.

similis, -e, adj. *like;* with gen. 10, 31; with dat. 22, 80; followed by *ut si*, 6, 17.

simplex, -icis, adj. *simple, single*. 10, 33; 21, 78.

simul, adv. *at the same time.*

sīn, see **sī**.

sine. prep. with abl. *without.*

siquidem, adv. see **sī**.

sitis, -is, f. *thirst*, 8, 26.

sīve [or **seu**], conj. *whether, or*, **sīve quis**, 12, 40.

socer, -erī, m. *a father-in-law,* 6, 15.

socius, -ī, m. *an ally*, 17, 59.

sodālis, -is, m. *a comrade, a member of the same club*, 13, 55.

sodālitās, -tātis, f. *a collection of comrades, a club*, 13, 45.

sōl, sōlis, m. *the sun*, 14, 49.

soleō, -ēre, solitus, *to be wont*, 2. 4, etc.

sollers, -rtis, adj. **sollertior**, -ius, *skilful*, 15, 54.

sollertia, -ae, f. *skill, cleverness*, 17, 59.

438

CATÒ MĀIOR.

sollicitō, -āre, -āvī, -ātum, *to trouble, to cause anxiety to*, 1, 1.

sōlum, adv. *only:* **nōn sōlum** . . . **vērum etiam**, 23, 84: **nōn sōlum** . . . **sed**, 1, 1; 3, 9; *or* **sed etiam**, 4, 12; 9, 28.

sōlus, -a, -um, gen. -īus, adj. *alone*, 11, 36, etc.

somniculōsus, -a, -um, adj. *sleepy, drowsy*, 11, 36.

somnus, -ī, m. *sleep*, 22, 80.

spargō, -ere, -rsī, -rsum, *to scatter*, 15, 51; 21, ⁷⁷.

spatium, -ī, n. *a space*, 17, 60; *a race-course*, 5, 14; 23, 83.

speciēs, -ēī, f. *appearance, beauty*, 16, 57.

spectō, -āre, -āvī, -ātum, *to look at, to examine*, 14, 48.

spernō, -ere, sprēvī, sprētum, *to spurn, to despise*, 3, 7; 13, 43.

spērō, -āre, -āvī, -ātum, *to hope for*, 19, 68, etc.

spēs, -ēī, f. *hope*, 20, 72.

spīcum, -ī, n. [collat. form of spīca] *an ear of corn*, 15, 51.

spīritus, -ūs, m. *breath*, 9, 27; 11, 38.

splendēscō, -ere, incept. *to shine, to become brilliant*, 9, 28.

splendidē, adv. *brilliantly*, 18, 64.

splendor, -ōris, m. *glory, splendor*, 3, 8.

sponte [abl. of spons], **suā sponte**, *for itself, on its own*

account, 13, 43; *voluntarily, spontaneously*, 19, 71.

stadium, -ī, n. *race-course*, 10, 33.

statiō, -ōnis, f. *post, guard*, 20, 72.

stercorō, -āvī, -ātum, *to dung, to manure*, 15, 54.

stīpendium, -ī, n. *military pay*, hence, *term of military service*, 14, 49.

stīpō, -āre, -āvī, -ātum, *to crowd, to surround*, 9, 28.

stirps, -pis, f. *a stock, stem*, 15, 51.

stō, stāre, stetī, statum, *to stand, to be firm*, 6, 16.

Stōicus, -ī, m. *a Stoic*, 7, 23; -a, -um, adj.

struō, -ere, -xī, -ctum, *to build, to construct*, 15, 51.

studiōsē, adv. *diligently, eagerly*, 17, 59.

studium, -ī, n. *study*, 14, 49; *a pursuit*, 5, 13; *zeal*, 7, 22, 3; *affection*, 9, 28.

stultitia, -ae, f. *folly*, 2, 4; 11, 36.

stuprum, -ī, n. *debauchery*, 12, 39.

suāda, -ae, f. *persuasiveness*, 15, 50.

suādeō -ēre, suāsī, suāsum, *to advise, to support a law*, 5, 14.

suāsor, -ōris, m. *an advisor, a supporter* (of a law), 4, 10.

suāvitās, -tātis, f. *sweetness, pleasant odor*, 10, 31; 17, 59; 19, 70.

sub, prep. [acc. and abl.] *under*.

subigō, -ere, -ēgī, -āctum, *to bring under, to subdue*, 15, 51; 17, 59.

subitō, adv. *suddenly*, 11, 38.

subveniō, -īre, -vēnī, -ventum, *to come to the aid of, to support*, 11, 36.

succīdia, -ae, f. *a flitch*, 16, 56.

succumbō -ere, -cubuī, -cubitum, *to succumb, to give way to*, 11, 37.

sūcus, -ī, m. *juice, sap*, 15, 53.

suī, sē, sibī, reflex. pron. *himself, herself, itself, themselves*, 2, 4, etc.

sum, es, est, esse, fuī, futūrus, *to be*, 1, 1, etc.; **futūrum est**, 2, 6.

summus, -a, -um (superus), superl. adj. *highest, greatest, most excellent*, 6, 19; 10, 34; 17, 59; 21, 77; *topmost*, ā **summō** sc. lectulō, 14, 46; *last*.

superior, -ōris [supra, superus], comp. adj. *former, preceding*, 8, 26; 6, 16; 18, 62.

superō, -āre, -āvī, -ātum, *to conquer, to overcome*, 12, 41.

supervacāneus, -a, -um, adj. *superfluous, extra, belonging to leisure hours*, 16, 56.

supplicium, -ī, n. *punishment, torture*, 20, 75.

suprēmus, -a, -um, superl. adj. [supra, superus] *last*, 5, 14.

suscipiō, -ere, -cēpī, -ceptum, *to undertake*, 12, 40; 23, 82.

Q

suspicor, -ārī, -ātus, *to suspect*, 1, 1.

sustentō, -āre, -āvī, -ātum, freq. *to support*, 6, 20.

sustineō, -ēre, -tinuī, -tentum, *to carry, to hold up, to support*, 2, 4; 10, 33; 11, 34.

suus, -a, -um, reflex. poss. pron. *his, her, its* or *their own*, 3, 8, etc.; *proper, peculiar*, 10, 33.

symposium (συμπόσιον), -ī, n. *a drinking together, a party*, 14, 46.

tālis, -e, adj. correlative of **quālis**, *such, of such sort*, 8, 26; 12, 40.

tālus, -ī, m. *a knuckle-bone*: **tālī**, *dice*, 16, 58.

tam, adv. *so much, so*: **tam multa**, 5, 13: **tam diū**, 5, 13; 12, 41: **tam . . . quam**, 9, 27.

tamen, adv. *nevertheless*.

tamquam, adv. *as though*, 2, 5; 19, 69, 70, etc.: **tamquam . . . sīc**, 11, 35.

tandem, adv. *at length*.

tantulus, -a, -um,. adj. *so little*, 15, 52.

tantum, adv. *only, so much*, 10, 33; 14, 48.

tantus, -a, -um, adj. *so great*, correlative of **quantus**, which see: **tantum**, as n. subst. *so much*, 13, 44.

tardus, -a, -um, adj. **tardior**, -ius, *slow*, 7, 21.

Tarentīnus, -a, -um, adj. *of Tarentum*, 12, 39.

440

taurus, -ī, m. *a bull*, 9, 27.
tēcum, see **tū**, 1, 2.
temerē, adv. *rashly*, 12, 39.
temeritās, -tātis, f. *audacity, rashness*, 6, 20; 20, 75.
temperantia, -ae, f. *temperance, self-control*, 10, 34; 12, 41.
tempestīvitās, -tātis, f. *seasonableness, timeliness*, 10, 33.
tempestīvus, -a, -um, adj. *seasonable, timely*, 2, 5; 14, 46.
tempus, -oris, n. *time*, 10, 33; **tempora**, *seasons*, 16, 55.
teneō, -ēre, -uī, -ntum, *to hold, to retain*, 4, 12; 11, 37; 12, 80; pass. *to be possessed by, to be affected*, 10, 33.
tenuis -e, adj. *slight, feeble*, 11, 35.
tepefaciō, -ere, -fēcī, -factum, *to make warm*, 15, 51.
tepor, -ōris, m. *warmth*, 15, 53.
terminō, -āre, -āvī, -ātum, *to limit, to put bounds to*, 23, 82.
terminus, -ī, m. *a limit, a boundary*, 20, 72.
terra, -ae, f. *earth*, 15, 51, etc.; *land* opposed to sea, 19, 71.
tertius, -a, -um, ordinal num. adj. *third*, 5, 15; 6, 19; 19, 66.
tessera, -ae, f. *a die*, 16, 58.
theātrum, -ī, n. *a theatre*, 18, 63.
thēsaurus, -ī, m. *a treasure*, 7, 21.
Thessalus, -a, -um, adj. *of Thessaly, Thessalian*, 13, 43.
tībicen, -inis, m. *a flute-player*, 13, 44.

timeō, -ēre, -uī, *to fear*, 19, 67.
tītillātiō, -ōnis, f. *relish*, 14, 47.
toga, -ae, f. *a toga*, a Roman's outer garment: as opposed to **arma**, *peace, peaceful occupations*, 4, 11.
tolerābilis, -e, adj. *tolerable, to be borne*, 3, 7.
tollō, -ere, sustulī, sublātum, *to take away*, 14, 46.
tot, indeclin. adj. *so many*, 21, 78, etc.
tōtus, -a, -um, gen. **tōtīus**, adj. *whole, entire*.
trāctō, -āre, -āvī, -ātum, *to treat, to handle*, 11, 38.
trādō, -ēre, -didī, -ditum, *to hand over, to hand down*, 9, 29.
trādūcō, -ere, -ūxī, -uctum, *to conduct to its end*, 23, 82.
tragoedia, -ae, f. *tragedy*, 7, 22.
tranquillus, -a, -um, adj. *tranquil, quiet*, 20, 74.
tribūnus, -ī, m. *a tribune of the Plebs*, 4, 11; *a military officer, a tribune*, 6, 8: **tribūnus mīlitāris**, 10, 32.
tribuō, -ere, -uī, -ūtum, *to give, to assign*, 1, 3; 18, 63.
tricēsimus, -a, -um, ordinal num. adj. *thirtieth*, 6, 19.
trīstius, compar. adv. [triste] *with more pain*, 19, 67.
triumphō, -āre, -āvī, -ātum, *to celebrate a triumph*, 16, 55.
triumphus, -ī, m. *a triumph*.
truncus, -ī, m. *a trunk*, 15, 52
tū, tuī, tibi, tē, pers. pron. *thou*, 1, 1, etc.

VOCABULARY.

tueor, -ērī, tuitus, *to defend,* 11, 38; *manage,* 17, 59; 21, 77; *to keep up,* 20, 72.

tum, adv. *then, moreover, next:* **cum ... tum,** *both ... and,* 3, 7, 15, 53; **tum dēnique,** *not till then,* 23, 82.

turba, -ae, f. *a crowd,* 23, 84.

tyrannus, -ī, m. *a tyrant,* 20, 72.

ūber, -eris, **ūberior,** -ius, adj. *fruitful,* 11, 35; 16, 57.

ultimus, -a, -um [ultra], superl. adj. *last,* 11, 38; 14, 48; 17, 60.

ultrō, adv. *uncalled for, of one's own act,* 11, 38.

umbra, -ae, f. *shade,* 22, 80.

umerus, ī, m. *shoulder,* 10, 33; 21, 77.

umquam, adv. *at any time, ever,* 9, 27.

ūnā, adv. *together, at the same time,* 22, 81.

unde, adv. *whence,* 22, 80; *from whom,* 4, 12.

ūndēvīcēsimus, -a, -um, ordinal num. adj. *nineteenth,* 5, 14.

ūnicus, -a, -um, adj. *unique, unexampled,* 17, 6.

ūnus, -a, -um, gen. **ūnīus,** num. adj. *one,* 5, 15, etc.

ūnusquisque, ūnaquaeque, ūnumquidque, adj. *each separately,* 5, 15.

urbs, -bis, f. *a city.*

urgeō, -ēre, ursī, *to press, to come close to,* 1, 2.

usque, adv. *even, ever;* **usque ad,** 17, 60.

ūsūra, -ae, f. *interest, usury,* 15, 51.

ūsus, -ūs, m. *use, experience;* **ūsū venīre,** *to happen,* 3, 7.

ut, conj. *in order that, so that, that,* 1, 2; 12, 42, etc.: **ut ita dīcam,** *so to speak,* 7, 24: *how,* 8, 26; adv. *when, how, as,* 18, 63, etc.; *considering that, for,* 4, 12; in comparisons, **ut ... sīc,** 6, 20; 11, 38; **sīc ... ut,** 22, 81.

uterque, utraque, utrumque, gen. utrīusque, adj. *both,* 1, 2, etc.

utervīs, -travīs, -trumvīs, gen. utrīusvis, *whichever of the two you wish,* 10, 33.

ūtilitās, -tātis, f. *usefulness, expediency,* 15, 53, 54.

utinam, adv. *would that!* 2, 5; 6, 18; 23, 86.

ūtor, -ī, ūsus, *to enjoy,* 1, 2; 10, 33; *to use, to employ,* 6, 9; 8, 26; 11, 38; *to indulge in,* 14, 47.

utrum, adv. asking a question *whether?* 10, 33; see **an.**

ūva, -ae, f. *a grape,* 15, 53.

vacō, -āre, -āvī, -ātum, *to be without, to be excused from,* 11, 34.

vadimōnium, -ī, n. *bail, security,* 7, 21.

vāgīna, -ae, f. *a sheath,* 15, 51.

vāgiō, -īre, -īvī, -ītum, *to cry, to wail* like a child, 23, 83.

valdē, adv. [validus] *certainly, strongly, very*, 23, 83.

valētūdō, -inis, f. *health, state of health*, 11, 35.

vallus, -ī, m. *a stockade, a rampart*, 15, 51.

vapor, -ōris, m. *heat*, 15, 51.

varietās, -tātis, f. *variety*, 15, 54.

varius, -a, -um, adj. *various*, 6, 18; 4, 46.

ve, enclit. conj. *or.*

vel, conj. *or, either; even*, 20, 75 : **vel māximē**, 2, 4.

vēlōcitas, -tātis, f. *swiftness*, 6, 17.

vēnātiō, -ōnis, f. *hunting*, 16, 56.

venerius, -a, -um, adj. *of passion, sexual*, 14, 47.

veniō, -īre, vēnī, ventum, *to come :* **veniendum est**, impers. 19, 70.

vēr, vēris [no plur.], n. *spring*, 15, 52; 19, 70.

verbum, -ī, n. *a word*, 15, 54.

vereor, -ērī, veritus, *to fear, to respect*, 11, 37; 22, 81: v. n. *to be afraid*, 6, 8; 10, 31.

vērnus, -a, -um, adj. *of spring, vernal*, 19, 70.

vērō, adv. *truly, indeed*, 4, 11; *however*, 6, 17 ; 14, 46.

versiculus, -ī, m. *a verse, a short poem*, 14, 50.

versō, -āre, -āvī, -ātum, *to torture*, 1, 1: **versārī**, *to be engaged*, 6, 17.

versus, -ūs, m. *a verse*, 1, 1; 6, 16; 8, 26.

vērum, conj. *but*, 23, 84, etc.

vērus, -a, -um, adj. *true*, 10, 31: **vērī simile**, *likely*, 2, 5.

vesper, -erī and -eris, m. *evening*, 19, 67 : **vesperī**, *in the evening*, 11, 38.

vester, -tra, -trum, poss. pron. *your*, 21, 77, etc.

vestiō, -īre, -īvī, -ītum, *to clothe*, 15, 53.

vestrūm, gen. plur. of **vōs**, *of you*, 2, 6.

vetō, -āre, -tuī, -titum, 1 v. a. *to forbid*, 20, 72.

vetustās, -tātis, f. *the being old, age*, 18, 65.

via, -ae [viai, 6, 16], f. *a road, a way, a journey*, 2, 6.

viāticum, -ī, n. *provision for a journey*, 18, 65.

viātor, -ōris, m. *a summoner, an officer employed by the state for taking messages, etc.*, 16, 56.

vīcīnus, -ī, m. *a neighbor*, 7, 24; 14, 46.

vicissim, adv. *in turns*, 14, 46; 16, 57.

victor, -ōris, adj. *victorious*, 5, 14; subst. m. *a conqueror.*

victus, -ūs, m. *food*, 11, 56.

vidēlicet, adv. *that is to say*, 6, 20; 13, 44.

video -ēre, vīdī, vīsum, *to see*, 23, 83, etc.: **vīsum est**, *it seemed good, I resolved*, 1, 1.

viētus, -a, -um [vieō], adj. *shrivelled, withered*, 2, 5.

vigeō, -ēre, -uī, *to flourish, to be strong*, 11, 37.

VOCABULARY.

vigilantia, -ae, f. *wakefulness, watchfulness*, 4, 11.

viginti, indeclin. num. adj. *twenty*, 9, 30.

villa, -ae, f. *a country house, a farmhouse*, 16, 55.

vinaceus, -ī, m. *a grapestone*, 15, 52.

vinarius, -a, -um, adj. *belonging to wine, of wine*, 16, 56.

vinculum, -ī, n. *a chain, a bond*, 3, 7; 12, 42; 22, 81.

vindicō, -āre, -āvī, -ātum, *to excuse, to claim exemption for*, 16, 55.

vinea, -ae, f. *a vineyard*, 15, 54; 16, 57.

vinulentia, -ae, f. *intoxication*, 13, 44.

vinum, -ī, n. *wine*, 18, 65.

vir, virī, m. *a man*, 1, 1, etc.

viriditās, -tātis, f. *greenness, greenery*, 15, 51; 16, 57.

viritim, adv. *singly, man by man*, 4, 11.

virtūs, -tūtis, f. *virtue*, 8, 26; 12, 39, etc.

vis [no gen. sing.], acc. vim, abl. vī, plur. vīres, vīrium, f. *force, power, strength*, 6, 15; 15, 51, etc.; *violence*, 19, 71, etc.

vita, -ae, f. *life*, 21, 77, etc.

vitiōsus, -a, -um, adj. *faulty, vicious;* **vitiōsior**, -ius, 8, 25; **vitiōsissimus**, -a, -um, 12, 29.

vitis, -is, f. *a vine*, 15, 52.

vitium, -ī, n. *vice*, 5, 14; *defect, fault*, 8, 25; 9, 27, 29; 11, 35, 36.

vituperātiō, -ōnis, f. *abuse, charge against*, 12, 39; 13, 44.

viviradix, -īcis, f, *a layer, a quickset*, 15, 52.

vivō, -ere, vīxī, vīctum, *to be alive, to live:* **vitam vivere**, 21, 77; in pass. impers. 19, 67: 20, 71.

vivus, -a, -um, adj. *alive*, 10, 33.

vocō, -āre, -āvī, -ātum, *to call, to name*, 13, 45; *to summon*, 7, 22.

volō, **vis**, **volt**, velle, voluī, *to wish, to be willing*, 1, 1, etc.: **sibi velle**, *to mean, to intend*, 18, 65.

voluntārius, -a, -um, adj. *voluntary, spontaneous*, 20, 75.

voluptās, -tātis, f. *pleasure*, especially *sensual pleasure*, 3, 7, etc.: **corporis voluptas**, 12, 39.

vox, vōcis, f. *voice*, 5, 14; 9 28; *a saying*, 9, 27.

INDEX OF PROPER NAMES.

[The numbers indicate sections.]

444

INDEX OF PROPER NAMES.

CATŌ MĀIOR.

Printed in the United States of America.